First edition October 2012
Edition 1.10 September 2013

Published by Design Community College Inc,

Design Community College Inc.
PO Box 1153
Topanga CA 90290 USA

info@curedale.com
Designed and illustrated by Robert Curedale

ISBN-10: 0988236206

ISBN-13: 978-0988236202

Cover Image: Copyright 2012 oriontrail, Used under license from Shutterstock.com

Structured Workshops
The author presents workshops online and in person in global locations for executives, engineers, designers, technology professionals and anyone interested in learning and applying these proven innovation methods. For information contact: info@curedale.com

Design Methods 1

200 ways to apply design thinking

Robert Curedale

Dedication

Dedicated to aidan, liam, ashton and clayton

introduction

The methods in this book are an evolution from the traditional approach to design education in a number of ways. The methods help make a designer more effective and efficient when working as part of a multidisciplinary team. They enable a designer to create more successful design by better understanding the outlook of those we are designing for. The methods allow a designer to make informed design decisions that are not only about physical things but also about complex interfaces, systems, services and experiences. In Western economies such as the United States the service sector now employs 90% of the population and organizations that employ designers need to create design that balances the requirements of complex ecosystems of products, environments, services and experiences both physical and virtual.

This is a new approach to design and a different way of seeing the world. These methods can help you work more efficiently and effectively. Four global trends in design require new approaches to designing. These are: the growing focus on people, systems and experiences beyond objects; the growing complexity of the design problems being faced; the trend towards working in cross disciplinary teams; and the growing need to design for distant unfamiliar cultures. These techniques can help you produce design that is innovative and more valuable. This approach is now called Design Thinking. These methods have been tested and successfully applied across disciplines, across cultures, across the globe. They will enable you to design products, systems buildings, interfaces and experiences with confidence that you have created the most informed design solutions for real people that is possible. We believe that this is the largest collection of design methods that is available and with the companion volume two is an indispensable resource for anyone practicing design.

These methods are becoming required skills for designers everywhere. These methods allow designers to decide what is most important and make informed design decisions in complex ecosystems of products services and experiences these methods help designers think in 4 dimensions instead of three. Designing experiences has the added dimension of time. These methods help the design team understand the response of customers to a proposed design and so reduce the subjectivity by providing evidence for design decisions. I have tried to convey the essence of each method in cookbook format that can be easily and quickly understood and applied. The collection is a resource for practicing designers, design team professionals, teachers and students in diverse fields of design and architecture and professionals working in design teams including managers, engineers and marketing professionals.

Few working designers today were trained in Design Thinking skills. These techniques supplement traditional design skills in the areas of design activity in the steadily growing areas where traditional skills are inadequate. The wide range of methods contained in this book will help you close the gap between your clients and organizations and the people that you are designing for to help you create more considered, informed, repeatable, innovative, empathetic design solutions that people need but may not yet know that they want. The methods have been selected to help you adopt and apply a design thinking approach to design.

The methods are necessary when working in multidisciplinary multinational collaboration. They include research methods, team alignment methods, creativity methods and design management and review methods selected to help your team work together efficiently. They combine analytical and creative thinking approaches for the complex and rapidly evolving global consumer behaviors and markets that designers now work in.

I have kept the descriptions simple to give readers the essential information to adapt, combine and apply the methods in their own way. I hope that you will gradually build a personal toolkit of favored methods that you have tried and found effective. Different design practitioners can select different methods for their toolkit and apply them in different ways. There is no best combination.

contents

Chapter 4
Information gathering frameworks 97

Chapter 5
Know people and context 107

Chapter 1
Design Thinking

design thinking

WHAT IS IT?

Design Thinking is a methodology or approach to designing that should help you be more consistently innovative. It involves methods that enable empathy with people, it focuses on people. It is a collaborative methodology that involves iterative prototyping. It involves a series of divergent and convergent phases. It combines analytical and creative thinking approaches. It involves a toolkit of methods that can be applied to different styles of problems by different types of people. Anyone can use Design Thinking. It can be fun.

WHO INVENTED IT?

The origins of new design methods date back to before the 1950s. 1987 Peter Rowe, Professor at the Harvard Graduate School of Design, published "Design Thinking" the first significant usage of the term "Design Thinking" in literature. After 2000 the term became widely used.

CHALLENGES

1. There has been little research to validate claims about Design Thinking by advocates.
2. Some critics of Design Thinking suggest that it is a successful attempt to brand a set of existing concepts and frameworks with a appealing idea.

WHY USE DESIGN THINKING?

Design Thinking is useful when you have:
1. A poorly defined problem.
2. A lack of information.
3. A changing context or environment
4. It should result in consistently innovative solutions.

Design Thinking seeks a balance of design considerations including:
1. Business.
2. Empathy with people.
3. Application of technologies.
4. Environmental consideration.

Design Thinking seeks to balance two modes of thinking:
1. Analytical thinking
2. Creative Thinking

Advocates of Design Thinking believe that the approach results in consistently innovative design solutions oriented towards people.

Design Thinking takes a cross disciplinary team approach. It rejects the idea of a designer being a lone expert artist working in a studio remote from people in favor of an approach where a designer collaborates with a multidisciplinary team. Design Thinking advocates making informed decisions based on evidence gathered from the people and context in place of designers working on a hunch.

WHEN TO USE DESIGN THINKING

Design Thinking is an approach that can be applied throughout the design process:

1. Define intent
2. Know Context
3. Know User
4. Frame insights
5. Explore Concepts
6. Make Plans
7. Deliver Offering

RESOURCES

1. Paper
2. Pens
3. Camera
4. Notebook
5. Post-it-notes
6. Cardboard
7. White board
8. Dry-erase markers

REFERENCES

1. Martin, Roger L. The Opposable Mind: How Successful Leaders Win through Integrative Thinking. Boston, MA: Harvard Business School, 2007.
2. Buchanan, Richard, "Wicked Problems in Design Thinking," Design Issues, vol. 8, no. 2, Spring 1992
3. Cross, Nigel. "Designerly Ways of Knowing." Design Studies 3.4 (1982): 221–27.
4. Brown, Tim, and Katz, Barry. Change by Design: How Design Thinking Transforms Organizations and Inspires Innovation. New York: Harper Business, 2009.
5. Florida, Richard L. The Rise of the Creative Class: and How It is Transforming Work, Leisure, Community and Everyday Life. New York, NY: Basic, 2002 Basic, 2002
6. Jones, John Christopher. Design Methods. New York: John Wiley & Sons, 1970.

design thinking approach

FOCUS ON PEOPLE:

Design is more about people than it is about things. It is important to stand in those people's shoes, to see through their eyes, to uncover their stories, to share their worlds. Start each design by identifying a problem that real people are experiencing. Use the methods in this book selectively to gain empathy, understanding. and to inform your design. Good process is not a substitute for talented and skilled people on your design team.

GET PHYSICAL

Make simple physical prototypes of your ideas as early as possible. Constantly test your ideas with people. Do not worry about making prototypes beautiful until you are sure that you have a resolved final design. Use the prototypes to guide and improve your design. Do a lot of low cost prototypes to test how Your Ideas physically work. using cardboard, paper, markers, adhesive tape, photocopies, string and popsicle sticks. The idea is to test your idea, not to look like the final product. Expect to change it again. Limit your costs to ten or twenty dollars. Iterate, test and iterate. Do not make the prototype jewelry. It can stand in the way of finding the best design solution. In the minds of some a high fidelity prototype is a finished design solution rather than a tool for improving a design. You should make your idea physical as soon as possible. Be the first to get your hands dirty by making the idea real.

BE CURIOUS

Ask why? Explore and Experiment. Go outside your comfort zone. Do not assume that you know the answer. Look for inspiration in new ways and places. Christopher Columbus and Albert Einstein followed their curiosity to new places.

SEEK TEAM DIVERSITY

A diverse design team will produce more successful design than a team that lacks diversity. Innovation needs a collision of different ideas and approaches. Your team should have different genders, different ages, be from different cultures, different socioeconomic backgrounds and have different outlooks to be most successful. With diversity expect some conflict. Manage conflict productively and the best ideas will float to the surface. Have team members who have lived in different countries and cultures and with global awareness. Cross cultural life experience enables people to be more creative.

TAKE CONSIDERED RISKS

Taking considered risks is helps create differentiated design. Many designers and organizations do not have the flexibility or courage to create innovative, differentiated design solutions so they create products and services that are like existing products and services and must compete on price.
"It takes a lot of courage to release the familiar and seemingly secure, to embrace the new, but there is no real security in what is no longer meaningful. There is more security in the adventurous and exciting, for in movement there is life, and in change, there is power."
Alan Cohen

USE THE TOOLS

To understand the point of view of diverse peoples and cultures a designer needs to connect with those people and their context. The tools in this book are an effective way of seeing the world through the eyes of those people.

LEARN TO SEE AND HEAR

Reach out to understand people. Interpret what you see and hear. Read between the lines. Make new connections between the things you see and hear.

COMBINE ANALYTICAL AND CREATIVE THINKING

Effective collaboration is part of effective design. Designers work like members of an orchestra. We need to work with managers, engineers, salespeople and other professions. Human diversity and life experience contribute to better design solutions.

LOOK FOR BALANCE

Design Thinking seeks a balance of design factors including:

1. Business.
2. Empathy with people.
3. Application OF technology.
4. Environmental consideration.

TEAM COLLABORATION

Design today is a more complex activity than it was in the past. Business, technology, global cultural issues, environmental considerations, and human considerations all need careful consideration. Design Thinking recognizes the need for designers to be working as members of multidisciplinary multi skilled teams.

The need for creative self expression for designers is important. For an artist the need for creative self expression is a primary need. For a designer this need must be balanced by an awareness and response to the needs of others. Balanced design needs analytical as well as creative thinking. The methods in this book balance a designer's creative thinking with analytical thinking. This balance comes most effectively from a team rather than from an individual. Designers must respond to the needs of the design team, the needs of the business needs of those who employ us to design and the needs of those people that we design for.

design thinking process

DEFINE THE VISION?
What are we looking for?

1. Meet with key stakeholders to set vision
2. Assemble a diverse team
3. Develop intent and vision
4. Explore scenarios of user experience
5. Document user performance requirements
6. Define the group of people you are designing for. What is their gender, age, and income range. Where do they live. What is their culture?
7. Define your scope and constraints
8. Identify a need that you are addressing. Identify a problem that you are solving.
9. Identify opportunities
10. Meet stakeholders

KNOW THE PEOPLE AND CONTEXT
What else is out there?

1. Identify what you know and what you need to know.
2. Document a research plan
3. Benchmark competitive products
4. Create a budgeting and plan.
5. Explore the context of use
6. Understand the risks
7. Observe and interview individuals, groups, experts.
8. Develop design strategy
9. Undertake qualitative, quantitative, primary and secondary research.
10. Talk to vendors

EXPLORE IDEAS
How is this for starters?

1. Brainstorm
2. Define the most promising ideas
3. Refine the ideas
4. Establish key differentiation of your ideas
5. Investigate existing intellectual property.

PROTOTYPE TEST AND ITERATE
How could we make it better?

1. Make your favored ideas physical.
2. Create low-fidelity prototypes from inexpensive available materials
3. Develop question guides
4. Develop test plan
5. Test prototypes with stakeholders
6. Get feedback from people.
7. Refine the prototypes
8. Test again
9. Build in the feedback
10. Refine again.
11. Continue iteration until design works.
12. Document the process.
13. When you are confident that your idea works make a prototype that looks and works like a production product.

DELIVER
Let's make it. Let's sell it.

1. Create your proposed production design
2. Test and evaluate
3. Review objectives
4. Manufacture your first samples
5. Review first production samples and refine.
6. Launch
7. Obtain user feedback
8. Conduct field studies
9. Define the vision for the next product or service.

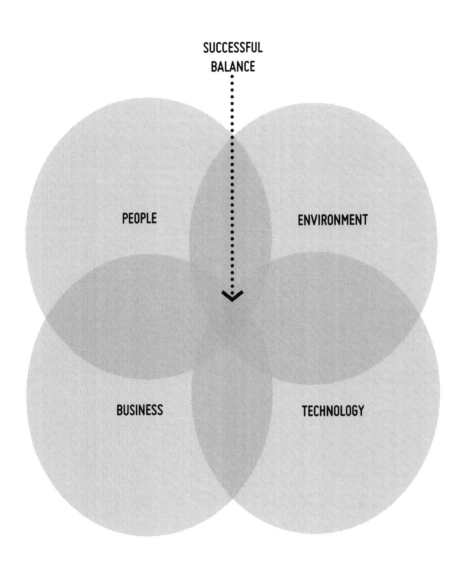

SUCCESSFUL
BALANCE

PEOPLE

ENVIRONMENT

BUSINESS

TECHNOLOGY

balanced design

WHAT IS IT?

Good design finds a balance between four factors.

1. **Business needs**, including return on investment, growth, price point, competitive advantage cash flow.
2. **Technology**. Selection of appropriate manufacturing methods and processes, materials and engineering approaches.
3. **People's needs and desires.** This includes the usability, and aesthetics.
4. **Environmental factors**. This includes environmental sustainability.

WHY CREATE BALANCED DESIGN?

Designers have often in the past oriented designs towards people's needs and desires but been less successful balancing business, environmental and technological factors. Many businesses have oriented their goals towards business factors. Companies that find a sustainable balance between these factors develop a competitive advantage over companies that tend to be oriented towards one factor.

WHEN TO USE THIS METHOD

1. Define goals
1. Know Context
2. Know User
3. Frame insights
4. Generate Concepts
5. Create Solutions

HOW TO USE THIS METHOD

1. Balanced design is more likely to evolve if the design and management team has diversity of nationality, gender, age, occupation and culture.
2. Companies that have individual VPs with specialization in each of these areas are more likely to be successful.

change

WHAT IS IT?

Design is change. The rate of change in the world is increasing. Changes in an organization can result from changes in global markets, new competitors, new technology, government legislation and customer feedback. Changes can be planned or unplanned. Planning for change is not a choice but a necessity.

WHY MANAGE CHANGE?

1. Productivity declines when change is poorly managed
2. Some resistance to change is inevitable.
3. Change creates conflict
4. Change involves risk
5. It is natural to resist change

CHALLENGES

1. Change can create resentment.
2. Not everyone reacts the same way to change. Some people prefer stability and others prefer change.
3. Change involves loss.
4. Needs and fears should be addressed when planning for change.

WHEN TO CONSIDER CHANGE

5. Define goals
1. Know Context
2. Know User
3. Frame insights
4. Generate Concepts
5. Create Solutions

HOW TO MANAGE CHANGE

1. Adjust your mindset from viewing change as a problem to an opportunity.
2. Keep sight of the long term vision
3. Have organizational structures that create long term solutions and short term solutions.
4. Be open to learning.
5. Provide others with information.
6. Be inclusive when discussing change.
7. Improve your ability to respond to change.
8. Communicate the desired changes and the need for change.
9. People undergoing change react in a cycle of emotions going through shock, denial, anger, bargaining, depression, testing, acceptance.
10. Involve the people resisting change in the in designing and implementing change.
11. Offer incentives for change.
12. Manage expectations realistically
13. Be consistent

REFERENCES

1. Marshak, R.J. (2005). Contemporary challenges to the philosophy and practice of organizational development. In David L. Bradford and W. Warner Burke. Reinventing organizational development: New approaches to change in organizations. San Francisco, CA: Pfeiffer.

Photo: photocase.com – pipp

context

WHAT IS IT?

Context is the environment situation or circumstances that surround a product or service in use.

The five w's of context

1. Who: Those who we design for
2. What: Human interactions and perceptions
3. Where: Physical location or path of activities.
4. When: The time or elapsed time.
5. Why: The purpose or meaning of the activity.

after Abowd & Mynatt 2000

WHO INVENTED IT?

The word first appeared in Late Middle English around 1375 and meant a joining together, scheme, structure or to join by weaving.

WHY USE THIS METHOD?

1. Every design is intended to accomplish goals, in a particular environment or context. Understanding the context is necessary in order to create a successful design.

CHALLENGES

1. A product or service may be used in diverse contexts.
2. A design can effect the context.
3. A designer needs to experience the context to create a successful design. This may be difficult, time consuming or expensive.

image: © F4f | Dreamstime.com

WHEN TO CONSIDER CONTEXT

1. Define goals
1. Know Context
2. Know User
3. Frame insights
4. Generate Concepts
5. Create Solutions

HOW TO USE THIS METHOD

1. Define contextual problem to address
2. Contextual inquiry
3. Discover insights
4. Create possible solutions
5. Create vision and scenarios
6. Prototype and test in context
7. Refine
8. Prototype and test in context
9. Deliver.

RESOURCES

1. Camera
2. Note pad
3. Pens
4. Digital voice recorder

REFERENCES

1. Albrecht Schmidt, Michael Beigl, and Hans-Werner Gellersen. There is more to context than location. Computers and Graphics, 23(6):893–901, 1999.
2. Peter Tarasewich. Towards a comprehensive model of context for mobile and wireless computing. In Proc. of AMCIS 2003, pages 114–124, 2003.

design ethnography

WHAT IS IT?

Ethnography is a collection of research methods that includes observing and interviewing people. Design ethnography helps create better more compelling and meaningful design. Ethnographers study and interpret culture, through fieldwork.

WHO INVENTED IT?

Bronisław Malinowski 1922 was an important pioneer of methods used today by designers.

WHY USE THIS METHOD?

1. To inform the design and innovation processes rather than basing your designs on intuition.
2. To ensure that your design solutions resonate with the people that you are designing for,

CHALLENGES

1. People may behave differently when they are in groups or alone.
2. Researchers should be aware that their research affects the people that they are studying.

WHEN TO USE THIS METHOD

1. Define intent
2. Know Context
3. Know User
4. Frame insights
5. Explore Concepts
6. Make Plans
7. Deliver Offering

HOW TO USE THIS METHOD

There are many different ethnographic techniques. Some of the general guidelines are:

1. Listen
2. Observe.
3. Be empathetic and honest.
4. Do research in context, in the environments that the people you are studying live or work.
5. Influence your subject's behavior as little as possible with your presence.
6. Beware of bias.
7. Take photos and notes.
8. Have clear goals related to understanding and prediction.
9. Study representative people

RESOURCES

1. Note pad
2. Pens
3. Post-it-notes
4. Video camera
5. Camera
6. Voice recorder
7. White board
8. Dry-erase pens.

REFERENCES

1. Erickson, Ken C. and Donald D. Stull (1997) Doing Team Ethnography : Warnings and Advice. Sage, Beverly Hills.
2. Westbrook, David A. Navigators of the Contemporary: Why Ethnography Matters. (2008). Chicago: University of Chicago Press.

experience design

WHAT IS IT?
Experience design is the practice of designing products, processes, services, events, and environments with a focus on the quality of the user experience. Experience design is concerned with moments of engagement, or touchpoints, between people and brand. Experience design requires a cross disciplinary approach.

WHO INVENTED IT?
Donald Norman 1990s

WHY USE THIS METHOD?
1.   A user experience is often more valuable than an individual product or service.

CHALLENGES
1.   Research methods are necessary to understand another person's experiences
2.   Observations can be subjective.

WHEN TO USE THIS METHOD
1.   Define intent
2.   Know Context
3.   Know User
4.   Frame insights
5.   Explore Concepts
6.   Make Plans
7.   Deliver Offering

HOW TO USE THIS METHOD
1.   Experience evaluation methods include:
2.   Diary Methods
3.   Experience sampling method
4.   Day reconstruction method
5.   Laddering interviews.

RESOURCES
6.   Cameras
7.   Video cameras
8.   Note pad
9.   Digital voice recorder
10.   Cell phones
11.   Tablets

REFERENCES
1.   Steve Diller, Nathan Shedroff, Darrel Rhea (2005): Making Meaning: How Successful Businesses Deliver Meaningful Customer Experiences. New Riders Press ISBN 0-321-37409-6
2.   Aarts, Emile H. L.; Stefano Marzano (2003). The New Everyday: Views on Ambient Intelligence. 010 Publishers. p. 46. ISBN 978-90-6450-502-7.
3.   Kuniavsky, M. 2003, Observing The User Experience — A Practitioner's Guide to User Research. Morgan Kaufmann Publishers, Elsevier Science, USA.

team collaboration

WHAT IS IT?

Collaboration is working together to achieve a goal. Designers today work as part of diverse multidisciplinary collaborative teams. In the past designers often worked independently. Designers need training to work effectively as part of a team. The internet has enabled new forms of collaboration such as crowd sourcing,and crowd funding.

WHO INVENTED IT?

Peter Watson dates the origin of long-distance commerce from around 150,000 years ago. Other forms of collaboration such as language possibly predating commerce.

WHY USE THIS METHOD?

1. Teams that work corroboratively can obtain greater resources, recognition and reward when facing competition by sharing knowledge, learning and building consensus.
2. Collaboration makes achieving goals possible that are not possible for an individual to achieve.

CHALLENGES

1. Complex products and services are designed by teams rather than by individuals.
2. Design of products such as airplanes may involve collaboration of thousands of people.

Photo: photocase.com - GoodwinDan

WHEN TO USE THIS METHOD

1. Define intent
2. Know Context
3. Know User
4. Frame insights
5. Explore Concepts
6. Make Plans
7. Deliver Offering

HOW TO USE THIS METHOD

1. Have a clear goal
2. Create a team that is appropriate for your goal
3. Each team member should have an assigned role.
4. Create a plan
5. Establish a system of communications
6. Establish a method of monitoring feedback and performance
7. Delegate tasks
8. Collaborate to achieve goal

REFERENCES

1. Axelrod, R. (1984). The Evolution Of Cooperation, Basic Books.
2. Schuman (Editor). Creating a Culture of Collaboration. Jossey-Bass, 2006. ISBN 0-7879-8116-8.
3. Schneider, Florian: Collaboration: Some Thoughts Concerning New Ways of Learning and Working Together., in: Academy, edited by Angelika Nollert and Irit Rogoff, 280 pages, Revolver Verlag, ISBN 3-86588-303-6.

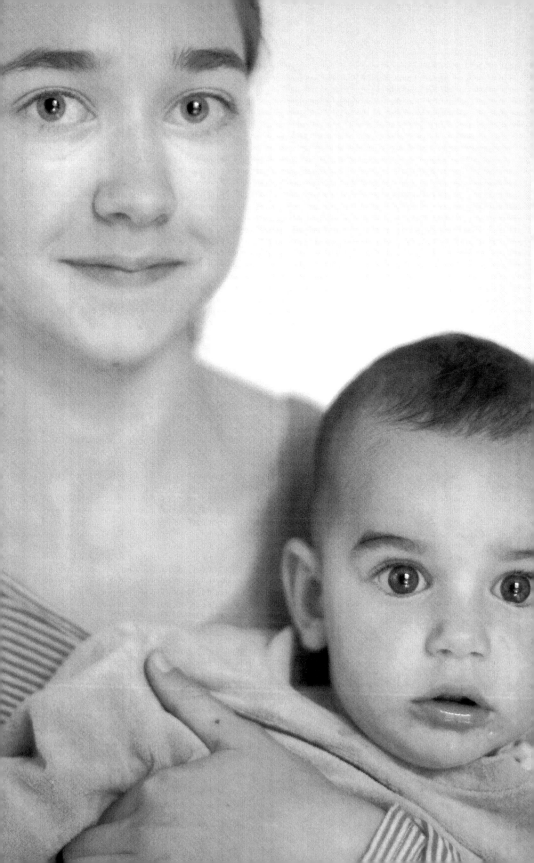

empathy

WHAT IS IT?

Empathy is sometimes defined as 'standing in someone else's shoes' or 'seeing through someone else's eyes'. It is The ability to identify and understand another's situation, feelings and motives. In design it may be defined as: identifying with others and, adopting their perspective. Empathy is different to sympathy. Empathy does not necessarily imply compassion. Empathy is a respectful understanding of what others are experiencing and their point of view.

WHO INVENTED IT?

E.B. Titchener invented the word in 1909 in an attempt to translate the German word "Einfühlungsvermögen".

WHY USE THIS METHOD?

1. Empathy is a core skill for designers to design successfully for other people.
2. Empathy is needed for business success.
3. Empathy is needed for products and services to be adopted by the people we design for.
4. Empathy builds trust.

CHALLENGES

1. Increasing use of teams
2. Rapid pace of globalization
3. Global need to retain talent

WHEN TO USE THIS METHOD

1. Define intent
2. Know Context
3. Know User
4. Frame insights
5. Explore Concepts
6. Make Plans
7. Deliver Offering

HOW TO USE THIS METHOD

1. Put yourself in contact and the context of people who you are designing for.
2. Ask questions and listen to the answers.
3. Read between the lines
4. Observe.
5. Listen
6. Ask questions.
7. Restating what you think you heard.
8. Recognize that people are individuals.
9. Notice body language. Most communication is non verbal
10. Withhold judgement when you hear views different to your own.
11. Take a personal interest in people

REFERENCES

1. Miyashiro, Marie R. (2011). The Empathy Factor: Your Competitive Advantage for Personal, Team, and Business Success. Puddledancer Press. p. 256. ISBN 1-892005-25-5.ment and Psychopathology 20: 1053—1080.

primary research

WHAT IS IT?

Primary research also called field research is collecting data that is created during the time of study. Primary research techniques include, questionnaires, interviews and direct observations.

WHO INVENTED IT?

Robert W. Bruere of the Bureau of Industrial Research 1921 may have been the first to use the term

WHY USE THIS METHOD?

You can collect this information yourself. There may be no secondary research available. It may be more reliable than secondary research. It may be more up to date than secondary research

CHALLENGES

1. May be more expensive than secondary research.
2. Information may become obsolete
3. Large sample can be time-consuming

WHEN TO USE THIS METHOD

1. Define intent
2. Know Context
3. Know User
4. Frame insights
5. Explore Concepts
6. Make Plans
7. Deliver Offering

Photos: photocase.com – Saimen

HOW TO USE THIS METHOD

Methods such as:

1. Diaries
2. E-mail
3. Interviews
4. News footage
5. Photographs
6. Raw research data
7. Questionnaires
8. Observation

RESOURCES

1. Camera
2. Notebook
3. Pens
4. Digital Voice recorder
5. Diaries
6. E-mail

REFERENCES

1. Creswell, John. Research Design: Qualitative, Quantitative, and Mixed Methods Approaches. 3rd ed. Sage publications, 2008. Print.
2. Rubin, Herbert and Irene Rubin. Qualitative Interviewing: The Art of Hearing Data. 2nd edition. Thousand Oaks, CA: Sage Publications, 2004. Print.
3. Fink, Arlene. How to Conduct Surveys: A Step-by-Step Guide. 4th ed. Thousand Oaks, CA: Sage Publications, 2008. Print.
4. Sanger, Jack. Compleat Observer? A Field Research Guide to Observation. New York: Routledge, 1996. Print.

secondary research

WHAT IS IT?

Secondary research is research that is existing and has been collected by others. Secondary research is the most widely used method for data collection. Secondary research accesses information that is already gathered from primary research.

WHO INVENTED IT?

Robert W. Bruere of the US Bureau of Industrial Research 1921 may have been the first to use the term secondary research.

WHY USE THIS METHOD?

1. Ease of access
2. Low cost
3. May be the only resource, for example historical documents
4. useful for studying trends.

CHALLENGES

1. Secondary resources always have some bias.
2. Secondary research has been collected in the past so it may not be as current as primary research.
3. May not be aligned with research goals
4. Lack of consistency of perspective
5. Biases and inaccuracies
6. Data affected by context of its collection

Photos: photocase.com – luxuz::.

WHEN TO USE THIS METHOD

1. Define intent
2. Know Context
3. Know User
4. Frame insights
5. Generate Concepts
6. Create Solutions
7. Implement solutions

HOW TO USE THIS METHOD

1. Define goals.
2. Define the context of the problem to be researched.
3. Frame research questions.
4. Develop procedure.
5. Select and retrieve appropriate data.
6. Analyze the data.
7. Review your findings by comparing them with other studies.
8. Summarize your insights.

RESOURCES

1. Books
2. Internet
3. Online search engines
4. Magazines
5. E-books
6. Bibliographies
7. Biographical works
8. Commentaries, criticisms
9. Dictionaries, Encyclopedias
10. Histories;
11. Newspaper articles
12. Web site

REFERENCES

1. Secondary Research: Information Sources and Methods. David W. Stewart, Michael A. Kamins Sage Publications, Inc; 2nd edition (December 18, 1992) ISBN-10: 0803950373 ISBN-13: 978-0803950375

qualitative research

WHAT IS IT?

Qualitative research seeks to understand people in the context of their daily experiences. Uses ethnographic methods including observation and interviews. Seeks to understand questions like why and how. Obtains insights about attitudes and emotions. Often uses small sample sizes. Seeks to see the world through the eyes of research subjects. Methods are flexible. Used to develop an initial understanding.

WHO INVENTED IT?

Bronisław Malinowski 1922

WHY USE THIS METHOD?

Methods commonly used by designers to gain empathy for the people they are designing for.

CHALLENGES

1. Concerned with validity
2. Subjective
3. Hard to recreate results
4. People may behave differently to the way they say they behave
5. Experiences can not be generalized.

WHEN TO USE THIS METHOD

1. Define intent
2. Know Context
3. Know User
4. Frame insights
5. Explore Concepts
6. Make Plans
7. Deliver Offering

HOW TO USE THIS METHOD

1. Define research question
2. Select research subjects and context to study.
3. Collect data
4. Interpret data.
5. Study data for insights
6. Collect more data
7. Analyze data

RESOURCES

1. Camera
2. Video camera
3. Note pad
4. Pens
5. Digital voice recorder
6. White board
7. Post-it-notes
8. Blank cards

REFERENCES

1. Holliday, A. R. (2007). Doing and Writing Qualitative Research, 2nd Edition. London: Sage Publications
2. Denzin, N. K., & Lincoln, Y. S. (2011). The SAGE Handbook of qualitative research (4th ed.). Los Angeles: Sage Publications.
3. Malinowski, B. (1922/1961). Argonauts of the Western Pacific. New York: E. P. Dutton.

quantitative research

WHAT IS IT?
Quantitative research uses mathematical and statistical methods. Sample sizes are often large. Findings may be expressed as numbers or percentages. Uses methods such as surveys and questionnaires. Asks questions like "How many?" Used to recommend a final course of action.

WHO INVENTED IT?
The Royal Statistical Society founded in 1834 pioneered the use of quantitative methods.

WHY USE THIS METHOD?
1. High level of reliability
2. Minimum personal judgement.
3. It is objective.

CHALLENGES
1. Methods are static. Real world changes.
2. Structured methods
3. Difficult to control the environment
4. Can be expensive if studying a large numb Er of people.

WHEN TO USE THIS METHOD
1. Define intent
2. Know Context
3. Know User
4. Frame insights
5. Explore Concepts
6. Make Plans
7. Deliver Offering

HOW TO USE THIS METHOD
1. Research design
2. Devise ways to measure hypothesis
3. Select subjects and context
4. Undertake research
5. Process data
6. Analyze data
7. Conclusions

REFERENCES
1. Bernard, H (1994) Research Methods in Anthropology: Qualitative and Quantitative Approaches, London, Sage
2. Creswell, J. W. (2009). Research design: Qualitative, quantitative, and mixed methods approaches (3rd ed.). Thousand Oaks, CA: Sage.

storytelling

WHAT IS IT?

A powerful story can help ensure the success of a new product, service or experience. Storytelling can be an effective method of presenting a point of view. Research methods can uncover meaningful stories from end users that illustrate needs or desires. These stories can become the basis of new designs and be used to support design decisions. Research shows that our attitudes, fears, hopes, and values are strongly influenced by story. Stories can be an effective way of communicating complex ideas and inspiring people to change.

WHO INVENTED IT?

1. Storytelling is one of the most ancient forms of human communication.

WHY USE THIS METHOD?

1. The stories help to get buy-in from people throughout the design process and may be used to help sell a final design.
2. Real life stories are persuasive.
3. They are different to advertising because they are able to influence a design if uncovered from users during the early research phases and provide authenticity.

CHALLENGES

1. A story with too much jargon will lose an audience.
2. Not everyone has the ability to tell vivid stories.
3. Stories are not always generalizable.

Photos: photocase.com - lube

WHEN TO USE THIS METHOD

1. Define intent
2. Know Context
3. Know User
4. Frame insights
5. Explore Concepts
6. Make Plans
7. Deliver Offering

HOW TO USE THIS METHOD

Answer in your story: What, why, when, who, where, how?
An effective story:

1. Is honest
2. Is real
3. Builds trust
4. Transmits values
5. Shares a vision
6. Shares knowledge
7. Helps Collaboration
8. Must differentiate you.
9. Uses humor
10. Engages the audience
11. Pose a problem and offer a resolution
12. Use striking imagery
13. Fit the audience
14. The audience must be able to act on it.

REFERENCES

1. Peter Guber Tell to Win: Connect, Persuade, and Triumph with the Hidden Power of Story. Publisher: Crown Business; 1ST edition (March 1, 2011) ISBN-10: 0307587959 ISBN-13: 978-0307587954

tacit knowledge

WHAT IS IT?

Tacit knowledge is knowledge that is gained through personal experience. Examples of tacit knowledge are the ability to ride a bicycle or recognizing someone's face. Tacit knowledge is difficult to pass on to another person by writing it down or describing it. Tacit knowledge is a form of intellectual property. Tacit knowledge includes best practices, stories, experience, wisdom, and insights.

WHO INVENTED IT?

Michael Polanyi 1958

WHY USE THIS METHOD?

1. Tacit knowledge is valuable to any organization.

CHALLENGES

1. Mapping tacit knowledge needs immersion in context.
2. A researcher can map behavior and perceptions.

WHEN TO USE THIS METHOD

1. Define intent
2. Know Context
3. Know User
4. Frame insights
5. Explore Concepts
6. Make Plans
7. Deliver Offering

Image Copyright Brocorwin, 2012
Used under license from Shutterstock.com

HOW TO USE THIS METHOD

The methods of capturing tacit knowledge include:
1. Interviews
2. Observation

RESOURCES

1. Camera
2. Note pad
3. Digital voice recorder

REFERENCES

1. Lam, A. (2000). Tacit Knowledge, Organizational Learning and Societal Institutions: An Integrated Framework. Organization Studies 21(3), 487–513.
2. Reber, Arthur S. 1993. Implicit learning and tacit knowledge: an essay on the cognitive unconscious. Oxford University Press. ISBN 0-19-510658-X
3. Reber, Arthur S. 1993. Implicit learning and tacit knowledge: an essay on the cognitive unconscious. Oxford University Press. ISBN 0-19-510658-X

Chapter 2
Warming up
get to know the team

team building exercises

WHAT IS IT?

An icebreaker is a short exercise at the beginning of a design project that helps the design team work productively together as quickly as possible. The duration of an icebreaker is usually less than 30 minutes.

They are an important component of collaborative or team based design. The Design Thinking approach recognizes the value of designers working productively as members of a diverse cross-disciplinary teams with managers, engineers, marketers and other professionals.

WHY USE THIS METHOD?

When a designer works with others in a new team it is important that the group works as quickly as possible in a creative constructive dialogue. An icebreaker is a way for team members to quickly start working effectively;y together. It is a worthwhile investment of half an hour at the beginning of a project and can be fun. Ice breakers help start people thinking creatively, exchanging ideas and help make a team work effectively. For meetings in a business setting in which contribute.

WHEN USE THIS METHOD

1. When team members do not know each other
2. When team members come from different cultures
3. When team needs to bond quickly
4. When team needs to work to a common gaol quickly.
5. When the discussion is new or unfamiliar.
6. When the moderator needs to know the participants.

ice breaker: desert island

WHAT IS IT?

An ice-breaker is an exercise that is used at the beginning of a design project or workshop to help to stimulate constructive interaction. It helps everyone to engage in the dialogue and contribute effectively.

WHY USE THIS METHOD?

1. Helps create a comfortable and productive environment.
2. Helps people get to know each other.
3. Helps participants engage the group and tasks.
4. Helps participants contribute effectively.
5. Creates a sense of community.

CHALLENGES

1. Be aware of time constraints. Should limit the time to 15 to 30 minutes
2. Make it simple
3. It should be fun
4. You should be creative
5. Consider your audience
6. Keep in mind technology requirements such as a microphone or projector.
7. Chairs can be arranged in a circle to help participants read body language.

WHEN TO USE THIS METHOD

1. Define intent
2. Explore Concepts

HOW TO USE THIS METHOD

1. Moderator introduces the warming up exercise.
2. Each person has 30 second to list all of the things that they should take. Each person should list at least 3 things.
3. Each person should defend why their 3 items should be one of the chosen items selected by their team.
4. Each team can vote for three items preferred by their team.
5. Each of the teams presents the 3 items that they have agreed upon to the larger group.

RESOURCES

1. A comfortable space.
2. A moderator

REFERENCES

1. Fergueson, S., & Aimone, L. (2002). Making people feel valued. Communication: Journalism Education Today, 36(1), 5-11
2. Sisco, B. R. (1991). Setting the climate for effective teaching and learning. New Directions for Adult and Continuing Education, (50), 41-50.

ice breaker: the interview

WHAT IS IT?

An ice-breaker is an exercise that is used at the beginning of a design project or workshop to help to stimulate constructive interaction. It helps everyone to engage in the dialogue and contribute effectively.

WHY USE THIS METHOD?

1. Helps create a comfortable and productive environment.
2. Helps people get to know each other.
3. Helps participants engage the group and tasks.
4. Helps participants contribute effectively.
5. Creates a sense of community.

CHALLENGES

1. Be aware of time constraints. Should limit the time to 15 to 30 minutes
2. Make it simple
3. It should be fun
4. You should be creative
5. Consider your audience
6. Keep in mind technology requirements such as a microphone or projector.
7. Chairs can be arranged in a circle to help participants read body language.

WHEN TO USE THIS METHOD

1. Define intent
2. Explore Concepts

HOW TO USE THIS METHOD

1. Moderator introduces the warming up exercise.
2. The group is paired into groups of two people who do not know each other.
3. The paired groups spend five minutes interviewing each other.
4. The interviewer introduces the interviewee to the group.
5. 3 minutes per person.

RESOURCES

1. A comfortable space.
2. A moderator

REFERENCES

1. Fergueson, S., & Aimone, L. (2002). Making people feel valued. Communication: Journalism Education Today, 36(1), 5-11
2. Sisco, B. R. (1991). Setting the climate for effective teaching and learning. New Directions for Adult and Continuing Education, (50), 41-50.

jumpstart storytelling

WHAT IS IT?

An ice-breaker is an exercise that is used at the beginning of a design project or workshop to help to stimulate constructive interaction. It helps everyone to engage in the dialogue and contribute effectively.

WHY USE THIS METHOD?

1. Stories reveal what is happening.
2. Stories inspire us to take action.
3. Stories are remembered.
4. Stories share and imbed values.
5. Stories connect people.

WHO INVENTED IT?

Seth Kahan

WHEN TO USE THIS METHOD

1. Helps create a comfortable and productive environment.
2. Helps people get to know each other.
3. Helps participants engage the group and tasks.
4. Helps participants contribute effectively.
5. Creates a sense of community narrative in the first 5 minutes of the project.

RESOURCES

1. Paper
2. Pens
3. White board
4. Dry-erase markers
5. Post-it-notes.

CHALLENGES

1. Be aware of time constraints. Should limit the time to 15 to 30 minutes
2. Make it simple
3. It should be fun
4. You should be creative
5. Consider your audience
6. Keep in mind technology requirements such as a microphone or projector.

Chairs can be arranged in a circle to help participants read body language.

HOW TO USE THIS METHOD

1. Divide the participants into groups of 5
2. Ask everyone to provide a story that is related to the objective of the workshop.
3. Each person gets 90 seconds.
4. Ask the participants to remember the story that resonated the most with them;
5. Reform the groups of 5 with different people.
6. Ask everyone to retell their story.
7. Note how the story improves with each retelling.
8. 90 seconds per story.
9. Ask each participant to reassess which story resonates with them the most.
10. Ask everyone to remember the person who told the most powerful, relevant, engaging story.
11. When clusters appear invite the people the group favored to retell their story to the whole group.

ice breaker: finish the sentence

WHAT IS IT?

An ice-breaker is an exercise that is used at the beginning of a design project or workshop to help to stimulate constructive interaction. It helps everyone to engage in the dialogue and contribute effectively.

WHY USE THIS METHOD?

1. Helps create a comfortable and productive environment.
2. Helps people get to know each other.
3. Helps participants engage the group and tasks.
4. Helps participants contribute effectively.
5. Creates a sense of community.

CHALLENGES

1. Be aware of time constraints. Should limit the time to 15 to 30 minutes
2. Make it simple
3. It should be fun
4. You should be creative
5. Consider your audience
6. Keep in mind technology requirements such as a microphone or projector.
7. Chairs can be arranged in a circle to help participants read body language.

WHEN TO USE THIS METHOD

1. Define intent
2. Explore Concepts

HOW TO USE THIS METHOD

1. Moderator introduces the warming up exercise.
2. The moderator writes a question on the board such as:

"I would give anything to."
"The best advice I ever had was."

3. Each participant then introduces themselves and answers the question.

RESOURCES

1. A comfortable space.
2. A moderator

REFERENCES

1. Fergueson, S., & Aimone, L. (2002). Making people feel valued. Communication: Journalism Education Today, 36(1), 5-11
2. Sisco, B. R. (1991). Setting the climate for effective teaching and learning. New Directions for Adult and Continuing Education, (50), 41-50.

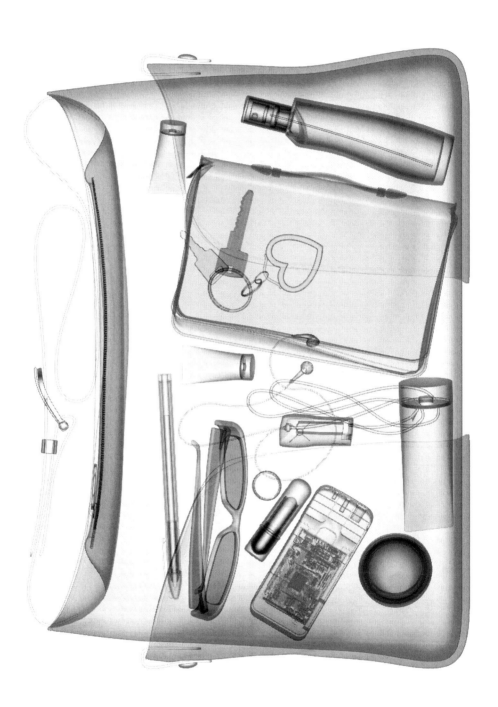

ice breaker: show and tell

WHAT IS IT?

An ice-breaker is an exercise that is used at the beginning of a design project or workshop to help to stimulate constructive interaction. It helps everyone to engage in the dialogue and contribute effectively.

WHY USE THIS METHOD?

1. Helps create a comfortable and productive environment.
2. Helps people get to know each other.
3. Helps participants engage the group and tasks.
4. Helps participants contribute effectively.
5. Creates a sense of community.
6. Helps group to collaborate and work as a team.

CHALLENGES

1. Be aware of time constraints.
2. Limit the time to 15 to 30 minutes
3. Make it simple
4. It should be fun
5. You should be creative
6. Consider your audience
7. Keep in mind technology requirements such as a microphone or projector.
8. Chairs can be arranged in a circle to help participants read body language.

WHEN TO USE THIS METHOD

1. Define intent
2. Explore Concepts

HOW TO USE THIS METHOD

1. Moderator introduces the warming up exercise.
2. Each person introduces themselves.
3. Each person selects one or two items from their pocket, wallet, purse or bag and explains why it is important to them.
4. 3 minutes per person.

RESOURCES

1. A comfortable space.
2. A moderator

REFERENCES

1. Fergueson, S., & Aimone, L. (2002). Making people feel valued. Communication: Journalism Education Today, 36(1), 5-11
2. Sisco, B. R. (1991). Setting the climate for effective teaching and learning. New Directions for Adult and Continuing Education, (50), 41-50.

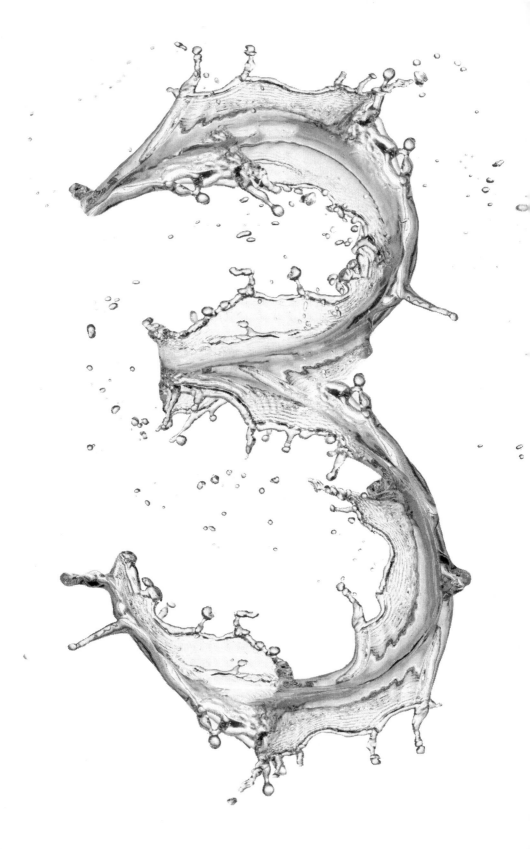

ice breaker: three in common

WHAT IS IT?

An ice-breaker is an exercise that is used at the beginning of a design project or workshop to help to stimulate constructive interaction. It helps everyone to engage in the dialogue and contribute effectively.

WHY USE THIS METHOD?

1. Helps create a comfortable and productive environment.
2. Helps people get to know each other.
3. Helps participants engage the group and tasks.
4. Helps participants contribute effectively.
5. Creates a sense of community.

CHALLENGES

1. Be aware of time constraints. Should limit the time to 15 to 30 minutes
2. Make it simple
3. It should be fun
4. You should be creative
5. Consider your audience
6. Keep in mind technology requirements such as a microphone or projector.
7. Chairs can be arranged in a circle to help participants read body language.

WHEN TO USE THIS METHOD

1. Define intent
2. Explore Concepts

HOW TO USE THIS METHOD

1. Moderator introduces the warming up exercise.
2. Break the larger group into groups of three participants.
3. Each group should find three things that they have in common.
4. After 15 minutes discussion each group should present to the larger group the three things that they have in common.

RESOURCES

1. A comfortable space.
2. A moderator

REFERENCES

1. Fergueson, S., & Aimone, L. (2002). Making people feel valued. Communication: Journalism Education Today, 36(1), 5-11
2. Sisco, B. R. (1991). Setting the climate for effective teaching and learning. New Directions for Adult and Continuing Education, (50), 41-50.

hopes and hurdles

WHAT IS IT?

Hopes and hurdles is a brainstorm that identifies factors that may help or hinder the success of a project:

1. Business drivers and hurdles
2. User and employee drivers and hurdles
3. Technology drivers and hurdles
4. Environmental drivers and hurdles.
5. Vendors
6. Competitive benchmarking.

WHY USE THIS METHOD?

1. This method helps identify where resources should be focused for most return on investment.
2. Enables stakeholders to understand other stakeholders expectations.

CHALLENGES

1. It provides a tangible focus for discussion.
2. It draws out tacit knowledge from your team.
3. It helps build team consensus.
4. It drives insights
5. Don't get too detailed
6. Some information may be sensitive.

WHEN TO USE THIS METHOD

1. Define intent
2. Know Context
3. Know User
4. Frame insights

HOW TO USE THIS METHOD

1. Define the problem.
2. Find a moderator
3. Brainstorm hopes and hurdles
   ◦ Which are our own advantages?
   ◦ What are we able to do quite well?
   ◦ What strategic resources can we rely upon?
   ◦ What could we enhance?
   ◦ What should we avoid to do?
   ◦ What are we doing poorly?
4. Collect the ideas on a white board or wall with post-it-notes.
5. Organize the contributions into two lists.
6. Prioritize each element
7. Use the lists to create strategic options.

RESOURCES

1. White board
2. Marker pens
3. Post-it notes
4. Flip chart
5. Video Camera
6. Camera

TASK	NAME	DATE	CONCERNS

allocating tasks

WHAT IS IT?

This method can be used in each meeting to ensure that the things that need to be done are assigned to someone and dates are assigned to each action. One of the most common problems with large projects can be overshooting due dates. This is a simple but effective method that helps keep a project on schedule and budget.

WHY USE THIS METHOD?

1. It ensures that things get done on time
2. It ensures that each person knows their responsibilities

CHALLENGES

3. Team members concerns can be included on the list.

WHEN TO USE THIS METHOD

1. Define intent
2. Know Context
3. Know User
4. Frame insights

HOW TO USE THIS METHOD

1. At the end of each meeting the moderator lists a number of things that need to be done. Each action has a team member assigned with a due date.
2. This list can be distributed after the meeting by e-mail.
3. At the start of the next meeting the list from the previous meeting is reviewed and each team member reports on progress.

RESOURCES

1. White board
2. Marker pens
3. Post-it notes
4. Flip chart
5. Camera

Chapter 3
Defining the vision
what are we looking for?

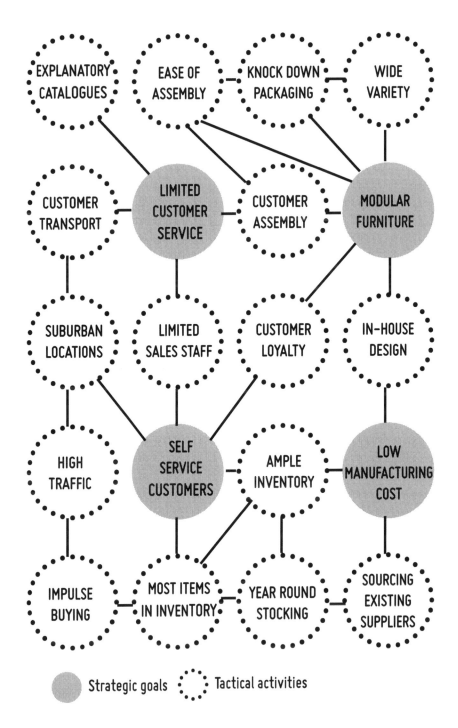

Activity map for Ikea (after Porter)

Strategic goals ⬤   Tactical activities ⚬

activity map

WHAT IS IT?

An activity map is a map that show a companies strategic position in relation to company activities. A number of higher order strategic themes are implemented through linked activities.

WHO INVENTED IT?

Walt Disney Corporation 1957

WHY USE THIS METHOD?

1. Activity maps are useful for understanding and strengthening organizational strategy.
2. The value of individual activities cannot be separated from the system of activities.
3. Helps develop a unique competitive position.
4. Helps align activities with strategy
5. Helps understand trade off and choices.

WHEN TO USE THIS METHOD

1. Define intent
2. Know Context
3. Know User
4. Frame insights

HOW TO USE THIS METHOD

1. Is each activity contributing positively to the overall strategy, and customer needs?
2. Are there ways of making the activities and the relationships of activities support strategy better?

REFERENCES

1. Michael E Porter. What is Strategy? Harvard Business Review November–December 1996

backcasting

WHAT IS IT?
Backcasting is a method for planning
the actions necessary to reach desired
future goals. This method is often applied
in a workshop format with stakeholders
participating. The future scenarios are
developed for periods of between 1 and 20
years in the future.

The participants first identify their goals and
then work backwards to identify the
necessary actions to reach those goals.

WHO INVENTED IT?
AT&T 1950s, Shell 1970s

WHY USE THIS METHOD?
1. It is inexpensive and fast
2. Backcasting is a tool for identifying,
   planning and reaching future goals.
3. Backcasting provides a strategy to reach
   future goals.

CHALLENGES
1. Need a good moderator
2. Needs good preparation

RESOURCES
1. Post-it-notes
2. White board
3. Pens
4. Dry-erase markers
5. Cameras

WHEN TO USE THIS METHOD
1. Define intent
2. Know Context
3. Know User
4. Frame insights
5. Explore Concepts
6. Make Plans
7. Deliver Offering

HOW TO USE THIS METHOD
A typical backcasting question is "How would
you define success for yourself in 2015?
1. Define a framework
2. Analyze the present situation in relation
   to the framework
3. Prepare a vision and a number of desirable
   future scenarios.
4. Back-casting: Identify the steps to
   achieve this goal.
5. Further elaboration, detailing
6. Step by step strategies towards achieving
   the outcomes desired.
7. Ask do the strategies move us in the right
   direction? Are they flexible strategies?.
   Do the strategies represent a good return
   on investment?
8. Implementation, policy, organization
   embedding, follow-up

REFERENCES
1. Quist, J., & Vergragt, P. 2006. Past and
   future of backcasting: The shift to
   stakeholder participation and a proposal
   for a methodological framework. Futures
   Volume 38, Issue 9, November 2006,
   1027-1045

banned

WHAT IS IT?

Banned is a method involving creating future scenarios based on imagining a world if a product, service system or experience did not exist and how people would possibly adapt.

WHO INVENTED IT?

Herman Kahn, Rand Corporation 1950, US

WHY USE THIS METHOD?

1. May uncover new design directions and possibilities not dependent on existing products services and systems.
2. Expose problems and opportunities.
3. Banned Scenarios become a focus for discussion related to a user experience. which helps evaluate and refine concepts. They can be used to challenge concepts through prototyping user interactions.

REFERENCES

1. "Scenarios," IDEO Method Cards. ISBN 0-9544132-1-0
2. Carroll, John M. Making Use: Scenario-based design of human-computer interactions. MIT Press, 2000.
3. Carroll J. M. Five Reasons for Scenario Based Design. Elsevier Science B. V. 2000.
4. Carroll, John M. Scenario-Based Design: Envisioning Work and Technology in System Development.

WHEN TO USE THIS METHOD

1. Know Context
2. Know User
3. Frame insights
4. Generate Concepts

HOW TO USE THIS METHOD

This exercise can be done individually or in group.

1. Decide the question to investigate.
2. Decide time and scope for the scenario process.
3. Identify stake holders.
4. Identify uncertainties.
5. Define the scenarios.
6. Can use with personas. Who is the persona? What is the experience? What is the outcome?
7. Create storyboards.
8. Analyze the scenarios through discussion.
9. Iterate as necessary.
10. Summarize insights

RESOURCES

1. Storyboard templates
2. Post-it-notes
3. Pens
4. Dry-erase markers
5. Video cameras
6. Empathy tools
7. Props

benefits map

WHAT IS IT?

The benefits map is a simple tool that helps your team decide what will give you the best return on investment for time invested

WHY USE THIS METHOD?

1. Aids communication and discussion within the organization.
2. It is human nature to do tasks which are not most urgent first.
3. To gain competitive advantage,
4. Helps build competitive strategy
5. Helps build communication strategy
6. Helps manage time effectively

CHALLENGES

1. Can be subjective

WHEN TO USE THIS METHOD

1. Know Context
2. Know User
3. Frame insights
4. Explore Concepts

HOW TO USE THIS METHOD

1. Moderator draws axes on whiteboard or flip chart.
2. Worthwhile activity at the start of a project.
3. Map individual tasks.
4. Interpret the map.
5. Create strategy.
6. Tasks which have high benefit with low investment may be given priority.

RESOURCES

1. Pen
2. Paper
3. White board
4. Dry erase markers

blue ocean strategy

WHAT IS IT?

Blue Ocean Strategy is a business strategy proposed by W. Chan Kim and Renée Mauborgne. The authors propose that companies can experience high growth and profits by exploiting "blue ocean" or uncontested, differentiated market spaces.

Blue Ocean strategy:

1. Create uncontested market space
2. Make competition irrelevant.
3. Create and capture new demand.
4. Break the value-cost trade off.
5. Align the whole system of a company's activities in pursuit of differentiation and low cost.

Red Ocean Strategy

6. Compete in existing market place.
7. Beat the competition.
8. Exploit existing demand.
9. Make the value-cost trade off.
10. Align the whole system of a company's activities with it's strategic choice of differentiation or low cost.

WHO INVENTED IT?

W. Chan Kim and Renée Mauborgne 2004

WHY USE THIS METHOD?

1. BOS contains a road map for assessing a company and its business and strategy.
2. Useful for mature companies that need new strategy.
3. A number of methods that help an an organization understand what value they are delivering.

CHALLENGES

1. Blue Ocean Strategy does not define where or how to find Blue Oceans.
2. Some critics of the Blue Ocean approach suggest that the strategy is a new way of packaging old ideas.

WHEN TO USE THIS METHOD

1. Define intent
2. Know Context
3. Know User
4. Frame insights
5. Explore Concepts
6. Make Plans
7. Deliver Offering

REFERENCES

1. Kim and Mauborgne. Blue Ocean Strategy. Harvard Business School Press. 2005.
2. Kim, Chan (2005). Blue Ocean Strategy. Boston: Harvard Business School Press. p. 210. ISBN 1-59139-619-0.

BRAND	BRAND A	BRAND B	BRAND C	BRAND D
BRAND STATEMENT				
VALUE PROPOSITION				
TARGET CUSTOMERS				
BUSINESS MODEL				
TECHNOLOGY				
ENVIRONMENTAL PERFORMANCE				
KEY DIFFERENTIATION				

competitive analysis

WHAT IS IT?

Competitor analysis is a strategic design tool that can identify opportunities and threats. Comparing competitors using one framework is an essential tool of corporate strategy. Most design is created based on less formal impressions and intuition creating blind spots due to lack of rigorous methodology.

WHY USE THIS METHOD?

1. Allows awareness and adoption of best practices.
2. Helps in strategy for differentiation of products and services.
3. Shows how products, services and experiences can be improved.
4. Identifies opportunities.
5. Identifies threats.
6. Allows an organization to be more flexible and agile in a changing environment.

WHEN TO USE THIS METHOD

1. Define intent
2. Know Context
3. Know User
4. Frame insights

HOW TO USE THIS METHOD

1. A competitive analysis includes five factors:
o   Your competitors.
o   Competitor product offerings.
o   Competitor weaknesses and strengths.
o   Competitor strategies.
o   The market trends
2. Track competitors performance over time to understand trends.

RESOURCES

1. Paper
2. Pens
3. Camera
4. Research data

REFERENCES

1. Craig Fleisher and Babette Bensoussan: "Business and Competitive Analysis: Effective Application of New and Classic Methods." FT Press, 2007.
2. Craig Fleisher and Babette Bensoussan: "Strategic and Competitive Analysis: Methods and Techniques for Analyzing Business Competition." Prentice Hall, 2003.
3. Ian Gordon: Beat the Competition. How to Use Competitive Intelligence to Develop Winning Business Strategies. Basil Blackwell Publishers, Oxford/UK 1989

TRENDS	POLITICAL	ECONOMIC	USER NEEDS	TECHNOLOGY	UNCERTAINTIES	TRENDS

context map

WHAT IS IT?

A context map is a tool for representing complex factors affecting an organization or design visually. Context maps are sometimes used by directors or organizations as a tool to enable discussion of the effects of change and related interacting business, cultural and environmental factors in order to create a strategic vision for an organization. A context map can be used to analyze trends

WHO INVENTED IT?

Joseph D. Novak Cornell University 1970s.

WHY USE THIS METHOD?

Uses include:
1. New knowledge creation
2. Documenting the knowledge existing informally within an organization.
3. Creating a shared strategic vision

WHEN TO USE THIS METHOD

1. Define intent
2. Know Context
3. Know User
4. Frame insights

RESOURCES

1. Template
2. White board
3. Paper flip chart
4. Pens
5. Dry-erase markers
6. Post-it-notes

HOW TO USE THIS METHOD

1. Put together a team of between 4 and 20 participants with diverse backgrounds and outlooks.
2. Appoint a good moderator
3. Prepare a space. Use a private room with a white board or large wall.
4. Distribute post-it notes to each participant.
5. Brainstorm the list of factors one at a time.
6. These can include Trends, technology, trends, political factors, economic climate customer needs, uncertainties.
7. Each participant can contribute.
8. All contributions are recorded on the white board or on the wall with the post-it-notes.
9. When all factors have been discussed prioritize each group of contributions to identify the most critical.
10. This can be done by rearranging the post-it-notes or white board notes.
11. Video the session and photograph the notes after the session.
12. Analyze the map and create strategy.

REFERENCES

1. Context Map: A Method to Represent the Interactions Between Students' Learning and Multiple Context Factors written by Gyoungho Lee and Lei Bao Physics Education Research Conference 2002

consistency inspections

WHAT IS IT?

Consistency inspections determine if multiple products, services or experiences from the same family are consistent in their design and operation.

WHY USE THIS METHOD?

Consistency across a family of products or services can:

1. Improve the usability,
2. Reduce necessary learning
3. Reduce errors.
4. Provide a consistent brand message.
5. They reduce the likelihood of confusion or negative transfer when using different products in the same suite of tools.

CHALLENGES

1. Defining the acceptable range of consistency.

WHEN TO USE THIS METHOD

1. Know Context
2. Know User
3. Frame insights
4. Know Context
5. Know User
6. Frame insights

HOW TO USE THIS METHOD

1. Select a team of 4 to 8 with diverse backgrounds.
2. Define the family of products, services or experiences to evaluate.
3. Define the attributes to evaluate for consistency.
4. Define the consistency reference for comparison such as a style guide.
5. Define the definition of consistency and the acceptable variation of consistency.
6. Categorize and prioritize the consistency issues

RESOURCES

1. Products for assessment
2. Camera
3. Notebook
4. Pens
5. White board

REFERENCES

1. Wixon, Dennis, et. al., "Inspections and Design Reviews: Framework, History, and Reflection," in Nielsen, Jacob, and Mack, R. ends, Usability Inspection Methods, 1994, John Wiley and Sons, New York, NY. ISBN 0-471-01877-5 (hardcover)
2. Nielsen, Jacob, Usability Inspection Tutorial, 1995, CHI '95 Proceedings

critical design

WHAT IS IT?

Critical design uses design as a vehicle for commentary on consumer culture. Both the design and the process of design promote thinking about existing values, practices and culture.

A critical design can challenge its audience's preconceptions and expectations. The approach is related to that of Italian Radical Design of the 1970s.

"Critical Design uses speculative design proposals to challenge narrow assumptions, preconceptions and givens about the role products play in everyday life. It is more of an attitude than anything else, a position rather than a method."

Anthony Dunne & Fiona Raby

WHO INVENTED IT?

The term Critical Design was first used in Anthony Dunne's book "Hertzian Tales" 1999

WHY USE THIS METHOD?

1. To raise awareness
2. Expose assumptions
3. Provoke action.
4. To spark debate,
5. A method of critiquing social, cultural, technical and economic systems through designing critical artefacts

CHALLENGES

1. Critical design works outside usual commercial framework of design.

WHEN TO USE THIS METHOD

1. Know Context
2. Know User
3. Frame insights
4. Explore Concept

REFERENCES

1. Dunne, Anthony (1999). Hertzian tales : electronic products, aesthetic experience and critical design. London: Royal College of Art computer related design research studio. pp. 117. ISBN 1-874175-27-6.
2. Flanagan, Mary (2009). Critical Play:Radical Game Design. Cambridge: MIT Press. ISBN 978-0-262-06268-8.
3. Raby, Fiona (2001). Design Noir: The Secret Life of Electronic Objects. Basel: Birkhäuser. ISBN 978-3-7643-6566-0.
4. Sanders, Elizabeth B.-N. (September 2006). "Design Research in 2006". Design Research Quarterly 1 (1): 1—8. ISSN 0142-694X.

design intent

WHAT IS IT?

Designs are created for a purpose. The design intent is a written statement of the creative objectives of the design While not describing the final design solution, the design intent provides the design team with a target for their efforts. It often gives a description of the problem to be sold, information about how the solution will be used.

WHY USE THIS METHOD?

1. A design intent statement provides a focus for design efforts throughout a project.

CHALLENGES

1. The statement of intent should be clear and unambiguous to all team members.

WHEN TO USE THIS METHOD

1. Define intent

HOW TO USE THIS METHOD

1. A design intent statement is best based on an understanding of a particular problem being addressed or a need identified.
2. This can be the result of research such as observation or interviews with the user group.
3. It includes information about the scope of the solution.

QUESTIONS FOR DESIGN INTENT

1. Is the problem clear?
2. Are the objectives clear?
3. Is there agreement on the design intent by all stakeholders?
4. What are the constraints?
5. Have assumptions been tested?
6. What are the risks?
7. What are the business objectives
8. What re the user objectives
9. What are the environmental objectives
10. What are the technology objectives?

Photo: photocase.com – complize

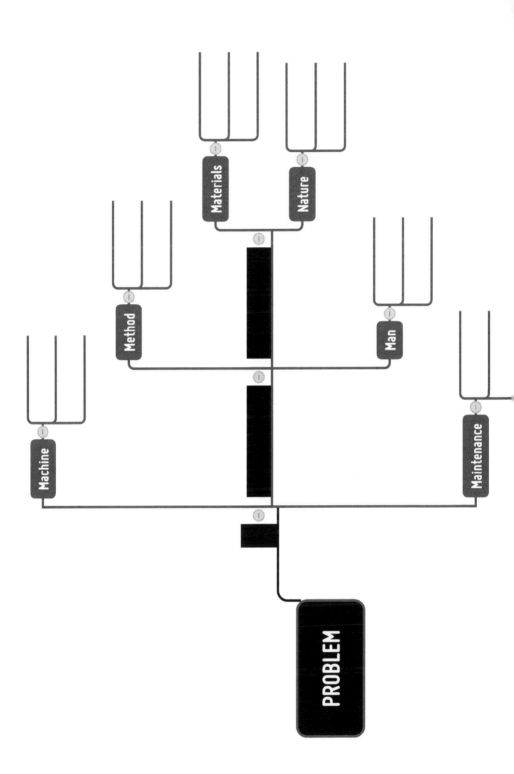

fishbone diagrams

WHAT IS IT?

Fishbone diagrams also called Ishikawa diagrams, are diagrams that show the causes of a specific event. Mazda Motors used an Ishikawa diagram to design the Miata sports car, The goal was "Jinba Ittai" Horse and Rider as One. Every factor identified in the diagram was included in the final design. Ishikawa described the process as fishboning your problem and letting it cook overnight.

WHO INVENTED IT?

Kaoru Ishikawa University of Tokyo 1968

WHY USE THIS METHOD?

1. People tend to fix a problem by responding to an immediately visible cause while ignoring the deeper issues. This approach may lead to a problem reoccurring.
2. Use in the predesign phase to understand the root causes of a problem to serve as the basis for design.
3. Identifies the relationship between cause and effect.

WHEN TO USE THIS METHOD

1. Define intent
2. Know Context
3. Know User
4. Frame insights

HOW TO USE THIS METHOD

1. Prepare the six arms of the Ishikawa Diagram on a white board.
2. Define the problem clearly as a short statement in the head of the diagram.
3. Describe the causes of each bone and write them at the end of each branch. Use the 4 M's as categories; Machine, Man Methods, Materials.
4. Conduct the brainstorming session using brainstorming guidelines Ask each team member to define the cause of the problem. You may list as many causes as necessary. Typically 3 to 6 are listed.
5. Minor causes are then listed around the major causes.
6. Interpret the Ishikawa Diagram once it's finished.

RESOURCES

1. White board
2. Dry-erase markers
3. Room with privacy
4. Paper
5. Pens

REFERENCES

1. Ishikawa, Kaoru, Guide to Quality Control, Asian Productivity Organization, UNIPUB, 1976, ISBN 92-833-1036-5
2. Ishikawa, Kaoru (1990); (Translator: J. H. Loftus); Introduction to Quality Control; 448 p; ISBN 4-906224-61-X OCLC 41428

goal hierarchy

WHAT IS IT?

This method is a model for organizing goals. This method helps an organization find the best balance between short-term goals, medium-term goals, and long-term goals

WHY USE THIS METHOD?

1. Allows stakeholder alignment on actions necessary to achieve goals
2. Assures that project goals are aligned with company goals.

WHEN TO USE THIS METHOD

1. Define intent

HOW TO USE THIS METHOD

1. Create a list of goals using a method such as SMART.
2. With your team describe the objectives to the two questions "How?" And "Why?"
3. Do the goals make sense?
4. Are they measurable and consistent with organizational goals?

RESOURCES

1. White board
2. Dry-erase markers
3. Room with privacy
4. Paper
5. Pens

scope

WHAT IS IT?

This is a method that helps your design team define what is inside and outside of the cope. It is a useful exercise early in the design process.

WHY USE THIS METHOD?

1. It helps define the scope
2. It helps define the problems too be addressed in a project.
3. It helps align the design team

WHEN TO USE THIS METHOD

1. Define intent

HOW TO USE THIS METHOD

2. The moderator starts with the wwwwwh method by asking the team.
3. Who, why, when, what, where and how?
4. Two lists are created on a white board headed "In Scope" and "Out of scope"
5. Review the two lists

RESOURCES

1. White board
2. Dry-erase markers
3. Room with privacy
4. Paper
5. Pens

literature review

WHAT IS IT?

A literature is a detailed review of books, articles dissertations, conference proceedings and other written sources relevant to a particular area of researcher design project providing a description, summary, and critical evaluation of each source. The purpose is to review and understand the body of knowledge that exists on a subject.

WHY USE THIS METHOD?

1. To create a summary of literature published on a topic.
2. To understand the body of knowledge that exists on a subject.
3. Place each work in the context of other works.
4. Identify gaps in previous research
5. Identify areas of existing research to prevent duplication of effort
6. To identify areas of possible further research

WHEN TO USE THIS METHOD

1. Know Context
2. Know User
3. Frame insights

HOW TO USE THIS METHOD

1. Define your area of interest
2. Plan your search.
3. Identify key authors
4. Define the scope
5. Define the style of your review
6. Identify sources and search tools.
7. Search the literature.
8. Manage your references
9. Critically analyze the information
10. Synthesize the information.
11. Write the review.

John Kinstler

RESOURCES

1. Computer
2. Literature sources

REFERENCES

1. Hart, C. (1998) Doing a Literature Review: Releasing the Social Science Research Imagination. United Kingdom. London: Sage ISBN 0-7619-5974-2
2. Hart, C. (2008) 'Literature Reviewing and Argumentation''. In The Postgraduate's Companion, (eds.) Gerard Hall and Jo Longman. UK Grad. United Kingdom. London: Sage ISBN 978-1-4129-3026-0
3. Machi, L.A. (2009). The Literature Review: Six Steps to Success. Thousand Oaks, California: Corwin Press. 1 Pages 194.
4. Book cover from Amazon.com
5. Fink, A (2009). Conducting research literature reviews : from the internet to paper. 3rd ed. Los Angeles : Sage. p.51-53

johari's window

WHAT IS IT?

The Johari window is a method of understanding relationships between people. Helps us understand how others see us and how we see ourselves. It helps communicate information about people and perceptions.

WHO INVENTED IT?

Joseph Luft and Harry Ingham 1955 combining their first names, Joe and Harry.

WHY USE THIS METHOD?

1. The Johari window is a way of representing information about people feelings, experiences, attitudes, skills,and motivation, from four perspectives.
2. Helps identify what are the gaps in knowledge and where further research needs to be undertaken.

WHEN TO USE THIS METHOD

1. Know Context
2. Know User
3. Frame insights

RESOURCES

1. Paper
2. Pens
3. White board
4. Dry erase markers

HOW TO USE THIS METHOD

1. Open: The team and participants select adjectives to place in this quadrant that describe the traits of the subjects that both are aware of.
2. Hidden: Adjectives are selected by subjects to describe the traits that the team are not aware of.
3. Blind Spot: These adjectives are selected by the team to describe things that the subjects are not aware of but others are.
4. Unknown: These are adjectives not selected by either the team or the subjects in other quadrants.

REFERENCES

1. Hase, Steward; Alan Davies, Bob Dick (1999). The Johari Window and the Dark Side of Organizations. Southern Cross University.

Photo: photocase.com – zabalotta

KNOWN TO SELF   NOT KNOWN TO SELF

KNOWN TO OTHERS

                              ARENA | BLIND SPOT
                             FACADE | UNKNOWN

NOT KNOWN TO OTHERS

johari's window

ADJECTIVES

able
accepting
adaptable
bold
brave
calm
caring
cheerful
clever
complex
confident
dependable
dignified
Energetic
extroverted
friendly
giving
happy
helpful
idealistic
independent
ingenious
intelligent
introverted
kind
knowledgeable
logical
loving

mature
modest
nervous
observant
organized
patient
powerful
proud
quiet
reflective
relaxed
religious
responsive
searching
self-assertive
self-conscious
sensible
sentimental
shy
silly
smart
spontaneous
sympathetic
tense
trustworthy
warm
wise
witty

MIND MAP

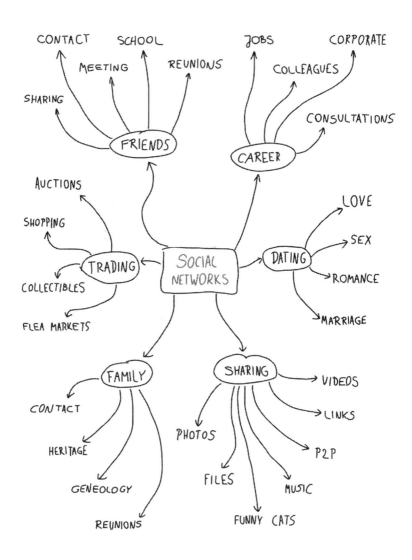

mind map

WHAT IS IT?

A mind map is a diagram used to represent the affinities or connections between a number of ideas or things. Understanding connections is the starting point for design. Mind maps are a method of analyzing information and relationships.

WHO INVENTED IT?

Porphry of Tyros 3rd century BC.
Allan Collins, Northwestern University 1960, USA

WHY USE THIS METHOD?

1. The method helps identify relationships.
2. There is no right or wrong with mind maps. They help with they help with memory and organization.
3. Problem solving and brainstorming
4. Relationship discovery
5. Summarizing information
6. Memorizing information

CHALLENGES

Print words clearly, use color and images for visual impact.

WHEN TO USE THIS METHOD

7. Know Context
8. Know User
9. Frame insights
10. Explore Concepts
11. Make Plans

HOW TO USE THIS METHOD

1. Start in the center with a key word or idea. Put box around this node.
2. Use images, symbols, or words for nodes.
3. Select key words.
4. Keep the key word names of nodes s simple and short as possible.
5. Associated nodes should be connected with lines to show affinities.
6. Make the lines the same length as the word/image they support.
7. Use emphasis such as thicker lines to show the strength of associations in your mind map.
8. Use radial arrangement of nodes.

RESOURCES

1. Paper
2. Pens
3. White board
4. Dry-erase markers

REFERENCES

1. Mind maps as active learning tools', by Willis, CL. Journal of computing sciences in colleges. ISSN: 1937-4771. 2006. Volume: 21 Issue: 4
2. Mind Maps as Classroom Exercises John W. Budd The Journal of Economic Education, Vol. 35, No. 1 (Winter, 2004), pp. 35-46 Published by: Taylor & Francis, Ltd.

objectives tree

WHAT IS IT?
Objective Tree method, also known as decision tree, is a tool for clarifying the goals of a project.

The objective tree method shows a structured hierarchy of goals with higher level goals branching into related groups of sub goals.

WHY USE THIS METHOD?
1. An objectives tree is a visual way of mapping your design objectives so that you can discuss and refine them.
2. Building a better understanding of the project objectives.
3. It is a way to refine vague goals into more concrete and achievable goals.
4. Build stakeholder consensus.
5. Identify potential constraints

CHALLENGES
1. Consider the likely stakeholders and constraints.
2. Be precise

SEE ALSO
1. Decision tree
2. Concept tree
3. Problem tree

WHEN TO USE THIS METHOD
1. Define intent

HOW TO USE THIS METHOD
1. Prepare a list of design objectives. This can be done by brainstorming within your team and by undertaking research of your customers, their needs and desires. You can create an objective tree from a problem tree. Convert each problem into an objective.
2. Create a written list of objectives.
3. Create lists of higher and lower level objectives by sorting your original list of objectives. This can be done with an affinity diagram.
4. Create an objectives tree, showing hierarchical relationships and interconnections
5. Place each task in a box.
6. Connect the boxes with lines show associations.
7. Iterate.
8. Make the task descriptions as simple as possible

RESOURCES
1. White board
2. Dry-erase markers.

REFERENCES
1. ODI (2009): Problem Tree Analysis. Successful Communication: Planning Tools. London: ODI
2. Campbell, K.l.i.; Garforth, C.; Heffernan, C.; Morton, J.; Paterson, R.; Rymer, C. ; Upton, M. (2006): The Problem Tree. Analysis of the causes and effects of problems. The Problem Tree. Analysis of the causes and effects of problems.

smart goals

WHAT IS IT?
SMART is a method of setting objectives.

WHY USE THIS METHOD?
1. SMART is a thorough and effective way of setting goals for a project.

WHO INVENTED IT?
George T. Doran 1981

WHEN TO USE THIS METHOD
1. Define intent

RESOURCES
1. White board
2. Dry-erase markers.
3. Paper
4. Pens

REFERENCES
1. Doran, G. T. (1981). There's a S.M.A.R.T. way to write management's goals and objectives. Management Review, Volume 70, Issue 11(AMA FORUM), pp. 35–36.

HOW TO USE THIS METHOD
1. Brainstorm with your team the goals of the project using the SMART mnemonic.
2. A moderator can list the headings on a white board and team members can contribute individual goals using post-it-notes.
3. A specific goal will usually answer the five "W" questions: what,why, where, when, which.
4. Letter: S. Major term Specific. Minor terms Significant, Stretching, Simple
5. Letter M Major term Measurable Minor term Meaningful, Motivational, Manageable
6. Letter: A. Major term Attainable. Minor terms: Appropriate, Achievable, Agreed, Assignable, Actionable, Adjustable, Ambitious, Aligned, Aspirational, Acceptable, Action-focused
7. Letter: R. Major term Relevant. Minor terms Result-Based, Results-oriented, Resourced, Resonant, Realistic
8. Letter: T. Major term Timely. Minor terms Time-oriented, Time framed, Timed, Time-based, Timeboxed, Time-bound, Time-Specific, Timetabled, Time limited, Trackable, Tangible

tasks and deliverables

WHAT IS IT?
One of the most useful activities at the start of a project is to define the objectives, tasks and deliverables

WHY USE THIS METHOD?
1. It is a critical planning tool that defines for the key stakeholders what are the objective of the project, what will be delivered and how this will be done.
2. This tool allows stakeholders to reach a common understanding early in the project.

CHALLENGES
1. An area of common misunderstanding between a client and designer is the precise nature of what will be delivered.

WHEN TO USE THIS METHOD
1. Define intent

HOW TO USE THIS METHOD
1. The moderator creates a list of each project objective and related deliverables, tasks, whether it is in scope, potential costs, resources and success and comments.
2. The group brainstorms to create a realistic lists of tasks and deliverables.
3. The list is photographed and documented after the meeting.

RESOURCES
1. White board
2. Dry erase markets
3. Pen
4. Paper
5. Camera

triptych

WHAT IS IT?

The triptych method is a triangulation method that obtains three different points of view on a question. Three different stakeholder groups for example the design team, the client stakeholders and a user group are asked the questions to see if the answers are the same.

WHY USE THIS METHOD?

1. The method identifies areas of misalignment early in a project which can save cost and time in realignment later in a project.

CHALLENGES

1. Major stakeholder groups sometimes not in alignment on key questions

WHEN TO USE THIS METHOD

1. Define intent

HOW TO USE THIS METHOD

1. Identify three stakeholder groups
2. Prep[are question guide
3. Arrange interview sessions
4. Conduct interviews
5. Analyze the results
6. Identify areas of alignment and areas of conflict between the views of the groups.

RESOURCES

1. Pen
2. Paper
3. Camera
4. Digital voice recorder

prediction markets

WHAT IS IT?

Prediction markets are speculative markets that make predictions. They are used by businesses and governments to harvest the wisdom of the crowd for forecasting the future. The model is similar to the stock exchange. Prediction markets may involve hundreds of thousands of participants. A famous example of a prediction market is the Hollywood stock exchange.

WHO INVENTED IT?

Robin Hanson 1990. In October 2007 companies from the US, and a number of European countries formed the Prediction Market Industry Association.

WHY USE THIS METHOD?

1. It is a way of predicting the future.
2. They motivate people to think about the future.

CHALLENGES

1. Because online gambling in the US is illegal due to federal and Sate laws, many prediction markets operate using play or virtual money.
2. Participants need to be informed about events and trends.

WHEN TO USE THIS METHOD

1. Defining a vision

RESOURCES

1. Pen
2. Paper
3. White board
4. Dry erase markers
5.

REFERENCES

1. Douglas W. Hubbard, *How to Measure Anything: Finding the Value of Intangibles in Business", John Wiley & Sons, July 2007
2. Graefe, A. & Armstrong, J.S. (2011). Comparing face-to-face meetings, nominal groups, Delphi and prediction markets on an estimation task, International Journal of Forecasting, 27(1), 183-195

PROBLEM TREE

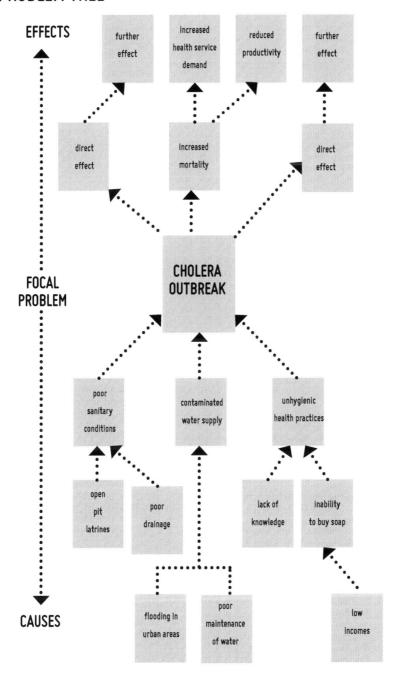

Source: Adapted from Water Supply and Sanitation Collaborative Council

problem tree

WHAT IS IT?

A problem tree is a tool for clarifying the problems being addressed by a design project. The problem tree shows a structured hierarchy of problems being addressed with higher level problems branching into related groups of sub-problems.

WHY USE THIS METHOD?

1. A problem tree is a visual way of mapping your design problems so that you can discuss and refine them.
2. It is useful for identify a core problem and it's and root causes
3. It is a way to refine vague problems into more concrete and solvable goals.
4. The problem tree often helps build a shared sense of understanding, purpose and action.

CHALLENGES

1. Consider the likely stakeholders and constraints.
2. It may be difficult to understand all effects and causes of a problem early in a project.

WHEN TO USE THIS METHOD

1. Define intent

HOW TO USE THIS METHOD

1. Imagine a large tree with its trunk, branches, leaves, primary and secondary roots.
2. Write the main problem/concern in the center of a large flip chart (trunk).
3. Add the causes of the main problem onto the chart below the main problem, with arrows leading to the problem (primary roots).
4. For each of the causes, write the factors that lead to them, again using arrows to show how each one contributes (secondary roots).
5. Draw arrows leading upwards from the main problem to the various effects/consequences of that problem (branches).
6. For each of these effects, add any further effects/consequences (leaves).

Source: Adapted from Water Supply and Sanitation Collaborative Council

RESOURCES

1. Pen
2. Paper
3. White board

REFERENCES

1. ODI (2009): Problem Tree Analysis. Successful Communication: Planning Tools. London: ODI
2. Campbell, K.l.i.; Garforth, C.; Heffernan, C.; Morton, J.; Paterson, R.; Rymer, C. ; Upton, M. (2006): The Problem Tree. Analysis of the causes and effects of problems. The Problem Tree. Analysis of the causes and effects of problems.

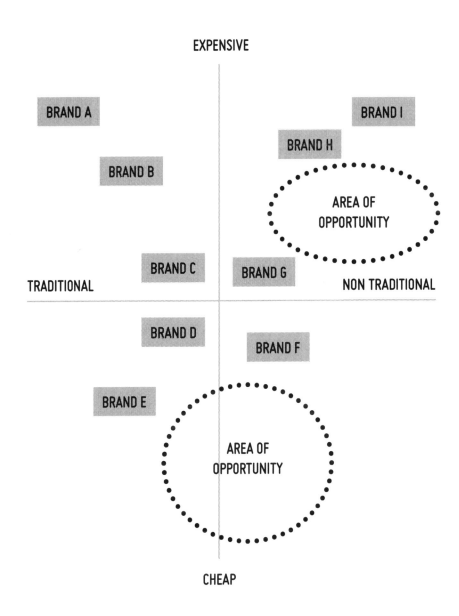

perceptual map

WHAT IS IT?

Perceptual mapping is a method that creates a map of the perceptions of people of competing alternatives to be compared.

WHO INVENTED IT?

Unknown

WHY USE THIS METHOD?

1. Aids communication and discussion within the organization
2. To gain competitive advantage,
3. Helps build competitive strategy
4. Helps build communication strategy
5. Helps identify potential new products
6. Helps build brand strategy

CHALLENGES

1. Because the position of a product or service on the map is subjective, you can ask several people to locate the position through group discussion.
2. Works well for clearly defined functional attributes such as price, product features

WHEN TO USE THIS METHOD

1. Know Context
2. Know User
3. Frame insights
4. Explore Concepts

HOW TO USE THIS METHOD

1. Define characteristics of product or service to map.
2. Identify competing brands, services or products to map.
3. Map individual items.
4. Interpret the map.
5. Create strategy.

RESOURCES

1. Pen
2. Paper
3. White board
4. Dry erase markers

pest analysis

WHAT IS IT?
PEST analysis is a type of situational analysis which reviews Political, Economic, Social, and Technological factors.

1. **Political.** These include government regulations in areas such as employment, environment and tax.
2. **Economic.** These include the health of the economy, the changing values of currencies and loan rates.
3. **Social.** Market size, demographics, customer needs and desires.
4. **Technological.** Materials and processes, automation, technological change.

WHO INVENTED IT?
Francis J. Aguilar 1967

WHY USE THIS METHOD?
PEST analysis is an audit of an organization's environmental influences to assist in strategic planning.

CHALLENGES
1. A PEST analysis can be used prior to undertaking a SWOT analysis to better understand opportunities and threats.

WHEN TO USE THIS METHOD
1. Know Context
2. Know User
3. Frame insights

HOW TO USE THIS METHOD
1. Appoint a moderator.
2. Brainstorm influences under the following headings
3. The moderator can record the teams suggestions on a white board under the four headings
4. Review and iterate
5. Record with camera.

RESOURCES
1. White board
2. Dry erase markers
3. Camera
4. Paper
5. Pens
6. Post-it-notes

REFERENCES
1. Porter, Michael. "The Five Competitive Forces That Shape Strategy". The Harvard Business Review. Retrieved March 28, 2012.

SOME SAMPLE PEST QUESTIONS

POLITICAL
1. Government trade policy
2. Government financial initiatives.
3. Political lobbyists.
4. Wars international relations
5. Government policies
6. Government electoral cycles
7. Political change
8. Political parties
9. Government organizations

ECONOMIC
1. National economy
2. National economic trends
3. Overseas economies and trends
4. Tax
5. Industrial economics
6. Market trends
7. International trade economics
8. Personal income
9. Employment levels
10. Exchange rates
11. Inflation
12. Interest rates
13. Consumer confidence levels
14. Imports and exports
15. Cost of living

SOCIAL
1. Consumer perceptions
2. Media
3. Social events
4. Purchasing trends
5. Advertising and marketing
6. Ethical issues
7. Demographics
8. Lifestyle
9. Demographic trends.
10. Education
11. Diversity
12. Income
13. Management strategies

TECHNOLOGICAL
1. Alternative technologies
2. Research
3. Related technologies
4. Maturity of technology
5. Manufacturing maturity and capacity
6. Information and communications
7. Consumer buying mechanisms/technology
8. Technology laws
9. Intellectual property issues
10. Communications
11. Innovation
12. Energy

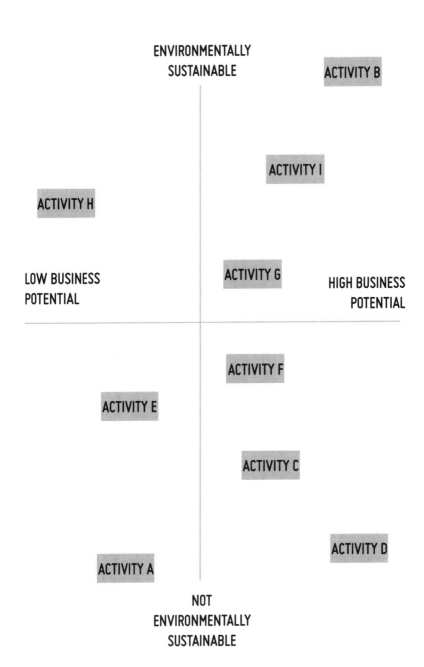

sustainability map

WHAT IS IT?

This method allows the team to assess the relative business potential and environmental impact of products and services.

WHY USE THIS METHOD?

1. Aids communication and discussion within the organization.
2. To gain competitive advantage with environmental sustainability,
3. Helps build competitive strategy
4. Helps build team alignment

CHALLENGES

1. Can be subjective

WHEN TO USE THIS METHOD

1. Know Context
2. Know User
3. Frame insights
4. Explore Concepts

HOW TO USE THIS METHOD

1. Moderator draws grid on whiteboard or flip chart.
2. Team brainstorms
3. Interpret the map.
4. Create strategy.
5. Products and services which have both high environmental sustainability and good business proposition are given priority.

RESOURCES

1. Pen
2. Paper
3. White board
4. Dry erase markers

swot analysis

WHAT IS IT?

SWOT Analysis is a useful technique for understanding your strengths and weaknesses, and for identifying both the opportunities open to you and the threats you face.

WHO INVENTED IT?

Albert Humphrey 1965 Stanford University

WHY USE THIS METHOD?

1. SWOT analysis can help you uncover opportunities that you can exploit.
2. You can analysis both your own organization, product or service as well as those of competitors.
3. Helps develop a strategy of differentiation.
4. It is inexpensive

CHALLENGES

1. Use only verifiable information.
2. Have system for implementation.

WHEN TO USE THIS METHOD

1. Define intent
2. Know Context
3. Know User
4. Frame insights

RESOURCES

1. Post-it-notes
2. SWOT template
3. Pens
4. White board
5. Video camera
6. Dry-erase markers

HOW TO USE THIS METHOD

1. Explain basic rules of brainstorming.
2. Ask questions related to the SWOT categories.
3. Record answers on a white board or video
4. Categorize ideas into groups
5. Consider when evaluating "What will the institution gain or lose?"

REFERENCES

1. Armstrong. M. A handbook of Human Resource Management Practice (10th edition) 2006, Kogan Page, London ISBN 0-7494-4631-5

SOME SAMPLE SWOT QUESTIONS

STRENGTHS

1. Advantages of proposition
2. Capabilities
3. Competitive advantages
4. Marketing – reach, distribution
5. Innovative aspects
6. Location and geographical
7. Price, value, quality?
8. Accreditation, certifications
9. Unique selling proposition
10. Human resources
11. Experience,
12. Assets
13. Return on investment
14. Processes, IT, communications
15. Cultural, attitudinal, behavioral
16. Management cover, succession

WEAKNESSES

1. Value of proposition
2. Things we cannot do.
3. Things we are not good at
4. Perceptions of brand
5. Financial
6. Own known vulnerabilities
7. Time scales, deadlines and pressures
8. Reliability of data, plan predictability
9. Morale, commitment, leadership
10. Accreditation,
11. Cash flow, start-up cash-drain
12. Continuity, supply chain robustness
13. Effects on core activities, distraction
14. Processes and systems
15. Management cover, succession

OPPORTUNITIES

1. Market developments
2. Competitors' vulnerabilities
3. New USP's
4. Tactics – surprise, major contracts
5. Business and product development
6. Information and research
7. Partnerships, agencies, distribution
8. Industrial trends
9. Technologies
10. Innovations
11. Global changes
12. Market opportunities
13. Specialized market niches
14. New exports or imports
15. Volumes, production, economies
16. Seasonal, weather, fashion influences

THREATS

1. Political effects
2. Legislative effects
3. Obstacles faced
4. Insurmountable weaknesses
5. Environmental effects
6. IT developments
7. Competitor intentions
8. Loss of key staff
9. Sustainable financial backing
10. Market demand
11. New technologies, services, ideas
12. Vital contracts and partners
13. Sustaining internal capabilities
14. Economy – home, abroad
15. Seasonality, weather effects

define the problem?

WHAT IS IT?

This is a method for defining the problem being addressed by the design.

WHY USE THIS METHOD?

1. A design needs to address a problem to be successful from all points of view.

CHALLENGES

1. Avoid vague definitions
2. Do not assume a solution
3. Be specific
4. Be aware of the difference between facts, opinions and guesses.

WHEN TO USE THIS METHOD

1. Define intent

HOW TO USE THIS METHOD

1. Hold a brainstorm with stakeholders to explore the question " What is the problem?"
2. Everyone should be able to understand the problem clearly.

Explore the following:

1. Initial problem description
2. Project brief
3. Who are the stakeholders?
4. What will determine our success?
5. What is the scope of the problem and solution?

RESOURCES

1. Pen
2. Paper
3. Whiteboard
4. Dry erase markers
5. Post it notes
6. Video camera.

wwwwwh

WHAT IS IT?

'Who, What, Where, When, Why, and How'? is a method for getting a thorough understanding of the problem, It is used to obtain basic information in police investigations. A well known golden rule of journalism is that if you want to know the full story about something you have to answer all the five W's. Journalists argue your story isn't complete until you answer all six questions.

1. Who is involved?
2. What occurred?
3. When did it happen?
4. Where did it happen?
5. Why did it occur?

"I keep six honest serving-men, They taught me all I knew; Their names are What and Why and When, And How and Where and Who" – *Rudyard Kipling*

WHO INVENTED IT?

Hermagoras of Temnos, Greece 1st century BC.

WHY USE THIS METHOD?

This method helps create a story that communicates clearly the nature of an activity or event to stakeholders.

CHALLENGES

1. The answers may be subjective.

WHEN TO USE THIS METHOD

1. Define intent
2. Know Context
3. Know User
4. Frame insights

HOW TO USE THIS METHOD

1. Ask the questions starting with the 5 w's and 1 h question words.
2. Identify the people involved
3. Identify the activities and make a list of them.
4. Identify all the places and make a list of them.
5. Identify all the time factors and make a list of them.
6. Identify causes for events of actions and make a list of them.
7. Identify the way events took place and make a list of them.
8. Study the relationships between the information.

RESOURCES

1. Pen
2. Paper

SOME SAMPLE
WWWWWH QUESTIONS

WHO
1. Is affected?
2. Who believes that the problem affects them?
3. Needs the problem solved?
4. Does not want the problem to be solved?
5. Could stand in the way of a solution?

WHEN
1. Does it happen
2. Doesn't it happen?
3. Did it start?
4. Will it end?
5. Is the solution needed?
6. Might it happen in the future?
7. Will it be a bigger problem?
8. Will it improve?

WHERE
1. Does it happen?
2. Doesn't it happen
3. Else does it happen?
4. Is the best place to solve the problem

WHY
1. Is this situation a problem?
2. Do you want to solve it?
3. Do you not want to solve it?
4. Does it not go away?
5. Would someone else want to solve it?
6. Can it be solved?
7. Is it difficult to solve?

WHAT
1. May be different in the future
2. Are its weaknesses?
3. Do you like?
4. Makes you unhappy about it?
5. Is flexible?
6. Is not flexible?
7. Do you know?
8. Do you not understand?
9. How have you solved similar problems?
10. Are the underlying ideas?
11. Are the values involved?
12. Are the elements of the problem and how are they related?
13. What can you assume to be correct
14. Is most important
15. Is least important
16. Are your goals?
17. Do you need to discover?

Chapter 4
Information gathering
how can we understand?

a(x4)

WHAT IS IT?

One of a number of ethnographic frameworks have been developed to give structure to observations and to ensure that the researcher doesn't miss important data.

1. Actors
2. Artifacts
3. Atmosphere
4. Actions

WHO INVENTED IT?

Paul Rothstein, Arizona State University 2001

WHY USE THIS METHOD?

1. To give structure to research
2. In order to collect most important information.
3. To provide some certainty in the uncertain environment of fieldwork

HOW TO USE THIS METHOD

Actors

Who are the people you are observing? Tell us through:

a. Photographs
b. Stories of them, their past
c. Simple data such as age, ethnicity,

Artifacts

Show us with photographs, and some annotation:

a. What kinds of objects do they choose to surround themselves with?
b. What objects are important to them? (why?)
c. What do they use on a daily basis?

d. Are there objects that they are dependent on?
e. Take a close look objects that you might be designing or redesigning, and show us through annotated image(s) how that object works or does not work. What does it look like, what needs does it meet? Or not?

Atmosphere

Spending on your project, this becomes more or less important/detailed. You can choose from a variety of approaches:

a. A floor plan of the space if this is relevant.
b. The general environment that you will be designing for (e.g. photographs of their home/work/travel experience).

Actions

This is very detailed. Some firms, advocate doing as second-by-second analysis of all of the steps involved in the activity you will be designing for. Consider the following methods for presenting the information:

a. Video or selected frames from a video
b. Series of photographs (numbered & timed)c. Re-enactment
d. Written list of steps along with noted times

Source: Rothstein, P. (2001). a(x 4): A user-centered method for designing experience. 2001

REFERENCES

1. Rothstein, P. (2001). a(x 4): A user-centered method for designing experience. 2001

aeiou

WHAT IS IT?

One of a number of ethnographic frameworks have been developed to give structure to observations and to ensure that the researcher doesn't miss important data.

Activities: Goal directed sets of actions which people want to accomplish.
Environments: where activities take place
Objects: located in an environment. Their use, function, meaning and context.
Users: The people and their behaviors, preferences and needs.

Source Recording ethnographic observations: palojono

WHO INVENTED IT?

The Doblin Group Elab 1997

WHY USE THIS METHOD?

1. To give structure to research
2. In order to collect most important information.
3. To provide some certainty in the uncertain environment of fieldwork

WHEN TO USE THIS METHOD

1. Know Context
2. Know User
3. Frame insights

RESOURCES

1. Computer
2. Notebook
3. Pens
4. Video camera
5. Digital camera
6. Digital voice recorder
7. Release forms
8. Interview plan or structure
9. Questions, tasks and discussion items

bringing the outside in

WHAT IS IT?

One of a number of ethnographic frameworks have been developed to give structure to observations and to ensure that the researcher doesn't miss important data.

1. Territory
2. Stuff
3. People
4. Authority
5. Talk

WHO INVENTED IT?

Patty Sotirin 1999

WHY USE THIS METHOD?

1. To give structure to research
2. In order to collect most important information.
3. To provide some certainty in the uncertain environment of fieldwork

WHEN TO USE THIS METHOD

1. Know Context
2. Know User
3. Frame insights

REFERENCES

1. Sotirin, P. (1999). Bringing the Outside In: Ethnography in/beyond the Classroom, Presented at the 85th Annual Meeting of the National Communication Association Conference, Ethnography Division, Chicago, Illinois, November 4-7, 1999

Territory:

How are work areas decorated? How are non-work areas designated?
How do people protect their own space?
Architecture: How is space arranged? Who gets more or less?

Stuff:

Who has what? What are private and what are communal possessions?
Furniture: what kinds and how is it arranged?
Visual signs: describe any graphics: what. Where, who looks at it. Who put it !here?
Technology: Who is using what for what purposes? How are access and use controlled and by whom?

People:

What categories do you observe? What flows of people do you observe Press: What are the consistencies and variations'? What patterns do you observe? Bodies: How are different bodies accommodated? Or not? What nonverbal behaviours do you observe?

Authority:

Who has it? Who is subjected to it and when/why? What interactions indicate differences in authority? Challenges to authority (subtle or not)? Affection: how. where, and between whom is it expressed? How often and intensely.,

Talk:

What is said and what vocabularies are in use? Conversation: who talks to whom about what? What kinds of talk rake place where, when,and with whom? How formal or informal'? Vocabularies: what technical or colloquial words ar distinct to this group? What words and names are used frequently?
Source: Soitrin, P. (1999). Bringing the outside in

nine dimensions

WHAT IS IT?

One of a number of ethnographic frameworks have been developed to give structure to observations and to ensure that the researcher doesn't miss important data.

Space: Layout of the physical setting, rooms outdoor spaces etc.
Actors: The names and details of the people involved
Activities: the various activities of the actors
Objects: Physical elements: furniture etc
Acts: Specific Individual actions
Events: Particular occasions Eg meetings
Time: The sequence of events
Goals: What actors are attempting to accomplish
Feelings: Emotions in particular contexts

Source Recording ethnographic observations: palojono

WHO INVENTED IT?

Spradley, J. P. 1980

WHY USE THIS METHOD?

1. To give structure to research
2. In order to collect most important information.
3. To provide some certainty in the uncertain environment of fieldwork

WHEN TO USE THIS METHOD

1. Know Context
2. Know User
3. Frame insights

RESOURCES

1. Computer
2. Notebook
3. Pens
4. Video camera
5. Digital camera
6. Digital voice recorder
7. Release forms
8. Interview plan or structure
9. Questions, tasks and discussion items

REFERENCES

1. Spradley, J. P. (1980). Participant Observation. New York: Holt, Rinehart & Winston.

poems

WHAT IS IT?

One of a number of ethnographic frameworks have been developed to give structure to observations and to ensure that the researcher doesn't miss important data.

the poems framework tags data in order to organize user observations.

1. **People**
2. **Objects**
3. **Environments**
4. **Messages**
5. **Services**

WHO INVENTED IT?

Kumar and Whitney 2003

WHY USE THIS METHOD?

1. To give structure to research
2. In order to collect most important information
3. The POEMS framework is able to be non-linear in time and can cross domains for larger projects.
4. To provide some certainty in the uncertain environment of fieldwork

WHEN TO USE THIS METHOD

1. Know Context
2. Know User
3. Frame insights

RESOURCES

1. Computer
2. Notebook
3. Pens
4. Video camera
5. Digital camera
6. Digital voice recorder
7. Release forms
8. Interview plan or structure
9. Questions, tasks and discussion items

REFERENCES

1. Kumar, V. & Whitney, P. (2003). Faster, Cheaper, Deeper User Research. Design Management Journal, Spring 2003, 50–57. Design Management Institute.

posta

WHAT IS IT?

One of a number of ethnographic frameworks have been developed to give structure to observations and to ensure that the researcher doesn't miss important data.

1. People
2. Objects
3. Settings
4. Time
5. Activities

WHO INVENTED IT?

May have been invented by Pat Sachs Social Solutions and Gitte Jordan Institute for Research on Learning

WHY USE THIS METHOD?

1. To give structure to research
2. In order to collect most important information
3. To provide some certainty in the uncertain environment of fieldwork

WHEN TO USE THIS METHOD

1. Know Context
2. Know User
3. Frame insights

HOW TO USE THIS METHOD

Observe participant in the work setting around, observing what they do and how they interact with other people and tools in their environment. Or they may focus on key objects or artifacts in the environment, with special attention to the various roles that they play (functional, psychological and social). During another observation, the team may take notes and photo-graphs of the work setting and try to understand how the configuration of space mediates the work. Finally, they chart activities, including both formal workflow and informal work practices.

RESOURCES

1. Computer
2. Notebook
3. Pens
4. Video camera
5. Digital camera
6. Digital voice recorder
7. Release forms
8. Interview plan or structure
9. Questions, tasks and discussion items

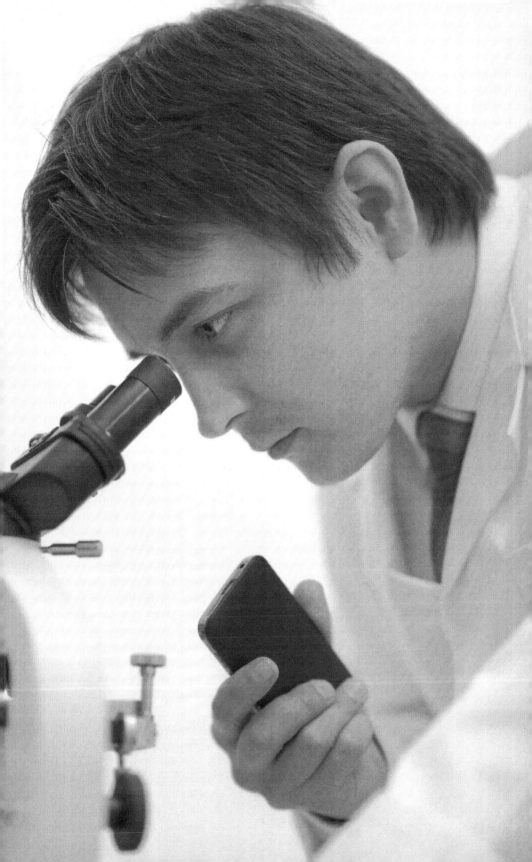

latch

WHAT IS IT?

One of a number of ethnographic frameworks have been developed to give structure to observations and to ensure that the researcher doesn't miss important data.

1. **Location**
   Compare information sources.
2. **Alphabet**
   Used for very large volume of data.
3. **Time**
   Used for events that occur over a measurable duration of time.
4. **Category**
   Grouped by similarity of characteristics.
5. **Hierarchy**
   Information is organized on a scale

WHO INVENTED IT?

Richard Saul Wurman, 1996

WHY USE THIS METHOD?

1. To give structure to research
2. In order to collect most important information.
3. To provide some certainty in the uncertain environment of fieldwork

WHEN TO USE THIS METHOD

1. Know Context
2. Know User
3. Frame insights

RESOURCES

1. Notebook
2. Pens
3. Video camera
4. Digital camera
5. Digital voice recorder
6. Release forms

Chapter 5
Know people and context
what is needed?

ACTORS MAP

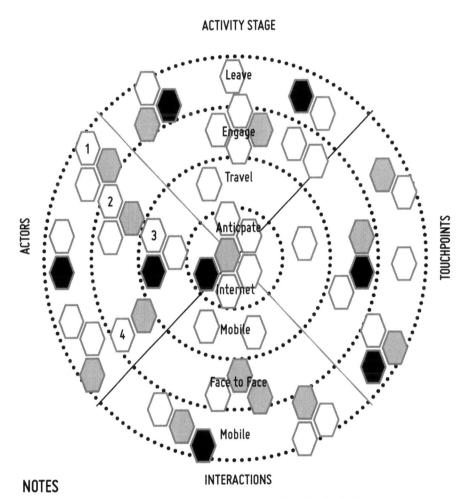

NOTES

1. **Activity Stage.** This is the timeline of stages in the activity that you are presenting
2. **Actors.** Each icon represents a person or stakeholder or group or organization involved in the activity at that particular stage
3. **Interactions.** This is the type of interaction such as face to face, mobile or online.
4. **Touchpoints.** Customer interaction channels such as call centers, web sites, automated teller machines and web kiosks.

actors map

WHAT IS IT?
The Actors Map represents the system of stakeholders and their relationships. It is a view of the service and its context. Stakeholders are organized by their function.

WHY USE THIS METHOD?
1. Understanding relationships is an important aspect of service design.

CHALLENGES
1. This is not a user centered method

WHY USE THIS METHOD?
1. Inexpensive and fast.
2. Connects to existing research tools and methods
3. Makes implicit knowledge explicit
4. Structures complex reality
5. Flexible for use in different contexts.

WHEN TO USE THIS METHOD
1. Know Context
2. Know User
3. Frame insights

SEE ALSO
1. Network map.

REFERENCES
1. (2007) Nicola Morelli, New representation techniques for designing in a systemic perspective, paper presented at Design Inquires, Stockholm.

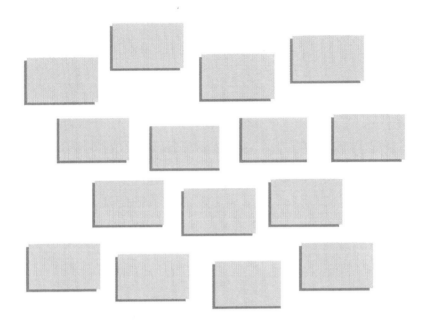

Put individual answers or ideas on post-it-notes Spread post-it-notes or cards on a wall or large table.

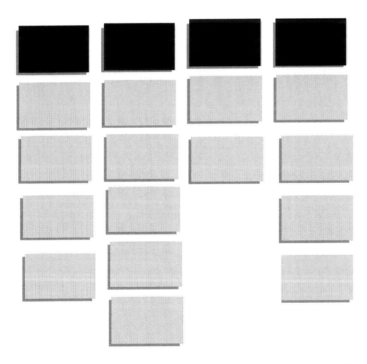

Group similar items and name each group with a different colored card or Post-it-note above the group.

affinity diagram

WHAT IS IT?

Affinity diagrams are a tool for analyzing large amounts of data and discovering relationships which allow a design direction to be established based on the affinities. This method may uncover important hidden relationships.

Affinity diagrams are created through consensus of the design team on how the information should be grouped in logical ways.

WHO INVENTED IT?

Jiro Kawaita, Japan, 1960

WHY USE THIS METHOD?

Traditional design methods are less useful when dealing with complex or chaotic problems with large amounts of data. This method helps to establish relationships of affinities between pieces of information. From these relationships insights and relationships can be determined which are the starting point of design solutions. It is possible using this method to reach consensus faster than many other methods.

RESOURCES

1. White board
2. Large wall spaces or tables
3. Dry-erase markers
4. Sharpies
5. Post-it notes
6. Digital camera

WHEN TO USE THIS METHOD

1. Know Context
2. Know User
3. Frame insights

HOW TO USE THIS METHOD

1. Select your team
2. Place individual opinions or answers to interview questions or design concepts on post-it-notes or cards.
3. Spread post-it-notes or cards on a wall or large table.
4. Group similar items.
5. This can be done silently by your design team moving them around as they each see affinities. Work until your team has consensus.
6. Name each group with a different colored card or Post-it-note above the group.
7. Repeat by grouping groups.
8. Rank the most important groups.
9. Photograph results
10. Analyze affinities and create insights.
11. 5 to 20 participants

REFERENCES

1. Brassard, M. (1989). The Memory Jogger Plus+, pp. 17 – 39. Methuen, MA: Goal/QPC.
2. King, R. (1989). Hoshin Planning, The Developmental Approach, pp. 4-2 – 4-5. Methuen, MA: Goal/QPC.

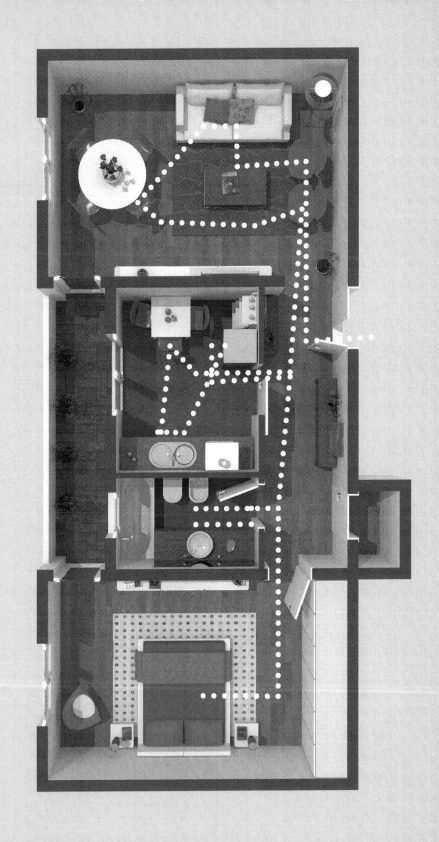

behavioral map

WHAT IS IT?

Behavioral mapping is a method used to record and analyze human activities in a location. This method is used to document what participants are doing and time spent at locations and travelling. Behavioral maps can be created based on a person or a space

WHO INVENTED IT?

Ernest Becker 1962

WHY USE THIS METHOD?

1. This method helps develop an understanding of space layouts, interactions and experiences and behaviors.
2. Helps understand way finding.
3. Helps optimize use of space.
4. A limitation of this method is that motivations remain unknown.
5. Use when you want to develop more efficient or effective use of space in retail environments, exhibits, architecture and interior design.

WHEN TO USE THIS METHOD

1. Define intent
2. Know Context
3. Know User
4. Frame insights
5. Explore Concepts
6.

Image: © Memendesig. | Dreamstime.com

HOW TO USE THIS METHOD

1. Decide who are the users.
2. Ask what is the purpose of the space?
3. Consider what behaviors are meaningful.
4. Consider different personas.
5. Participants can be asked to map their use of a space on a floor plan and can be asked to reveal their motivations.
6. Can use shadowing or video ethnographic techniques.
7. Create behavioral map.
8. Analyze behavioral map
9. Reorganize space based on insights.

RESOURCES

1. A map of the space.
2. Video camera
3. Digital still camera
4. Notebook
5. Pens

REFERENCES

1. Nickerson 1993: Bnet. Understanding your consumers through behavioral mapping.
2. A Practical Guide to Behavioral Research Tools and Techniques. Fifth Edition Robert Sommer and Barbara Sommer ISBN13: 9780195142099ISBN10: 0195142098

   Aug 2001

CRITERIA	A	B	C	D	E	F	G	H	I
USABILITY	1	2	3	1	4	1	1	2	3
SPEED TO MARKET	2	1	1	2	2	4	2	1	4
BRAND COMPATIBILITY	3	3	4	1	3	0	3	1	2
RETURN ON INVESTMENT	3	3	5	3	0	3	2	1	3
FITS STRATEGY	2	3	1	1	4	1	1	3	3
AESTHETIC APPEAL	1	1	1	4	0	3	1	2	2
DIFFERENTIATION	2	4	0	2	2	4	0	4	4
TOOLING COST	2	2	2	0	1	1	3	3	0
FITS DISTRIBUTION	2	2	1	1	1	2	0	4	3
USES OUR FACTORY	2	2	3	1	2	1	4	0	3
FITS TRENDS	1	3	2	2	1	3	4	3	2
TOTAL	21	26	23	18	20	23	21	24	29

Sample benchmarking matrix for products

benchmarking

WHAT IS IT?
Benchmarking is a method for organizations to compare their products, services or customer experiences with other industry products, services and experiences in order to identify the best practices.

WHO INVENTED IT?
Robert Camp Xerox, 1989
Benchmarking: the search for industry best practices that lead to superior performance.

WHY USE THIS METHOD?
1. A tool to identify, establish, and achieve standards of excellence.
2. A structured process of continually searching for the best methods, practices, and processes and either adopting them
3. The practice of measuring your performance against world-class organizations.

WHEN TO USE THIS METHOD
1. Define intent
2. Know Context
3. Know User
4. Frame insights

CHALLENGES
1. Can be expensive
2. Organizations often think their companies were above the average for the industry when they are not.

HOW TO USE THIS METHOD
1. Identify what you would like to be bench marked,
2. Define the process,
3. Identify potential partners
4. Identify similar industries and organizations.
5. Identify organizations that are leaders.
6. Identify data sources
7. Identify the products or organizations to be bench marked
8. Select the benchmarking factors to measure.
9. Undertake benchmarking
10. Visit the "best practice" companies to identify leading edge practices
11. Analyze the outcomes
12. Target future performance
13. Adjust goal
14. Modify your own product or service to conform with best practices identified in benchmarking process.

RESOURCES
1. Post-it-notes
2. Pens
3. Dry-erase markers
4. White board
5. Paper

REFERENCES
1. Benchmarking for Competitive Advantage. Robert J Boxwell Jr, New York: McGraw-Hill. 1994. pp. 225. ISBN 0-07-006899-2.
2. Beating the competition: a practical guide to Benchmarking. Washington, DC: Kaiser Associates. 1988. pp. 176. ISBN 978-1-56365-018-5.

	ACTIVITY PHASE	ACTIVITY PHASE	ACTIVITY PHASE	ACTIVITY PHASE	ACTIVITY PHASE	ACTIVITY PHASE
CUSTOMER ACTIONS	What does user do?					
TOUCHPOINTS	moments places customer contact					
LINE OF INTERACTION						
DIRECT CONTACT	What your Staff do					
LINE OF VISIBILITY						
BACK OFFICE	What your Staff do					
EMOTIONAL EXPERIENCE	+ −					

blueprint

WHAT IS IT?
A blueprint is a process map often used to describe the delivery of services information is presented as a number of parallel rows of activities. These are sometimes called swim lanes. They may document activities over time such as:
1. Customer Actions
2. Touch points
3. Direct Contact visible to customers
4. Invisible back office actions
5. Support Processes
6. Physical Evidence
7. Emotional Experience for customer.

WHO INVENTED IT?
Lynn Shostack 1983

WHEN TO USE THIS METHOD
1. Know Context
2. Know User
3. Frame insights

WHY TO USE THIS METHOD
1. Can be used for design or improvement of existing services or experiences.
2. Is more tangible than intuition.
3. Makes the process of service development more efficient.
4. A common point of reference for stakeholders for planning and discussion.
5. Tool to assess the impact of change.

HOW TO USE THIS METHOD
1. Define the service or experience to focus on.
2. A blueprint can be created in a brainstorming session with stakeholders.
3. Define the customer demographic.
4. See though the customer's eyes.
5. Define the activities and phases of activity under each heading.
6. Link the contact or customer touchpoints to the needed support functions
7. Use post-it-notes on a white board for initial descriptions and rearrange as necessary drawing lines to show the links.
8. Create the blueprint then refine iteratively.

RESOURCES
1. Paper
2. Pens
3. White board
4. Dry-erase markers
5. Camera
6. Blueprint templates
7. Post-it-notes

REFERENCES
1. (1991) G. Hollins, W. Hollins, Total Design: Managing the design process in the service sector, Trans Atlantic Publications
2. (2004) R. Kalakota, M.Robinson, Services Blueprint: Roadmap for Execution, Addison-Wesley, Boston.

bodystorming

WHAT IS IT?
Bodystorming is method of prototyping experiences. It requires setting up an experience – complete with necessary artifacts and people – and physically "testing" it. A design team play out scenarios based on design concepts that they are developing. The method provides clues about the impact of the context on the user experience.

WHO INVENTED IT?
Buchenau, Fulton 2000

WHY USE THIS METHOD?
1. You are likely to find new possibilities and problems.
2. Generates empathy for users.
3. This method is an experiential design tool. Bodystorming helps design ideation by exploring context.
4. It is fast and inexpensive.
5. It is a form of physical prototyping
6. It is difficult to imagine misuse scenarios

CHALLENGES
1. Some team members may find acting a difficult task.

RESOURCES
1. Empathy tools
2. A large room
3. White board
4. Video camera

WHEN TO USE THIS METHOD
1. Know Context
2. Know User
3. Frame insights
4. Explore Concepts

HOW TO USE THIS METHOD
1. Select team.
2. Define the locations where a design will be used.
3. Go to those locations and observe how people interact. the artifacts in their environment.
4. Develop the prototypes and props that you need to explore an idea. Identify the people, personas and scenarios that may help you with insight into the design directions.,
5. Bodystorm the scenarios.
6. Record the scenarios with video and analyze them for insights.

REFERENCES
Understanding contexts by being there: case studies in bodystorming. Personal and Ubiquitous Computing, Vol. 7, No. 2. (July 2003), pp. 125-134, doi:10.1007/s00779-003-0238-7 by Antti Oulasvirta, Esko Kurvinen, Tomi Kankainen

boundary shifting

WHAT IS IT?

Boundary shifting involves identifying features or ideas outside the boundary of the system related to the defined problem and applying to them to the problem being addressed.

WHY USE THIS METHOD?

1. It is fast and inexpensive.

RESOURCES

1. Pen
2. Paper
3. White board
4. Dry-erase markers

WHEN TO USE THIS METHOD

1. Know Context
2. Know User
3. Frame insights

HOW TO USE THIS METHOD

1. Define the problem.
2. Research outside systems that may have related ideas or problems to the defined problem.
3. Identify ideas or solutions outside the problem system.
4. Apply the outside idea or solution to the problem being addressed.

REFERENCES

1. Walker, D. J., Dagger, B. K. J. and Roy, R. Creative Techniques in Product and Engineering Design. Woodhead Publishing Ltd 1991. ISBN 1 85573 025 1

camera journal

WHAT IS IT?

The research subjects record their activities with a camera and notes. The researcher reviews the images and discusses them with the participants.

WHY USE THIS METHOD?

1. Helps develop empathy for the participants.
2. Participants are involved in the research process.
3. Helps establish rapport with participants.
4. May reveal aspects of life that are seldom seen by outsiders.

CHALLENGES

1. Should obtain informed consent.
2. May not be ideal for research among particularly vulnerable people.
3. May be a relatively expensive research method.
4. May be time consuming.
5. Best used with other methods.
6. Technology may be unreliable.
7. Method may be unpredictable'.
8. Has to be carefully analyzed

WHEN TO USE THIS METHOD

1. Know Context
2. Know User
3. Frame insights

HOW TO USE THIS METHOD

1. Define subject of study
2. Define participants
3. Gather data images and insight statements.
4. Analyze data.
5. Identify insights
6. Rank insights
7. Produce criteria for concept generation from insights.
8. Generate concepts to meet needs of users.

RESOURCES

1. Cameras
2. Voice recorder
3. Video camera
4. Note pad
5. Pens

REFERENCES

1. Latham, A. (2003). Researching and Writing Everyday Accounts ofthe City: An Introduction to the Diary-Photo Diary-interview Method in Knowles, C and Sweetmen, P (eds) Picturing the Social Landscape: Visual Methods and the Sociological Imagination. London, Routledge.
2. Latham,A.R.(2003)'Research, performance, and doing human geography: some reflections on the diary-photo diary-interview method', Environment and Planning A,35(11),1993-2017

closed card sorting

WHAT IS IT?

This is a method for understanding the relationships of a number of pieces of data. Participants asked to arrange individual, unsorted items into groups. A closed sort involves the cards being sorted into groups where the group headings may be defined by the researcher. There are a number of tools available to perform card sorting activities with survey participants via the internet.

Card sorting is applied when:
1. When there is a large number pieces of data.
2. The individual pieces of data are similar.
3. Participants have different perceptions of the data.

WHO INVENTED IT?

Jastrow 1886

Nielsen & Sano 1995

WHY USE THIS METHOD?

1. It is a simple method using index cards,
2. Used to provide insights for interface design.

CHALLENGES

1. Ask participants to fill out a second card if they feel it belongs in two groups.

REFERENCES

1. Jakob Nielsen (May 1995). "Card Sorting to Discover the Users' Model of the Information Space".
2. Jakob Nielsen (July 19, 2004). "Card Sorting: How Many Users to Test".

WHEN TO USE THIS METHOD

1. Know Context
2. Know User
3. Frame insights
4. Explore Concepts

HOW TO USE THIS METHOD

1. Recruit 15 to 20 participants representative of your user group.
2. Provide a deck of cards using words and or images relevant to your concept.
3. Provide clear instructions. Ask your participants to arrange the cards in ways that make sense to them. 100 cards takes about 1 hour to sort.
4. The user sorts labelled cards into groups by under header cards defined by the researcher.
5. The user can generate more card labels.
6. If users do not understand a card ask them to exclude it. Ask participants for their rationale for any dual placements of cards.
7. Discuss why the cards are placed in a particular pile yields insight into user perceptions.
8. Analyze the data. Create a hierarchy for the information
9. Use post cards or post-it notes.

RESOURCES

1. Post cards
2. Pens
3. Post-it-notes
4. Laptop computer
5. A table

coaching method

WHAT IS IT?

An expert coaches the participant. The expert answers the participant's questions while a researcher observes the participant's interaction with the product or service.

WHY USE THIS METHOD?

1. The method prototypes the user interaction with the system.
2. Information obtained can be used to refine the design or documentation.

WHEN TO USE THIS METHOD

1. Know Context
2. Know User
3. Frame insights
4. Explore Concepts

HOW TO USE THIS METHOD

1. Select the participants
2. Select the tasks and design scenarios.
3. Ask the participant to perform the interaction with the expert coach.
4. During the interaction the participant will ask the expert questions about the interaction.
5. Video and record the questions and interactions.
6. Refine the design based on the questions and interactions.

RESOURCES

1. Video camera
2. Computers

REFERENCES

1. J. Nielsen "Usability Engineering", pp.199-200, Academic Press, 1993

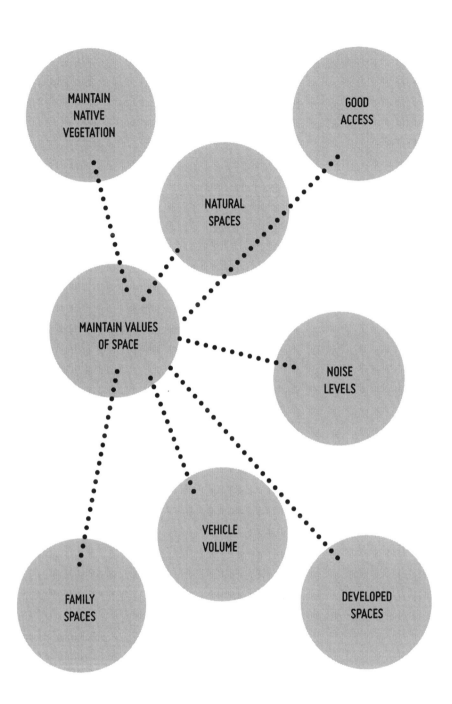

cognitive map

WHAT IS IT?

A cognitive map is a mental map of an environment. Cognitive maps are a method by which people remember and recall a physical or virtual environment and spatial knowledge.

WHO INVENTED IT?

Edward Tolman 1948.
Trowbridge 1913

WHY USE THIS METHOD?

1. Useful to discover how people navigate in a real or virtual space.
2. Used to understand a problem space.
3. Cognitive maps uncover how people make decisions.
4. Cognitive maps uncover how people perceive spaces

WHEN TO USE THIS METHOD

1. Know Context
2. Know User
3. Frame insights
4. Explore Concepts

SEE ALSO

1. Mind maps

HOW TO USE THIS METHOD

1. Ask a subject to create a map showing how they navigate in a real or a virtual space.
2. Select participants
3. Ask the participant to describe how they get to a location and how they return referencing the obstacles.
4. Maps can be created by a group of people to incorporate different viewpoints.

RESOURCES

1. Note pad
2. Paper
3. Pens
4. Video camera

REFERENCES

5. Eden, C. (1992). On the nature of cognitive maps. Journal of Management Studies, 29, 261-265.
6. Kitchin RM (1994). "Cognitive Maps: What Are They and Why Study Them?". Journal of Environmental Psychology 14 (1): 1—19. DOI:10.1016/S0272-4944(05)80194-X.
1. Tolman E.C. (July 1948). "Cognitive maps in rats and men". Psychological Review 55 (4): 189—208. DOI:10.1037/h0061626. PMID 18870876.

cognitive task analysis

WHAT IS IT?

The purpose of a cognitive task analysis is to define the decision requirements and psychological processes used by expert individuals. Task analysis makes it possible to design and develop strategy for tasks related to a system or service being designed.

Factors analyzed could include:
1. Task duration and variability
2. Task frequency
3. Task sequence
4. Task allocation
5. Task complexity
6. Environmental conditions
7. Data and information dependencies
8. Tools needed for the activity
9. User knowledge and skills

WHO INVENTED IT?

IBM circa 1985

WHY USE THIS METHOD?

1. Generates detailed data
2. Analyze the participant's perceptions and motivations related to tasks.

CHALLENGES

1. Can be time intensive and costly.

Photo: photocase.com – daumenkino

WHEN TO USE THIS METHOD

1. Define intent
2. Know Context
3. Know User
4. Frame insights
5. Explore Concepts

HOW TO USE THIS METHOD

1. Develop some general understanding of the domain area in which the cognitive task analysis will be conducted,
2. Identify experts
3. Identify the activity's knowledge structures with observations and interviews
4. Develop a strategy for each of the tasks.
5. Analyze and verify data

RESOURCES

1. Computers
2. Workstations
3. Video Cameras
4. White board
5. Notebook
6. Pens

REFERENCES

1. Crandall, B., Klein, G., and Hoffman, R. (2006). Working minds: A practitioner's guide to cognitive task analysis. MIT Press.
2. Kirwan, B. and Ainsworth, L. (Eds.) (1992). A guide to task analysis. Taylor and Francis.

collage

WHAT IS IT?

A collage involves gluing images or words onto paper. Research participants are given a large and diverse supply of images and words. The images and words chosen should be abstract so as not to influence the participants too much but may include images of objects and people and interactions. The moderator provides the participants with guidelines for the activity. They are a useful medium for communicating emotions and ideas and starting a conversation.

WHO INVENTED IT?

Invented in China, around 200 BC
Pablo Picasso and Georges Braque 1912
The word collage comes from the French word "coller" which means to glue.

WHY USE THIS METHOD?

1. Collages can enhance discourse, illustrate theses, and to anchor scientific observations in human experience.
2. The creation of a collage is a process that is both creative and analytical.
3. Collages can provide clues to the researcher about the participants lifestyle, aesthetic likes and dislikes.
4. A collage can give direction in selecting colors for a manufactured product
5. Collages are very suitable to present a particular atmosphere or context that you want to capture in the form of the new product ideas and concepts.

Image Copyright Leigh Prather, 2012 Used under license from Shutterstock.com

WHEN TO USE THIS METHOD

1. Know Context
2. Know User
3. Frame insights
4. Explore Concepts

HOW TO USE THIS METHOD

1. Define the theme.
2. Define the scope of the study such as number of words or images.
3. Print words and images onto sticker sheets.
4. Distribute scissors.
5. Group creates collages.
6. Subjects tell own stories through the collages.
7. Collect the stories.
8. Analyze the stories.

RESOURCES

1. Scissors
2. Magazines or preprinted stickers
3. Paper
4. Glue

REFERENCES

1. Brandon Taylor. Urban walls : a generation of collage in Europe & America : Burhan Dogançay with François Dufrêne, Raymond Hains, Robert Rauschenberg, Mimmo Rotella, Jacques Villeglé, Wolf Vostell ISBN 978-1-55595-288-4; ISBN 1-55595-288-7New York : Hudson Hills Press ; [Lanham, MD] : Distributed in the United States by National Book Network, 2008

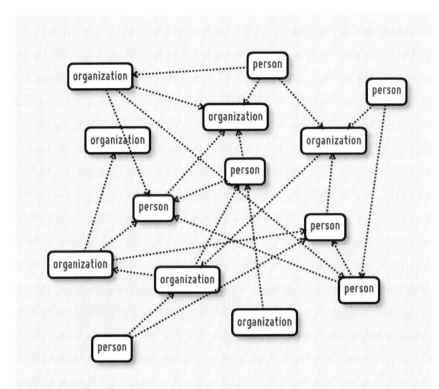

It is possible to show existing and planned relationships on your communications map

communications map

WHAT IS IT?

A communications map is a tool to study and create strategy for communications. It may be used in a project to understand where there are gaps which could affect the project outcomes. The project communication map processes documents the critical links among people and information that are necessary for successful project outcomes.

WHY USE THIS METHOD?

1. It may show where there are gaps in communications which need to be addressed.
2. Assists the project team to provide timely and accurate information to all stakeholders.

WHEN TO USE THIS METHOD

1. Know Context
2. Know User
3. Frame insights

RESOURCES

1. Pens
2. Paper
3. White board
4. Dry-erase markers

HOW TO USE THIS METHOD

1. Identify stakeholders.
2. Identify those with whom
3. Your organization needs the strongest communications linkages.
4. Identify Internal audiences.
5. Identify Peer groups or sub groups.
6. Identify Strong and frequent communications
7. Connectivity needed to a primary audience.
8. Identify less frequent communications connectivity needed to a secondary audience.
9. Determine stakeholder needs.
10. Identify communication methods and resources.
11. Prepare communication map showing existing and desired communications.
12. Distribute to stakeholders for feedback.
13. Incorporate Changes
14. Implement.

cradle to cradle

WHAT IS IT?

Cradle-to-Cradle is is a biometic approach to the design of products and systems proposed by the authors William McDonough and Michael Braungart based on the intelligence of natural systems. it is an industrial and social framework that proposes systems that are efficient and waste free.

The basis for the Cradle-to-Cradle approach involves three guiding principles:

1 Use current solar income.
2 Waste equals Food.
3 Celebrate diversity.

WHO INVENTED IT?

William McDonough and Michael Braungart
2002

WHY USE THIS METHOD?

1. The Cradle-to-Cradle approach is a framework for global economic and natural stainability

CHALLENGES

1. Cradle to Cradle is often criticized for its lack of attention to energy.
2. Some critics see the approach as utopian.
3. Even the highest Cradle to cradle certification requires only 50 % of energy for production to come from solar sources.

WHEN TO USE THIS METHOD

1. Define intent
2. Know Context
3. Know User
4. Frame insights
5. Explore Concepts
6. Make Plans
7. Deliver Offering

HOW TO USE THIS METHOD

1. Do not specify environmentally damaging materials processes and systems.
2. Follow informed personal preferences.
3. Create a 'passive positive' list of substances known to be healthy and safe for use.
4. Eliminate waste
5. Use solar energy.
6. Respect human and natural systems.
7. Design the product from beginning to end to become food for either biological or technical metabolisms.
8. Reinvent. Recast the design assignment. Towards environmentally sustainable ends.

REFERENCES

Braungart, Michael; & McDonough, William (2002). Cradle to Cradle: Remaking the Way We Make Things. North Point Press. ISBN 0-86547-587-3.

Photo: photocase.com – alwayshappy

cultural immersion

WHAT IS IT?
The design team spends a period of time exploring a location or environment to gain a deeper understanding of the design context.

WHY USE THIS METHOD?
1. To gain a deeper understanding of the design context
2. To gain empathy

RESOURCES
1. Note book
2. Digital camera
3. Video Camera
4. Digital Voice recorder

WHEN TO USE THIS METHOD
Most often used in the early stages of a design process

HOW TO USE THIS METHOD
Activities may involve
1. Interviews
2. Photography
3. Observations
4. Video
5. Note taking
6. Sketching
7. Recordings
8. Collecting objects.

cultural inventory

WHAT IS IT?

It is a survey focused on the cultural assets of a location or organization.

WHO INVENTED IT?

Julian Haynes Steward may have been the first to use the term in 1947.

WHY USE THIS METHOD?

1. Can be used in strategic planning
2. Can be used to solve problems.

CHALLENGES

1. Requires time and resources

WHEN TO USE THIS METHOD

1. Know Context
2. Know User
3. Frame insights
4. Explore Concepts

HOW TO USE THIS METHOD

1. Create your team
2. Collect existing research
3. Review existing research and identify gaps
4. Host a meeting of stakeholders
5. Promote the meeting
6. Ask open-ended questions about the culture and heritage
7. Set a time limit of 2 hours for the meeting.
8. Plan the collection phase
9. Compile inventory. This can be in the form of a web site
10. Distribute the inventory and obtain feedback.

RESOURCES

1. Diary
2. Notebooks
3. Pens
4. Post-it notes
5. Voice recorder
6. Post cards
7. Digital Camera

REFERENCES

1. Spradley, James P. Participant Observation. Holt, Rinehart and Winston, 1980.

cultural probes

WHAT IS IT?

A cultural probe is a method of collecting information about people, their context and their culture. The aim of this method is to record events, behaviors and interactions in their context. This method involves the participants to record and collect the data themselves.

WHO INVENTED IT?

Bill Gaver Royal College of Art London 1969

WHY USE THIS METHOD?

1. This is a useful method when the participants that are being studied are hard to reach for example if they are travelling.
2. It is a useful technique if the activities being studied take place over an extended period or at irregular intervals.
3. The information collected can be used to build personas.

CHALLENGES

4. It is important with this method to select the participants carefully and give them support during the study.

SEE ALSO

1. Diary study

WHEN TO USE THIS METHOD

1. Define intent
2. Know Context
3. Know User
4. Frame insights

HOW TO USE THIS METHOD

1. Define the objective of your study.
2. Recruit your participants.
3. Brief the participants
4. Supply participants with kit. The items in the kit are selected to collect the type of information you want to gather and can include items such as notebooks, diary, camera, voice recorder or post cards.
5. You can use an affinity diagram to analyze the data collected

RESOURCES

1. Diary
2. Notebooks
3. Pens
4. Post-it notes
5. Voice recorder
6. Post cards
7. Digital Camera

REFERENCES

1. Bailey, Kathleen M. (1990) The use of diary studies in teacher education programs In Richards, J. C. & Nunan, D. (org.). Second Language Teacher Education (pp. 215-226). Cambridge: Cambridge University Press.

customer experience audit

WHAT IS IT?

A customer experience audit is a method of systematically analyzing an organization's with their customers. It is a systematic way of understanding how your customers see your organization.

WHY USE THIS METHOD?

1. Increase employee engagement
2. Establish a baseline of Customer Experience
3. Provide insights into opportunities
4. Prepare a team for Customer Journey Mapping
5. Reveal customer perspective to employees
6. A customer perspective allows your organization to shift its culture from opinion to
7. Fact based thinking.
8. Audit findings get people on the same page.

CHALLENGES

1. When your customer experience has evolved over time, rather than being intentionally designed, product and company performance suffer.
2. Which customers are your most valuable
3. Which interactions these key customers most value

Image Copyright LuckyPhoto, 2012 Used under license from Shutterstock.com

WHEN TO USE THIS METHOD

1. Know Context
2. Know User
3. Frame insights

HOW TO USE THIS METHOD

Will depend on your organization anf customer base, but could typically include;

1. Customer surveys and interviews with; existing and past customers as well as potential customers
2. Mystery shopping
3. Focus groups
4. Interviews with staff who interact with your customers.
5. Review of customer interactions and literature including face-to-face interviews, telephone and online surveys
6. Prospective, current, and lost customers.
7. Signs
8. Advertisements
9. Website
10. E-mail or Newsletters
11. Facebook or other social pages
12. Retail Space
13. Marketing Materials
14. Information Forms

REFERENCES

1. Rubin, Herbert and Irene Rubin. Qualitative Interviewing: The Art of Hearing Data. 2nd edition. Thousand Oaks, CA: Sage Publications, 2004. Print.
2. Kvale, Steinar. Interviews: An Introduction to Qualitative Research Interviewing, Sage Publications, 1996

	ANTICIPATE	ENTER	ENGAGE	EXIT	REVIEW
CUSTOMER MORE POSITIVE EXPERIENCES					
CUSTOMER POSITIVE EXPERIENCES					
BASELINE					
CUSTOMER NEGATIVE EXPERIENCES					
CUSTOMER MORE NEGATIVE EXPERIENCES					
EMOTIONAL EXPERIENCE					

customer experience map

WHAT IS IT?

Customer experience also called customer journey mapping is a method of documenting and visualizing the experiences that customers have as they use a product or service and their responses to their experiences.

It allows your team to access and analyze the interacting factors that form a customer experience.

WHY USE THIS METHOD?

1. Helps develop a consistent, predictable customer experience,
2. Presents an overview of your customer's experience from their point of view.
3. Helps reduce the number of dissatisfied customers
4. Can be used with different personas.

WHEN TO USE THIS METHOD

1. Know Context
2. Know User
3. Frame insights

HOW TO USE THIS METHOD

1. Identify your team.
2. Identify the customer experience to be analyzed. Identify the context. Identify personas.
3. Define the experience as a time line with stages such as anticipation, entry, engagement, exit, and reflection.
4. Use post-it notes to add positive and negative experiences to the relevant parts of the time line.
5. Order the experiences around a baseline by how positive or negative the experience were.
6. Analyze the parts of the time line and activities that have the most negative experiences. These are opportunities for design.

RESOURCES

1. Post-it-notes
2. Printed or projected template
3. White board
4. Markers

REFERENCES

1. Joshi, Hetal. "Customer Journey Mapping: The Road to Success." Cognizant. (2009) Web. 26 Jul. 2012.
2. World Class Skills Programme. "Customer Journey Mapping." Developing Responsive Provision. (2006): n. page. Web. 27 Jul. 2012.

After scanning the daily British newspapers, The Queen reviews her correspondence.

If there is an Investiture – a ceremony for the presentation of honours and decorations – it begins at 11.00am and lasts just over an hour

The Queen will often lunch privately. Every few months, she and The Duke of Edinburgh will invite a dozen guests from a wide variety of backgrounds to an informal lunch.

7 am 8 am 9 am 10 am 11 am 12 pm 1 pm 2 pm

Every day, 200–300 letters from the public arrive. The Queen chooses a selection to read herself and tells members of her staff how she would like them to be answered

A series of official meetings or 'audiences' will often follow. The Queen will see a number of important people.

In the afternoons, The Queen goes out on public engagements. The Queen prepares for each visit by briefing herself on whom she will be meeting and what she will be seeing and doing

day in the life

WHAT IS IT?

A study in which the designer observes the participant in the location and context of their usual activities, observing and recording events to understand the activities from the participant's point of view. This is sometimes repeated. Mapping a 'Day in the Life' as a storyboard can provide a focus for discussion.

WHO INVENTED IT?

ALex Bavelas 1944

WHY USE THIS METHOD?

1. This method informs the design process by observation of real activities and behaviors.
2. This method provides insights with relatively little cost and time.

CHALLENGES

1. Choose the participants carefully
2. Document everything. Something that seems insignificant may become significant later.

WHEN TO USE THIS METHOD

1. Know Context
2. Know User
3. Frame insights

HOW TO USE THIS METHOD

1. Define activities to study
2. Recruit participants
3. Prepare
4. Observe subjects in context.
5. Capture data,
6. Create storyboard with text and timeline.
7. Analyze data
8. Create insights.
9. Identify issues
10. Identify needs
11. Add new/more requirements to concept development

RESOURCES

1. Camera
2. Notebook
3. Video camera
4. Voice recorder
5. Pens

REFERENCES

1. Shadowing: And Other Techniques for Doing Fieldwork in Modern Societies [Paperback] Barbara Czarniawska. Publisher: Copenhagen Business School Pr (December 2007) ISBN-10: 8763002159 ISBN-13: 978-8763002158

diary study

WHAT IS IT?

This method involves participants recording specific events, feelings or interactions, in a diary supplied by the researcher. User Diaries help provide insight into behavior. Participants record their behavior and thoughts. Diaries can uncover behavior that may not be articulated in an interview or easily visible to outsiders.

WHO INVENTED IT?

Gordon Allport, may have been the first to describe diary studies in 1942.

WHY USE THIS METHOD?

1. Can capture data that is difficult to capture using other methods.
2. Useful when you wish to gather information and minimize your influence on research subjects.
3. When the process or event you're exploring takes place intermittently or
4. When the process or event you're exploring takes place over a long period.

CHALLENGES

1. Process can be expensive and time consuming.
2. Needs participant monitoring.
3. Diary can fit into users' pocket.
4. It is difficult to get materials back.

WHEN TO USE THIS METHOD

1. Know Context
2. Know User
3. Frame insights

HOW TO USE THIS METHOD

1. A diary can be kept over a period of one week or longer.
2. Define focus for the study.
3. Recruit participants carefully.
4. Decide method: preprinted, diary notebook or online.
5. Prepare diary packs. Can be preprinted sheets or blank 20 page notebooks with prepared questions or online web based diary.
6. Brief participants.
7. Distribute diaries directly or by mail.
8. Conduct study. Keep in touch with participants.
9. Conduct debrief interview.
10. Look for insights.

RESOURCES

1. Diary
2. Preprinted diary sheets
3. Online diary
4. Pens
5. Disposable cameras
6. Digital camera
7. Self addressed envelopes

REFERENCES

1. Bailey, Kathleen M. (1990) The use of diary studies in teacher education programs In Richards, J. C. & Nunan, D. (org.). Second Language Teacher Education (pp. 215–226). Cambridge: Cambridge University Press.

SEE ALSO

Empathy probe

day experience method

WHAT IS IT?

The method requires participants to record answers to questions during a day. The person's mobile phone is used to prompt them The participants use a notebook, a camera or a voice recorder to answer your questions. The interviews are followed by a focus group.

WHO INVENTED IT?

Intille 2003

WHY USE THIS METHOD?

1. The participants are co-researchers.
2. Reduces the influence of the researcher on the participant when compared to methods such as interviews or direct observation.

CHALLENGES

1. Cost of devices.
2. This method should be used with other methods.

WHEN TO USE THIS METHOD

1. Know Context
2. Know User
3. Frame insights

HOW TO USE THIS METHOD

1. Conduct a preliminary survey to focus the method on preferred questions.
2. Recruit participants.
3. The experience sampling takes place over one day.
4. The participants are asked to provide answers to questions at irregular intervals when promoted by a SMS message via the participant's mobile phone.
5. The interval can be 60 to 90 minutes.
6. The participant can record the activity with a camera, notebook or voice recorder.
7. Soon after the day organize a focus group with the participants.
8. The participants describe their day using the recorded material.

RESOURCES

1. Mobile phone
2. Automated SMS messaging
3. Notebook
4. Camera
5. Software

REFERENCES

1. Hektner, J.M., Schmidt, J.A. & Csikszentmihalyi, M (2006). Experience Sampling Method: Measuring the Quality of Everyday Life, London: Sage.
2. Kahneman, D., Krueger, A. B., Schkade, D. A., Schwarz, N., & Stone, A. A. (2004). 'A Survey Method for Characterizing Daily Life Experience: The Day Reconstruction Method'. Science, 306(5702), 1776-1780.

design workshops

WHAT IS IT?

A design workshop is a strategic design method that involves bringing the design team together with stakeholders to explore issue related to explore issues related to the people who are being designed for or to create design solutions.

WHY USE THIS METHOD?

1. Fast and inexpensive.
2. Increased probability of implementation.
3. Stakeholders can share information.
4. Promotes trust.

CHALLENGES

1. Managing workflow can be challenging.
2. Stakeholders may have conflicting visions.

WHEN TO USE THIS METHOD

1. Know Context
2. Know User
3. Frame insights
4. Explore Concepts

HOW TO USE THIS METHOD

1. See charettes and creative toolkits.

RESOURCES

1. Paper flip chart
2. White board
3. Colored markers
4. Cards
5. Masking tape
6. Rolls of butcher paper
7. Post-it notes
8. Adhesive dots
9. Glue
10. Pins
11. Pens
12. Scissors
13. Spray adhesive
14. Screen
15. Laptop
16. Projector
17. Extension leads
18. Video Camera
19. Digital Camera
20. Chairs
21. Tables

workshops: creative toolkits

WHAT IS IT?

Collections of modular objects that can be used for participatory modeling and prototyping to inform and inspire design teams. Often used in creative codesign workshops. It is a generative design method which facilitates creative play. The elements can be reused in a number of research sessions in different geographic locations.

WHO INVENTED IT?

Pioneered by Liz Sanders and Lego Johan Roos and Bart Victor 1990s.

WHY USE THIS METHOD?

Helps develop:

1. Problem solving
2. Change management
3. Strategic thinking
4. Decision making
5. Services, product and experience redesign
6. Can be fun
7. Identify opportunities
8. Re frame challenges
9. Leverages creative thinking of the team

WHEN TO USE THIS METHOD

1. Know Context
2. Know User
3. Frame insights
4. Explore Concepts

image: © Grandeduc | Dreamstime.com

HOW TO USE THIS METHOD

1. Form cross-disciplinary team 5 to 20 members. It's best to have teams of not more than 8
2. Identify design problem. Create agenda.
3. Start with a warming up exercise.
4. Write design problem in visible location such as white board.
5. Workshop participants first build individual prototypes exploring the problem.
6. Divide larger group into smaller work groups of 3 to 5 participants.
7. Ask each participant to develop between 1 and 5 design solutions. Can use post-it notes or cards.
8. Through internal discussion each group should select their preferred group design solution.
9. The group builds a collective model incorporating the individual contributions.
10. Each group build a physical model of preferred solution and presents it to larger group.
11. Larger group selects their preferred design solutions by discussion and voting.
12. Capture process and ideas with video or photographs.
13. Debriefing and harvest of ideas.

REFERENCES

1. Statler, M., Roos, J., and B. Victor, 2009, 'Ain't Misbehavin': Taking Play Seriously in Organizations,' Journal of Change Management, 9(1): 87-107.

design charette

WHAT IS IT?

A design charette is a collaborative design workshop usually held over one day or several days. Charettes are a fast way of generating ideas while involving diverse stakeholders in your decision process. Charettes have many different structures and often involve multiple sessions. The group divides into smaller groups. The smaller groups present to the larger group.

WHO INVENTED IT?

The French word, "charrette" spelt with two r's means "cart" This use of the term is said to originate from the École des Beaux Arts in Paris during the 19th century, where a cart, collected final drawings while students finished their work.

WHY USE THIS METHOD?

1. Fast and inexpensive.
2. Increased probability of implementation.
3. Stakeholders can share information.
4. Promotes trust.

CHALLENGES

1. Managing workflow can be challenging.
2. Stakeholders may have conflicting visions.

WHEN TO USE THIS METHOD

1. Define intent
2. Know context and user
3. Frame insights
4. Explore concepts
5. Make Plans

RESOURCES

1. Large space
2. Tables
3. Chairs
4. White boards
5. Dry-erase markers
6. Camera
7. Post-it-notes

REFERENCES

1. Day, C. (2003). Consensus Design: Socially Inclusive Process. Oxford, UK, and Burlington, MA: Elsevier Science, Architectural Press.

1.5 day mini charette

HOW TO USE THIS METHOD

Day 1

1. Evening mixer night before event.
2. Breakfast 30 minutes.
3. Moderator introduces participants expectations and goals.
4. Overview of project 30 mins
5. Break 15 minutes
6. Individual presenters present information about aspects of project 1 hour
7. Lunch 1 hour
8. Further presentations related to aspects of project 1 hour
9. Question and answer session 15 minutes
10. Multi disciplinary breakout groups 2.5 hours
11. Group size preferred 4 to 8 participants.
12. Groups explore strategies and issues.
13. Groups present strategies and goals to larger group 30 minutes. Larger group brainstorms goals.
14. Site tour 1 hour – for urban or architectural projects.

Day 2

1. Breakfast 30 minutes
2. Review of Day 1, 30 minutes.
3. Breakout groups explore concept solutions as sketches 2.5 hours.
4. Groups present to larger group 30 minutes.
5. Larger group brainstorms next steps 30 minutes
6. Lunch 1 hour

RESOURCES

1. Large space
2. Tables
3. Chairs
4. White boards
5. Dry-erase markers
6. Camera
7. Post-it-notes

2.0 day design charette

HOW TO USE THIS METHOD

Day 1

1. Evening mixer night before event.
2. Breakfast 30 minutes.
3. Moderator introduces participants expectations and goals.
4. Overview of project 30 mins
5. Break 15 minutes
6. Individual presenters present information about aspects of project 1 hour
7. Lunch 1 hour
8. Further presentations related to aspects of project 1 hour
9. Question and answer session 15 minutes
10. Multi disciplinary breakout groups 2.5 hours
11. Group size preferred 4 to 8 participants.
12. Groups explore strategies and issues.
13. Groups present strategies and goals to larger group 30 minutes. Larger group brainstorms goals.
14. Site tour 1 hour – for urban or architectural projects.

Day 2

1. Breakfast 30 minutes
2. Review of Day 1, 30 minutes.
3. Breakout groups explore concept solutions as sketches 2.5 hours.
4. Groups present to larger group 30 minutes.
5. Lunch 1 hour
6. Breakout groups refine concept solutions as sketches 2.5 hours.
7. Groups present to larger group 30 minutes.
8. Wrap up and next steps 30 minutes

RESOURCES

1. Large space
2. Tables
3. Chairs
4. White boards
5. Dry-erase markers
6. Camera
7. Post-it-notes

4.0 day architectural charette

HOW TO USE THIS METHOD

1. Define problem
2. Public meeting Vision
3. Brief group
4. Alternative concepts generated
5. Small groups work
6. Small groups present.
7. Whole group discussion
8. Public meeting input
9. Preferred concepts developed
10. Small groups work
11. Small groups present.
12. Whole group discussion
13. Open house review
14. Small groups work
15. Small groups present.
16. Whole group discussion
17. Further plan development.
18. Public meeting confirmation of final design.

RESOURCES

1. Large space
2. Tables
3. Chairs
4. White boards
5. Dry-erase markers
6. Camera
7. Post-it-notes

635 method design charette

HOW TO USE THIS METHOD

1. Choose a problem to focus on.
2. Select moderator.
3. Select and invite participants.
4. Team size of 4 to 20 participants preferred representing users, managers, design and diverse group of stakeholders.
5. Break down teams into groups of 3 participants.
6. Each group of 3 should sit at a separate table.
7. Brief participants in advance by e-mail.
8. Allow one hour per problem
9. Use creative space such as a room with a large table and whiteboard.
10. Brief participants allow 15 minutes to one hour for individual concept exploration.
11. Can use egg timer to time sessions.
12. Give each participant a goal such as 5 concepts.
13. At end of concept exploration time group selects the best 3 concepts from the session and two participants move to another table. One participant stays at table.
14. The session is repeated each group combines the best ideas from two tables.
15. Repeat this process five times.
16. At the end of these concept exploration session pin all the drawings on a wall and group by affinities.
17. Moderator and group can evaluate the concepts using a list of heuristics.
18. Dot vote each category to determine best ideas to carry forward.
19. Do another round of sketching focusing of 3 best ideas.
20. Record session with digital images.
21. Smaller group can take preferred ideas and develop them after the session.

RESOURCES

1. Large space
2. Tables
3. Chairs
4. White boards
5. Dry-erase markers
6. Camera
7. Post-it-notes

0.5 day product design charette

HOW TO USE THIS METHOD

1. Choose a problem to focus on.
2. Select moderator.
3. Select and invite participants.
4. Team size of 4 to 20 participants preferred representing users, managers, design and diverse group of stakeholders.
5. Break down teams over 8 into smaller groups of 4 or 5 participants.
6. Brief participants in advance by e-mail.
7. Allow one hour per problem
8. Use creative space such as a room with a large table and whiteboard.
9. Brief participants allow 15 minutes to one hour for individual concept exploration.
10. Give participants a goal such as 5 concepts.
11. Output can be sketches or simple models using materials such as cardboard or toy construction kits.
12. Each individual presents their concepts to the group.
13. In larger groups each group of 4 can select 3 favored ideas in smaller group to present to larger group. Each smaller group selects a presenter.
14. Moderator and group can evaluate the concepts using a list of heuristics.
15. Put all the sketches or post it notes on a wall.
16. Group concepts into categories of related ideas.
17. Dot vote each category to determine best ideas to carry forward.
18. Do another round of sketching focusing of 3 best ideas.
19. Iterate this process as many times as necessary.
20. Record session with digital images.
21. Smaller group can take preferred ideas and develop them after the session.

RESOURCES

1. Large space
2. Tables
3. Chairs
4. White boards
5. Dry-erase markers
6. Camera
7. Post-it-notes
8. Materials such as cardboard, children's construction kits

0.5 day ux charette

HOW TO USE THIS METHOD

1. Choose a problem to focus on.
2. Select moderator.
3. Select and invite participants.
4. Team size of 4 to 20 participants preferred representing users, managers, design and diverse group of stakeholders.
5. Break down teams over 8 into smaller groups of 4 or 5 participants.
6. Brief participants in advance by email.
7. Allow one hour per problem
8. Use creative space such as a room with a large table and whiteboard.
9. Brief participants allow 15 minutes to one hour for individual concept exploration.
10. Give participants a goal such as 5 concepts.
11. Output can be wireframes or storyboards.
12. Each individual presents their concepts to the group.
13. Moderator and group can evaluate the concepts using a list of heuristics.
14. Put all the sketches or post it notes on a wall.
15. Group concepts into categories of related ideas.
16. Dot vote each category to determine best ideas to carry forward.
17. Do another round of sketching focusing of 3 best ideas.
18. Iterate this process as many times as necessary.
19. Record session with digital images.
20. Smaller group can take preferred ideas and develop them after the session.

RESOURCES

1. Large space
2. Tables
3. Chairs
4. White boards
5. Dry-erase markers
6. Camera
7. Post-it-notes

desirability testing

WHAT IS IT?

Desirability testing are a number of qualitative and quantitative attitudinal methods that assess people's attitudes to a product or service.

WHY USE THIS METHOD?

1. A manager often feels his or her perception of a design is just as valid as the designer's
2. These methods help the design team understand the response of customers to a proposed design.
3. Reduces the subjectivity of design decisions.

CHALLENGES

1. This method measures attitude rather than behavior.

WHEN TO USE THIS METHOD

1. Define intent
2. Know Context and user
3. Frame insights
4. Explore Concepts

HOW TO USE THIS METHOD

1. Participants are given cards that have words on each card such as desirable, high quality, valuable, useful, reliable, fun confusing, complex, familiar.
2. The participants select the cards that go with each design.
3. The researcher asks the participants why they made the selections.

RESOURCES

1. Word cards
2. Table
3. Prototype products or services

digital ethnography

WHAT IS IT?

Digital Ethnography is research that is undertaken in online, virtual or digitally enabled environments. It uses digital tools to gather, analyze, and present ethnographic data.

WHY USE THIS METHOD?

1. Can be faster and less expensive than non-digital methods.
2. Data collected real time
3. Access to people may be easier
4. People carry digital devices such as smart phones, cameras, laptops and tablets
5. Data can be gathered in context

CHALLENGES

1. Can miss non verbal feedback.
2. Technology may be unreliable

WHEN TO USE THIS METHOD

1. Define intent
2. Know Context
3. Know User
4. Frame insights
5. Explore Concepts
6. Make Plans
7. Deliver Offering

HOW TO USE THIS METHOD

There are many different methods which use or access:

1. Audio conferences
2. Web conferences
3. Virtual in depth interviews
4. Focus groups
5. Mobile diaries
6. Online forums
7. Private online communities

RESOURCES

1. Smart phones,
2. Cameras,
3. Laptops and
4. Tablets

REFERENCES

1. Coover, R. (2004) 'Using Digital Media Tools and Cross-Cultural Research,Analysis and Representation', Visual Studies19(1): 6—25.
2. Dicks, B., B. Mason, A. Coffey and P. Atkinson (2005) Qualitative Research and Hypermedia: Ethnography for the Digital Age. London: SAGE.
3. Kozinets R.V. (2010a), Netnography. Doing Ethnographic Research Online, Sage, London.

EMOTIONAL JOURNEY MAP

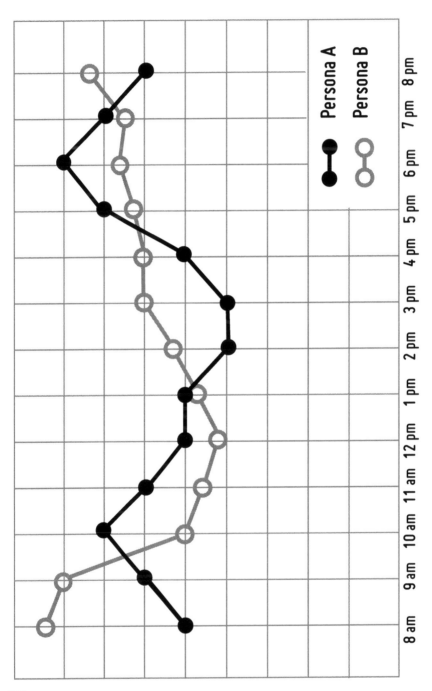

emotional journey map

WHAT IS IT?

An emotional journey map is a map that visually illustrates people's emotional experience throughout an interaction with an organization or brand.

WHY USE THIS METHOD?

1. It provides a focus for discussion
2. It focusses on what may make your customers unhappy
3. Provides a visually compelling story of customer experience.
4. Customer experience is more than interaction with a product.
5. By understanding the journey that your customers are making, you will be in a position to make informed improvements.

CHALLENGES

1. Customers often do not take the route in an interaction that the designer expects.
2. Failure to manage experiences can lead to lost customers.

WHEN TO USE THIS METHOD

1. Know Context
2. Know User
3. Frame insights
4. Explore Concepts
5. Make Plans

HOW TO USE THIS METHOD

1. Define the activity of your map. For example it could be a ride on the underground train.
2. Collect internal insights
3. Research customer perceptions
4. Analyze research
5. Map journey.
6. Across the top of the page do a time line Break the journey into stages using your customer's point of view
7. Capture each persona's unique experience
8. Use a scale from 0 to 10. The higher the number, the better the experience.
9. Plot the emotional journey.
10. Analyze the lease pleasant emotional periods and create ideas for improving the experience during those periods.
11. Create a map for each persona.

RESOURCES

1. Paper
2. Pens
3. White board
4. Post-it-notes

REFERENCES

1. Joshi, Hetal. "Customer Journey Mapping: The Road to Success." Cognizant. (2009) Web. 26 Jul. 2012.
2. World Class Skills Programme. "Customer Journey Mapping." Developing Responsive Provision. (2006): n. page. Web. 27 Jul. 2012.

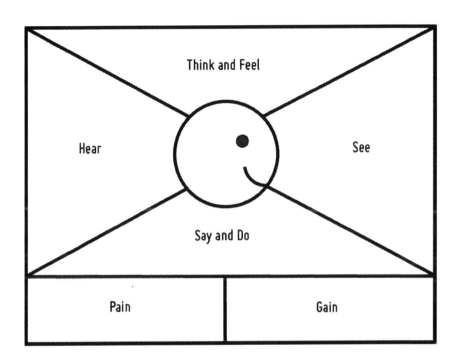

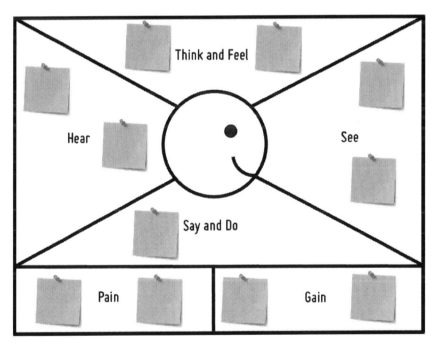

empathy map

WHAT IS IT?

Empathy Map is a tool that helps the design team empathize with people they are designing for, You can create an empathy map for a group of customers or a persona.

WHO INVENTED IT?

Scott Matthews and Dave Gray at PLANE now Dachis Group.

WHY USE THIS METHOD?

This tool helps a design team understand the customers and their context.

CHALLENGES

1. Emotions must be inferred by observing clues.
2. This method does not provide the same level of rigor as traditional personas but requires less investment.

WHEN TO USE THIS METHOD

1. Know Context
2. Know User
3. Frame insights

RESOURCES

1. Empathy map template
2. White board
3. Dry-erase markers
4. Post-it-notes
5. Pens
6. Video Camera

HOW TO USE THIS METHOD

1. A team of 3 to 10 people is a good number for this method.
2. This method can be used with personas.
3. Draw a cirle to represent your target persona.
4. Divide the circle into sections that represent aspects of that person's sensory experience.
5. Ask your team to describe from the persona's point of view their experience.
6. What are the persona's needs and desires?
7. Populate the map by taking note of the following traits of your user as you review your notes, audio, and video from your fieldwork: What are they thinking, feeling, saying, doing, hearing, seeing?
8. Fill in the diagram with real, tangible, sensory experiences.
9. 20 minutes to one hour is a good duration for this exercise.
10. Ask another group of people to look at your map and suggest improvements or refinements.

REFERENCES

1. Gray, Dave; Brown, Sunni; Macanufo, James (2010). Gamestorming: A Playbook for Innovators, Rulebreakers, and Changemakers. O'Reilly Media, Inc

empathy probes

WHAT IS IT?

This method involves participants recording specific events, feelings or interactions, in a diary supplied by the researcher. User Diaries help provide insight into behavior. Participants record their behavior and thoughts. Diaries can uncover behavior that may not be articulated in an interview or easily visible to outsiders.

WHO INVENTED IT?

Gordon Allport, may have been the first to describe diary studies in 1942.

WHY USE THIS METHOD?

1. Can capture data that is difficult to capture using other methods.
2. Cultural probes are appropriate when you need to gather information from users with minimal influence on their actions,
3. When the process or event you're exploring takes place intermittently or
4. When the process or event you're exploring takes place over a long period.

CHALLENGES

1. Process can be expensive and time consuming.
2. Needs participant monitoring.
3. Diary can fit into users' pocket.
4. It is difficult to get materials back.

WHEN TO USE THIS METHOD

1. Know Context
2. Know User
3. Frame insights

HOW TO USE THIS METHOD

1. A diary can be kept over a period of one week or longer.
2. Define focus for the study.
3. Recruit participants carefully.
4. Decide method: preprinted, diary notebook or online.
5. Prepare diary packs. Can be preprinted sheets or blank 20 page notebooks with prepared questions or online web based diary.
6. Brief participants.
7. Distribute diaries directly or by mail.
8. Conduct study. Keep in touch with participants.
9. Conduct debrief interview.
10. Look for insights.

RESOURCES

1. Diary
2. Preprinted diary sheets
3. Online diary
4. Pens
5. Disposable cameras
6. Digital camera
7. Self addressed envelopes

REFERENCES

1. Bailey, Kathleen M. (1990) The use of diary studies in teacher education programs In Richards, J. C. & Nunan, D. (org.). Second Language Teacher Education (pp. 215-226). Cambridge: Cambridge University Press.

SEE ALSO

Diary study

empathy tools

WHAT IS IT?

Empathy tools are aids or tools that help designers empathize with the people they are designing for. They can be used to test a prototype design or in activities such as role playing or body storming.

WHO INVENTED IT?

Brandt, E. and Grunnet, C 2000

WHY USE THIS METHOD?

1. To help a designer understand the experiences of people that they are designing for.

CHALLENGES

1. Empathy tools are imperfect approximations of user experiences.

WHEN TO USE THIS METHOD

1. Know Context
2. Know User
3. Frame insights
4. Explore Concept

HOW TO USE THIS METHOD

1. Wear heavy gloves to experience less sensitivity in your hands
2. Wear fogged glasses to experience less acute vision
3. Wear black glasses to eat to experience issues locating food and utensils.
4. Spend a day in a wheelchair.
5. Wear earplugs to experience diminished hearing

RESOURCES

1. Wheelchair
2. Fogged glasses
3. Blackened glasses
4. Gloves
5. Earplugs
6. Crutches
7. Walking stick

REFERENCES

1. Brandt, E. and Grunnet, C., "Evoking the Future: Drama and Props in User-centered Design", PDC 2000

EVALUATION MATRIX

CRITERIA	WEIGHT	DESIGN A		DESIGN B		DESIGN C		DESIGN D	
		SCORE	WEIGHTED	SCORE	WEIGHTED	SCORE	WEIGHTED	SCORE	WEIGHTED
TOTAL									

evaluation matrix

WHAT IS IT?

A simple tool used for planning and conducting an evaluation that aids the team in making informed decisions by comparing many options. The use of an evaluation matrix is a method of evaluating a number of options against a number of criteria. A Weighted Alternatives Evaluation Matrix, or Weighted Matrix, assigns weighting factors to criteria when comparing alternatives

WHY USE THIS METHOD?

1. Control costs by focusing resources
2. Answer/discover critical questions.
3. Fast and cost effective method.
4. Allows you to identify strengths and weaknesses.
5. An efficient way of conveying information.

CHALLENGES

1. Can emphasize data which is not most important.
2. Assignment of weights and scores is subjective

WHEN TO USE THIS METHOD

1. Know Context
2. Know User
3. Frame insights
4. Explore Concepts
5. Make Plans

HOW TO USE THIS METHOD

1. Establishing Evaluation Criteria.
2. Prioritizing criteria
3. List mandatory criteria
4. List desirable criteria
5. The simplest Alternatives Evaluation Matrix indicates with a yes or no whether each criterion was met.
6. Weighting factors are used to define the level of importance of criteria. Assigning meaning to weighting factors is subjective. Keep the number of weighting factors small
7. You can have the members of a group do their own ranking and then combine the results onto one summary report.
8. Analyze the criteria rankings

RESOURCES

1. Paper
2. Pens
3. White board
4. Dry-erase markers

eyetracking

WHAT IS IT?
Eye tracking is a group of methods of studying and recording a person's eye movements over time. The most widely used current designs are video-based eye trackers. One of the most prominent fields of commercial eye tracking research is web usability but this method is also used widely for evaluating retail interiors and products.

WHO INVENTED IT?
Louis Émile Javal 1879
Alfred L. Yarbus 1950s

WHY USE THIS METHOD?
1. Examine which details attract attention.
2. To record where a participant's attention is focussed for example on a supermarket shelf which products and parts of products attract the most attention from shoppers.

CHALLENGES
1. Each method of eye tracking has advantages and disadvantages, and the choice of an eye tracking system depends on considerations of cost and application.
2. A poorly adjusted system can produce unreliable information.

WHEN TO USE THIS METHOD
1. Know Context
2. Know User
3. Frame insights
4. Explore Concepts

TYPES OF SYSTEMS
1. Measures eye movement with a device attached to the eye. For example a contact lens with a magnetic field sensor.
2. Non contact measurement of eye movement. For example infrared, is reflected from the eye and sensed by a video camera.
3. Measures eye movement with electrodes placed around the eyes.

TYPES OF OUTPUTS
1. Heat maps
2. Gaze plots
3. Gaze replays

RESOURCES
1. Eye tracking device
2. Software
3. Laptop computer

REFERENCES
1. Bojko, A. (2006). Using Eye Tracking to Compare Web Page Designs: A Case Study. Journal of Usability Studies, Vol.1, No. 3.
2. Chandon, Pierre, J. Wesley Hutchinson, and Scott H. Young (2001), Measuring Value of Point-of-Purchase Marketing with Commercial Eye-Tracking Data.
3. Wedel, M. & Pieters, R. (2000). Eye fixations on advertisements and memory for brands: a model and findings. Marketing Science, 19 (4), 2000, 297–312.

field study

WHAT IS IT?
A field study is a study carried on in the context of people rather than in design studio or a laboratory. A field study is primary research It involves observing or interviewing people in their natural environments.

WHO INVENTED IT?
James Cowles Prichard 1841
Margaret Mead, 1928
Bronisław Malinowski, 1929
Pierre Bourdieu 1958-1962

WHY USE THIS METHOD?
1. A field study can be used to inform design and to create more successful outcomes for design by better informing the designer of the behaviors, desires and needs of the people being designed for.

CHALLENGES
1. May be more expensive than secondary research.
2. Information may become obsolete

WHEN TO USE THIS METHOD
1. Define intent
2. Know Context
3. Know User
4. Frame insights
5. Explore Concepts
6. Make Plans
7. Deliver Offering

HOW TO USE THIS METHOD
1. Define goals.
2. Develop plan
3. Create study materials such as question guides, release forms,
4. Prepare for site visits
5. Perform observations and interviews.
6. Analyze data
7. Develop insights
8. Make recommendations.

RESOURCES
1. Note pads
2. Pens
3. Digital camera
4. Video camera
5. Post-it notes

REFERENCES
1. Jarvie, I. C. (1967) On Theories of Fieldwork and the Scientific Character of Social Anthropology, Philosophy of Science, Vol. 34, No. 3 (Sep., 1967), pp. 223-242.
2. Marek M. Kaminski. 2004. Games Prisoners Play. Princeton University Press. ISBN 0-691-11721-7

fly-on-the-wall

WHAT IS IT?

Observation method where the observer remains as unobtrusive as possible and observes and collects data relevant to a research study in context with no interaction with the participants being observed. The name derived from the documentary film technique of the same name.

WHO INVENTED IT?

ALex Bavelas 1944
Lucy Vernile, Robert A. Monteiro 1991

WHY USE THIS METHOD?

1. Low cost
2. No setup necessary
3. Can observe a large number of participants.
4. Objective observations
5. Compared to other methods such as focus groups, setup, data collection, and processing are much faster.

CHALLENGES

1. No interaction by the observer.
2. Requires that the observer be silent during the presentation without asking questions or making suggestions.
3. Observer cannot delve deeper during a session.
4. No interruption allowed
5. Observer cannot obtain details on customer comments during a session

Photo: photocase.com – FreyaSapphire

WHEN TO USE THIS METHOD

1. Know Context
2. Know User
3. Frame insights

HOW TO USE THIS METHOD

1. Define activity to study
2. Select participants thoughtfully
3. Choose a context for the observation
4. Carefully observe the interaction or experience. This is best done by members of your design team.
5. It is important to influence the participants as little as possible by your presence.
6. Observe but do not interact with participants while observing them in context.
7. Capture Data
8. Identify issues
9. Identify needs
10. Create design solutions based on observed and experienced human needs.

RESOURCES

1. Digital camera
2. Video camera
3. Notebook
4. Pens
5. Voice recorder

REFERENCES

1. McDonald, Seonaidh. "Studying Actions in Context: A Qualitative Shadowing Method for Organizational Research." Qualitative Research. The Robert Gordon University. SAGE Publications. London. 2005. p455–473.

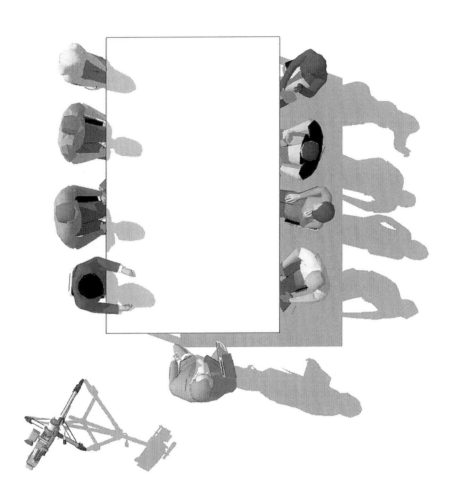

focus groups

WHAT IS IT?

Focus groups are discussions usually with 6 to 12 participants led by a moderator. Focus groups are used during the the design of products, services and experiences to get feedback from people

Powell defined a focus group as "A group of individuals selected and assembled by researchers to discuss and comment on, from personal experience, the topic that is the subject of the research."

WHO INVENTED IT?

Robert K. Merton 1940 Bureau of Applied Social Research.

WHY USE THIS METHOD?

1. To identify the expectations, needs and desires of customers.
2. It is useful to gain several different perspectives about a design problem.
3. A disadvantage of this method is that it removes the subjects from their context.

CHALLENGES

1. Focus group study results may not be not be generalizable.
2. Focus group participants can influence each other.

WHEN TO USE THIS METHOD

1. Know Context
2. Know User
3. Frame insights
4. Explore Concepts

HOW TO USE THIS METHOD

1. Select a good moderator.
2. Prepare a screening questionnaire.
3. Decide incentives for participants.
4. Select facility.
5. Recruit participants. Invite participants to your session well in advance and get firm commitments to attend. Remind participants the date of the event.
6. Participants should sit around a large table. Follow discussion guide.
7. Describe rules. Provide refreshments.
8. First question should encourage talking and participation.
9. The moderator manages responses and asks important questions
10. Moderator collects forms and debriefs focus group.
11. Analyze results while still fresh.
12. Summarize key points.
13. Run additional focus groups to deepen analysis.

RESOURCES

1. Focus group space.
2. Sound and video recording equipment
3. White board
4. Pens
5. Post-it-notes

REFERENCES

1. Nachmais, Chava Frankfort; Nachmais, David. 2008. Research methods in the Social Sciences: Seventh Edition New York, NY: Worth Publishers

FREE LIST TEMPLATE

Name of List ....

Prepared for ....

Date ....

Number	Name	Category	Use	Status	Checklist
1					
2					
3					
4					
5					
6					
7					
8					
9					
10					

Signature ....

free list

WHAT IS IT?
A free list is a list all words and concepts related to a particular area that is created by a participant. Because free lists are used to understand group culture frequency is important.

WHO INVENTED IT?
Trotter & Schensul 1998

WHY USE THIS METHOD?
1. Uncovers common perceptions meanings and classification systems
2. Low- cost
3. Little training required
4. Good source for baseline data
5. Works with individuals and groups
6. It is simple.
7. Can be used to compare different groups.
8. Can be used with brainstorming.
9. Helps researchers from using appropriate terms.
10. This method can be used when you have limited time with a group.

CHALLENGES
1. Not a stand alone method
2. Danger of making false associations
3. No accepted ways to check reliability of the procedure.

WHEN TO USE THIS METHOD
1. Know Context
2. Know User
3. Frame insights

HOW TO USE THIS METHOD
1. Consider what information would be valuable
2. Decide which domains you would like to define.
3. Formulate the question.
4. Test your question on several people to ensure the wording is coherent and appropriate.
5. Develop a short set of instructions.
6. Ask the free listing question.
7. It may be necessary to probe your informant for a more comprehensive list.
8. Ask informants to clarify items.
9. Collect data from multiple participants
10. Tally items to calculate the response frequency.
11. Combine the data collected through free listing with other methods to enrich your understanding.

RESOURCES
1. Pens
2. Laptop
3. Paper
4. Note pad.

REFERENCES
1. Borgatti, S. (1998). Elicitation Techniques for Cultural Domain Analysis. In Ethnographer's Toolkit, edited by J. Schensul. Newbury Park: Sage.
2. Weller, S.C. & Romney, A.K. (1988). Systematic Data Collection, Thousand Oaks, CA: Sage.

generative research

WHAT IS IT?

Generative research is research where participants make things to help express their ideas. Generative research can include methods from workshops where participants articulate their ideas by creating models using construction kits to diary methods.

WHO INVENTED IT?

Liz Sanders has been a pioneer of some generative methods.

WHY USE THIS METHOD?

1. Insights come from creative play.
2. Non designers can express their ideas creatively using generative tools.

CHALLENGES

1. Interpretation can be subjective.

WHEN TO USE THIS METHOD

1. Know Context
2. Know User
3. Frame insights

SEE ALSO

1. Diary studies
2. Creative toolkits
3. Photo diaries

RESOURCES

1. Construction kits
2. Diaries
3. White board
4. Pens
5. Creative space

REFERENCES

1. Sanders, E.B.-N. (2001) Virtuosos of the experience domain. In Proceedings of the 2001 IDSA Education Conference.

guerilla ethnography

WHAT IS IT?
Guerrilla ethnography is a collection of low cost responsive and flexible creative research methods. Examples include man on the street interviews, rapid iterative prototypes. remote usability testing. and empathy maps.

WHO INVENTED IT?
Jay Conrad Levinson 1984

WHY USE THIS METHOD?
1. Guerrilla methods are fast,
2. Guerrilla methods are less expensive.
3. Provide direction and data rather than opinions and speculation.
4. Uncover how people think and behave.
5. Provides sufficient insight to make more informed design decisions and guide design decisions.

CHALLENGES
1. Sometime the information gathered is more like a compass for design decisions rather than a road map.

WHEN TO USE THIS METHOD
1. Know Context
2. Know User
3. Frame insights

HOW TO USE THIS METHOD
1. Start by defining an activity, context, and time frame to focus on.
2. Create a plan.
3. Recruit from online sources like Facebook, Mechanical Turk, Ethnio, Craigslist, Twitter, or friends and family.
4. Observe real people in real-life situations
5. Capture Data
6. Reflection and Analysis
7. Brainstorming for solutions
8. Develop prototypes of possible solutions
9. Evaluate and refine the prototypes. Test several iterative refinements.
10. Ask for them to show and tell
11. Listen for pain points and seek opportunities.
12. Don't lead the user to the "right" path
13. Allow for exploration and discovery
14. Make simple prototypes of your favored designs.Only build what you need. No more.

RESOURCES
1. Digital camera
2. Notebook
3. Pens
4. Video camera

REFERENCES
1. Holtzblatt, K., Wendell, J.B., & Wood, S. 2005. Rapid Contextual Design: A How-to guide to key techniques for user-centered design. San Francisco: Morgan-Kaufmann.

ASSESSMENT CRITERIA	CONCEPT 1				CONCEPT 2				CONCEPT 3			
	-2	-1	+1	+2	-2	-1	+1	+2	-2	-1	+1	+2
AESTHETICS	X				X		X	X				X
COST	X	X									X	X
TIME TO MARKET							X		X		X	
ROI							X					
EASE OF MAINTENANCE	X	X		X	X		X	X				X
ENVIRONMENTAL IMPACT				X								
BRAND COMPLIANCE	X				X		X	X	X		X	
DISTRIBUTION	X	X			X					X		
USABILITY			X		X							
COMPLIANCE WITH REGULATIONS	X	X				X						
USE OF EXISTING RESOURCES								X				X

harris profile

WHAT IS IT?
A Harris Profile is a method for evaluating a number of design alternatives. A four-scale scoring method is used

WHO INVENTED IT?
J. S. Harris, 1961

WHY USE THIS METHOD?
1. One chosen/selected alternative from a group of alternatives.
2. Overview of the advantages and disadvantages of the selected alternative.
3. More understanding of the problem and criteria.

WHEN TO USE THIS METHOD
1. Define intent
2. Know Context
3. Know User
4. Frame insights

RESOURCES
1. Pen
2. Paper
3. White board
4. Dry erase markers

HOW TO USE THIS METHOD
1. Select criterion for evaluation.
2. Rate each criteria for each product, service or experience. The scale is coded – 2, – 1, + 1, and + 2.
3. Total the scores.

REFERENCES
1. Harris, J.S. (1961) 'New Product Profile Chart', Chemical and Engineering News, Vol. 39, No. 16, pp.110–118.
2. Roozenburg, N.F.M. and Eekels, J. (1995) Product Design: Fundamentals and Methods, Utrecht: Lemma.

heuristic evaluation

WHAT IS IT?

Also known as expert evaluation.
A technique used to identify user problems.
Experts judge whether a user interface follows
a list of established usability heuristics

WHO INVENTED IT?

Jacob Nielsen, 1990 Denmark

WHY USE THIS METHOD?

1. Inexpensive and fast.
2. Can be used early in the design process.
3. Fast feedback.
4. Reliable data.
5. Apply this method before testing
   prototypes with users.

CHALLENGES

1. Focuses on problems
2. Use before research subjects are studied
   for further testing.
3. This method will not uncover all problems.

WHEN TO USE THIS METHOD

1. Know Context
2. Know User
3. Frame insights
4. Explore Concepts

HOW TO USE THIS METHOD

1. Establish a panel of experts.
2. Establish an agreed set of evaluative
   criteria.
3. Brief experts and agree on criteria for the
   evaluation.
4. Each expert inspects the interface alone.
5. After the evaluations the individual
   results are aggregated.
6. A report is prepared which identifies
   a prioritized list of problems with the
   interface.
7. Action the findings of evaluation

RESOURCES

1. A panel of experts
2. A list of heuristic criteria for evaluation.

REFERENCES

1. Nielsen, J., and Molich, R. (1990).
   Heuristic evaluation of user interfaces,
   Proc. ACM CHI'90 Conf. (Seattle, WA, 1–5
   April), 249–256
2. Nielsen, J. (1994). Heuristic evaluation. In
   Nielsen, J., and Mack, R.L. (Eds.), Usability
   Inspection Methods, John Wiley & Sons,
   New York, NY

image: © Aniram | Dreamstime.com

historical method

WHAT IS IT?

Compare something today with something in history. Research the development of a product, service or experience.

Some areas of interest for designers are:

1. An understanding of the origin of an idea.
2. Knowledge of the author of an idea.
3. Local differences

WHO INVENTED IT?

Herodotus 5th century BC, was one of the earliest historians.

WHY USE THIS METHOD?

1. A review of history often uncovers insights relevant to a current design project.
2. Good ideas are sometimes forgotten and need to be rediscovered.
3. We want to avoid revisiting old but unsuccessful solutions

CHALLENGES

1. All constructed histories are written with a viewpoint or bias.
2. Choose sources that have no apparent benefit from presenting a biased account of events.

RESOURCES

1. Primary and secondary historical sources
2. Notebook
3. Pens
4. Digital voice recorder
5. Post-it-notes
6.

Photo: photocase.com - bobot

WHEN TO USE THIS METHOD

1. Know Context
2. Know User
3. Frame insights
4. Explore Concepts

HOW TO USE THIS METHOD

1. Define your subject of research.
2. Find out what secondary sources exist.
3. Create a research plan.
4. Create a goal for your research.
5. Make a list of necessary equipment, people, and materials.
6. Define a schedule for the research.
7. Plan tasks deliverable and milestones with dates.
8. Explore primary Sources.
9. Conduct primary source research.
10. Compile a list of citations.
11. Write the history.
12. Archive the data.

REFERENCES

1. Gilbert J. Garraghan, A Guide to Historical Method, Fordham University Press: New York (1946). ISBN 0-8371-7132-6
2. Martha Howell and Walter Prevenier, From Reliable Sources: An Introduction to Historical Methods, Cornell University Press: Ithaca (2001). ISBN 0-8014-8560-6.
3. R. J. Shafer, A Guide to Historical Method, The Dorsey Press: Illinois (1974). ISBN 0-534-10825-3.

interview methods

WHAT IS IT?
An interview is a conversation where questions are asked to obtain information.

WHY USE THIS METHOD?
Contextual interviews uncover tacit knowledge about people's context that the people may not be consciously aware of. The information gathered can be detailed.

CHALLENGES
1. Keep control
2. Be prepared
3. Be aware of bias
4. Be neutral
5. Select location carefully

RESOURCES
6. Note pad
7. Confidentiality agreement
8. Digital voice recorder
9. Video camera
10. Digital still camera

WHEN TO USE THIS METHOD
1. Know Context
2. Know User
3. Frame insights

HOW TO USE THIS METHOD
1. Contextual inquiry may be structured as 2 hour one on one interviews.
2. The researcher does not usually impose tasks on the user.
3. Go to the user's context. Talk, watch listen and observe.
4. Understand likes and dislikes.
5. Collect stories and insights.
6. See the world from the user's point of view.
7. Take permission to conduct interviews.
8. Do one-on-one interviews.
9. The researcher listens to the user.
10. 2 to 3 researchers conduct an interview.
11. Understand relationship between people, product and context.
12. Document with video, audio and notes.

RESOURCES
1. Computer
2. Notebook
3. Pens
4. Video camera
5. Release forms
6. Interview plan or structure
7. Questions, tasks and discussion items
8. Confidentiality agreement

REFERENCES
1. Kvale, Steinar. Interviews: An Introduction to Qualitative Research Interviewing, Sage Publications, 1996
2. Foddy, William. Constructing Questions for Interviews, Cambridge University Press, 1993

interview: contextual inquiry

WHAT IS IT?

Contextual inquiry involves one-on-one observations and interviews of activities in the context. Contextual inquiry has four guiding principles:

1. Context
2. Partnership with users.
3. Interpretation
4. Focus on particular goals.

WHO INVENTED IT?

Whiteside, Bennet, and Holtzblatt 1988

WHY USE THIS METHOD?

1. Contextual interviews uncover tacit knowledge about people's context.
2. The information gathered can be detailed.
3. The information produced by contextual inquiry is relatively reliable

CHALLENGES

1. End users may not have the answers
2. Contextual inquiry may be difficult to challenge even if it is misleading.

SEE ALSO

1. Questionnaire
2. Interview
3. Affinity diagram
4. Scenario
5. Persona
6. Ethnography
7. Contextual design

WHEN TO USE THIS METHOD

1. Know Context
2. Know User
3. Frame insights

HOW TO USE THIS METHOD

1. Contextual inquiry may be structured as 2 hour one on one interviews.
2. The researcher does not usually impose tasks on the user.
3. Go to the user's context. Talk, watch listen and observe.
4. Understand likes and dislikes.
5. Collect stories and insights.
6. See the world from the user's point of view.
7. Take permission to conduct interviews.
8. Do one-on-one interviews.
9. The researcher listens to the user.
10. 2 to 3 researchers conduct an interview.
11. Understand relationship between people, product and context.
12. Document with video, audio and notes.

REFERENCES

1. Beyer, H. and Holtzblatt, K., Contextual Design: Defining Customer-Centered Systems, Morgan Kaufmann Publishers Inc., San Francisco (1997).
2. Wixon and J. Ramey (Eds.), Field Methods Case Book for Product Design. John Wiley & Sons, Inc., NY, NY, 1996.

Photo: photocase.com – AlexAlex

interview: contextual interviews

WHAT IS IT?

Contextual inquiry is a user-centered research method. A contextual interview is conducted with people in their own environment. Contextual interviews with users can be conducted in environments such as homes, offices, trains, hospitals or factories. People and researchers collaborate to understand the context.

WHO INVENTED IT?

Whiteside, Bennet, and Holtzblatt 1988

WHY USE THIS METHOD?

Contextual interviews uncover tacit knowledge about people's context that the people may not be consciously aware of. The information gathered can be detailed.

CHALLENGES

1. Keep control
2. Be prepared
3. Be aware of bias
4. Be neutral
5. Select location carefully

WHEN TO USE THIS METHOD

1. Know Context
2. Know User
3. Frame insights

HOW TO USE THIS METHOD

Contextual inquiry is often structured as 2 hour one on one interviews. The researcher does not usually impose tasks on the user. The researcher listens to the user. A contextual interview has three phases:.

1. The introduction. The researcher gives information about the length of the interview, content, confidentiality and method of recording.
2. The body of the interview. The researcher investigates the user in context and documents the information gathered.
3. Wrap up. The researcher goes through the data gathered for verification and clarification by the person being interviewed.

RESOURCES

1. Computer
2. Notebook
3. Pens
4. Video camera
5. Release forms
6. Interview plan or structure
7. Questions, tasks and discussion items
8. Confidentiality agreement

REFERENCES

1. Rubin, Herbert and Irene Rubin. Qualitative Interviewing: The Art of Hearing Data. 2nd edition. Thousand Oaks, CA: Sage Publications, 2004. Print.
2. Kvale, Steinar. Interviews: An Introduction to Qualitative Research Interviewing, Sage Publications, 1996

interview: contextual laddering

WHAT IS IT?

Contextual laddering is a one-on-one interviewing technique done in context. Answers are further explored by the researcher to uncover root causes or core values.

WHO INVENTED IT?

Gutman 1982, Olsen and Reynolds 2001.

WHY USE THIS METHOD?

1. Laddering can uncover underlying reasons for particular behaviors.
2. Laddering may uncover information not revealed by other methods.
3. Complement other methods
4. Link features and product attributes with user/customer values

CHALLENGES

1. Analysis of data is sometimes difficult.
2. Requires a skilled interviewer who can keep the participants engaged.
3. Laddering can be an unpleasant experience for participants because of it's repetitive nature.
4. Sometimes information may not be represented hierarchically.

WHEN TO USE THIS METHOD

1. Know Context
2. Know User
3. Frame insights
4. Explore Concepts

HOW TO USE THIS METHOD

1. Interviews typically take 60 to 90 minutes.
2. The introduction. The researcher gives information about the length of the interview, content, confidentiality and method of recording.
3. The body of the interview. The researcher investigates the user in context and documents the information gathered.
4. Ask participants to describe what kinds of features would be useful in or distinguish different products.
5. Ask why.
6. If this answer doesn't describe the root motivation ask why again.
7. Repeat step 3. until you have reached the root motivation.
8. Wrap up. Verification and clarification

RESOURCES

1. Note pad
2. Confidentiality agreement
3. Digital voice recorder
4. Video camera
5. Digital still camera
6. Interview plan or structure
7. Questions, tasks and discussion items

REFERENCES

1. Reynolds TJ, Gutman J (2001) Laddering theory, method, analysis, and interpretation. In: Reynolds TJ et al (eds) Understanding consumer decision making. The means-end approach to marketing and advertising strategy. Lawrence Erlbaum associates, New Jersey, pp 25—62

interview: conversation cards

WHAT IS IT?
Cards used for initiating conversation in a contextual interview and to help subjects explore.

WHO INVENTED IT?
Originator unknown. Google Ngram indicates the term first appeared around 1801 in England for a collection of "Moral and Religious Anecdotes particularly adapted for the entertainment and instruction of young persons, and to support instead of destroying serious conversation"

WHY USE THIS METHOD?
1. Questions are the springboard for conversations.
2. Can be used to initiate sensitive conversations.

CHALLENGES
1. How will data from the cards be used?
2. How will cards be evaluated?
3. How many cards are necessary to be representative?
4. What are potential problems relating card engagement
5. Use one unit of information per question.

WHEN TO USE THIS METHOD
1. Know Context
2. Know User
3. Frame insights

HOW TO USE THIS METHOD
1. Decide on goal for research.
2. Formulate about 10 questions related to topic
3. Create the cards.
4. Recruit the subjects.
5. Undertake pre interview with sample subject to test.
6. Use release form if required.
7. Carry light equipment.
8. Record answers verbatim.
9. Communicate the purpose and length of the interview.
10. Select location. It should not be too noisy or have other distracting influences
11. Work through the cards.
12. Video or record the sessions for later review.
13. Analyze
14. Create Insights

RESOURCES
1. Conversation Cards.
2. Notebook
3. Video Camera
4. Pens
5. Interview plan or structure
6. Questions, tasks and discussion items

REFERENCES
1. Rubin, Herbert and Irene Rubin. Qualitative Interviewing: The Art of Hearing Data. 2nd edition. Thousand Oaks, CA: Sage Publications, 2004. Print.
2. Kvale, Steinar. Interviews: An Introduction to Qualitative Research Interviewing, Sage Publications, 1996

interview: emotion cards

WHAT IS IT?

Emotion cards are a field method of analyzing and quantifying peoples emotional response to a design. The method classifies emotions into sets of emotions which each can be associated with a specific recognizable facial expression.

The emotion card tool consists of sixteen cartoon-like faces, half male and half female, each representing distinct emotions. Each face represents a combination of two emotion dimensions,Pleasure and Arousal. Based on these dimensions, the emotion cards can be divided into four quadrants: Calm-Pleasant, Calm-Unpleasant, Excited-Pleasant, and Excited-Unpleasant.

WHO INVENTED IT?

Bradley 1994
Pieter Desmet 2001

WHY USE THIS METHOD?

1. It is an inexpensive method.
2. The results are easy to analyze.
3. Emotional responses are subtle and difficult to measure.
4. Emotion cards is a cross-cultural tool.
5. Facial emotions are typically universally recognized

CHALLENGES

1. Emotions of male and female faces are interpreted differently.
2. Sometimes users want to mark more than one picture to express a more complex emotional response.

WHEN TO USE THIS METHOD

1. Know Context
2. Know User
3. Frame insights
4. Explore Concepts

HOW TO USE THIS METHOD

1. Decide the goal of the study.
2. Recruit the participants.
3. Brief the participants.
4. When each interaction is complete the researcher asks the participant to select one of a number of cards that shows facial expressions that they associate with the interaction.

RESOURCES

1. Emotion cards
2. Notebook
3. Pens
4. Video camera
5. Release forms
6. Interview plan or structure
7. Questions, tasks and discussion items

REFERENCES

1. Bradley and Lang. Measuring emotion: the Self-Assessment Manikin and the Semantic Differential. Journal of Behavior Therapy and Experimental Psychiatry, 25, 1 (1994).
2. Desmet, P.M.A. Emotion through expression;designing mobile telephones with an emotional fit. Report of Modeling the Evaluation Structure of KANSEI, 3 (2000), 103-110.

interview: e-mail

WHAT IS IT?

With this method an interview is conducted via an e-mail exchange.

WHY USE THIS METHOD?

1. Extended access to people.
2. Background noises are not recorded.
3. Interviewee can answer the questions at his or her own convenience
4. It is not necessary to take notes
5. It is possible to use online translators.
6. Interviewees do not have to identify a convenient time to talk.

CHALLENGES

1. Interviewer may have to wait for answers.
2. Interviewer is disconnected from context.
3. Lack of communication of body language.

WHEN TO USE THIS METHOD

1. Know Context
2. Know User
3. Frame insight

HOW TO USE THIS METHOD

1. Choose a topic
2. Identify a subject.
3. Contact subject and obtain approval.
4. Prepare interview questions.
5. Conduct interview
6. Analyze data.

RESOURCES

1. Computer
2. Internet connection
3. Notebook
4. Pens
5. Interview plan or structure
6. Questions, tasks and discussion items
7. Confidentiality agreement

REFERENCES

1. Foddy, William. Constructing Questions for Interviews, Cambridge University Press, 1993

interview: extreme user

WHAT IS IT?

Interview experienced or inexperienced users of a product or service. in order to discover useful insights that can be applied to the general users.

WHY USE THIS METHOD?

Extreme user's solutions to problems can inspire solutions for general users. Their behavior can be more exaggerated than general users so it is sometimes easier to develop useful insights from these groups.

CHALLENGES

1. Keep control
2. Be prepared
3. Be aware of bias
4. Be neutral
5. Select location carefully

WHEN TO USE THIS METHOD

1. Know Context
2. Know User
3. Frame insights
4. Explore Concepts

HOW TO USE THIS METHOD

1. Do a timeline of your activity and break it into main activities
2. Identify very experienced or very inexperienced users of a product or service in an activity area.
3. Explore their experiences through interview.
4. Discover insights that can inspire design.
5. Refine design based on insights.

RESOURCES

1. Computer
2. Notebook
3. Pens
4. Video camera
5. Release forms
6. Interview plan or structure
7. Questions, tasks and discussion items
8. Confidentiality agreement

REFERENCES

1. Rubin, Herbert and Irene Rubin. Qualitative Interviewing: The Art of Hearing Data. 2nd edition. Thousand Oaks, CA: Sage Publications, 2004. Print.
2. Kvale, Steinar. Interviews: An Introduction to Qualitative Research Interviewing, Sage Publications, 1996
3. Foddy, William. Constructing Questions for Interviews, Cambridge University Press, 1993

Photo: photocase.com – gregpeppers

interview: group

WHAT IS IT?
This method involves interviewing a group of people.

WHY USE THIS METHOD?
People will often give different answers to questions if interviewed on=on=-one and in groups. If resources are available it is useful to interview people in both situations.

CHALLENGES
1. Group interview process is longer than an individual interview

WHEN TO USE THIS METHOD
1. Know Context
2. Know User
3. Frame insight

RESOURCES
1. Computer
2. Notebook
3. Pens
4. Video camera
5. Release forms
6. Interview plan or structure
7. Questions, tasks and discussion items
8. Confidentiality agreement

HOW TO USE THIS METHOD
1. Welcome everyone and introduce yourself
2. Describe the process.
3. Ask everyone to introduce themselves.
4. Conduct a group activity or warming-up exercise.
5. Break the larger group into smaller groups of 4 or 5 people and give them a question to answer. Ask each participant to present their response to the larger group.
6. Allow about 25 minutes.
7. Ask each interviewee to write a summary
8. Collect the summaries.
9. Ask if have any further comments.
10. Thank everyone and explain the next steps.
11. Give them your contact details.

REFERENCES
12. Kvale, Steinar. Interviews: An Introduction to Qualitative Research Interviewing, Sage Publications, 1996
13. Foddy, William. Constructing Questions for Interviews, Cambridge University Press, 1993

interview: guided storytelling

WHAT IS IT?

Guided storytelling is interview technique, where the designer asks a participant to walk you through a scenario of use for a concept. Directed story telling guides participants to describe their experiences and thoughts on a specific topic.

WHO INVENTED IT?

Whiteside, Bennet, and Holtzblatt 1988

WHY USE THIS METHOD?

1. Guided storytelling uncovers tacit knowledge.

CHALLENGES

1. Keep control
2. Be prepared
3. Be aware of bias
4. Be neutral
5. Select location carefully

WHEN TO USE THIS METHOD

1. Know Context
2. Know User
3. Frame insight

RESOURCES

1. Computer
2. Notebook
3. Pens
4. Video camera
5. Release forms
6. Interview plan or structure
7. Questions, tasks and discussion items
8. Confidentiality agreement

HOW TO USE THIS METHOD

1. Contextual inquiry may be structured as 2 hour one on one interviews.
2. The researcher does not usually impose tasks on the user.
3. Go to the user's context. Talk, watch listen and observe.
4. Understand likes and dislikes.
5. Collect stories and insights.
6. See the world from the user's point of view.
7. Take permission to conduct interviews.
8. Do one-on-one interviews.
9. The researcher listens to the user.
10. 2 to 3 researchers conduct an interview.
11. Understand relationship between people, product and context.

REFERENCES

1. Rubin, Herbert and Irene Rubin. Qualitative Interviewing: The Art of Hearing Data. 2nd edition. Thousand Oaks, CA: Sage Publications, 2004. Print.
2. Kvale, Steinar. Interviews: An Introduction to Qualitative Research Interviewing, Sage Publications, 1996
3. Foddy, William. Constructing Questions for Interviews, Cambridge University Press, 1993

interview: man in the street

WHAT IS IT?
Man in the street interviews are impromptu interviews usually recorded on video. They are usually conducted by two people, a researcher and a cameraman.

WHY USE THIS METHOD?
1. Contextual interviews uncover tacit knowledge.
2. The information gathered can be detailed.

CHALLENGES
1. Keep control
2. Be prepared
3. Be aware of bias
4. Be neutral
5. Ask appropriate questions
6. Select location carefully
7. Create a friendly atmosphere, interviewee to feel relaxed.
8. Clearly convey the purpose of the interview.
9. This method results in accidental sampling which may not be representative of larger groups.

WHEN TO USE THIS METHOD
1. Know Context
2. Know User
3. Frame insights

HOW TO USE THIS METHOD
1. Decide on goal for research.
2. Formulate about 10 questions related to topic
3. Use release form if required.
4. Conduct a preliminary interview.
5. Select location. It should not be too noisy or have other distracting influences
6. Approach people, be polite. Say, "Excuse me, I work for [your organization] and I was wondering if you could share your opinion about [your topic]."
7. If someone does not wish to respond, select another subject to interview.
8. Limit your time. Each interview should be no be longer than about 10 minutes.
9. Conduct 6 to 10 interviews

RESOURCES
1. Video camera
2. release forms

REFERENCES
1. Rubin, Herbert and Irene Rubin. Qualitative Interviewing: The Art of Hearing Data. 2nd edition. Thousand Oaks, CA: Sage Publications, 2004. Print.
2. Kvale, Steinar. Interviews: An Introduction to Qualitative Research Interviewing, Sage Publications, 1996
3. Foddy, William. Constructing Questions for Interviews, Cambridge University Press, 1993

interview: one-on-one

WHAT IS IT?
The one-on-one interview is an interview that is between a researcher and one participant in a face-to-face situation.

WHY USE THIS METHOD?
1. The best method for personal information
2. Works well with other methods in obtaining information to inform design.
3. Can be used to exchange ideas or to gather information to inform design

CHALLENGES
1. Keep control
2. Be prepared
3. Be aware of bias
4. Be neutral
5. Select location carefully
6. Record everything
7. Combine one on one interviews with group interviews.

WHEN TO USE THIS METHOD
1. Know Context
2. Know User
3. Frame insights

RESOURCES
4. Notebook
5. Pens
6. Video camera
7. Release forms
8. Interview plan
9. Questions, and tasks

image: © Kuzma | Dreamstime.com

HOW TO USE THIS METHOD
1. May be structured as 2 hour one on one interviews.
2. Select the questions and the subjects carefully.
3. Create interview guide,
4. Conduct a preinterview to refine the guide.
5. The researcher does not usually impose tasks on the user.
6. Go to the user's context. Talk, watch listen and observe.
7. Understand likes and dislikes.
8. Collect stories and insights.
9. See the world from the user's point of view.
10. Take permission to conduct interviews.
11. Understand relationship between person, product and context.
12. Document with video, audio and notes.

REFERENCES
1. Rubin, Herbert and Irene Rubin. Qualitative Interviewing: The Art of Hearing Data. 2nd edition. Thousand Oaks, CA: Sage Publications, 2004. Print.
2. Kvale, Steinar. Interviews: An Introduction to Qualitative Research Interviewing, Sage Publications, 1996
3. Foddy, William. Constructing Questions for Interviews, Cambridge University Press, 1993

interview: structured

WHAT IS IT?

In a structured interview the researcher prepares a list of questions, script or an interview guide that they follow during the interview. Most interviews use a structured method.

WHY USE THIS METHOD?

1. A structured interview is often used for for phone interviews.
2. It is easy to analyze the results.
3. Structured interviews are often used by quantitative researchers.

CHALLENGES

1. Respondents may be less likely to discuss sensitive experiences.

WHEN TO USE THIS METHOD

1. Know Context
2. Know User
3. Frame insight

HOW TO USE THIS METHOD

1. The researcher should follow the script exactly.
2. The interviewer is required to show consistency in behavior across all interviews

RESOURCES

1. Computer
2. Notebook
3. Pens
4. Video camera
5. Release forms
6. Interview plan
7. Questions, and tasks
8. Confidentiality agreement

REFERENCES

1. Rubin, Herbert and Irene Rubin. Qualitative Interviewing: The Art of Hearing Data. 2nd edition. Thousand Oaks, CA: Sage Publications, 2004. Print.
2. Kvale, Steinar. Interviews: An Introduction to Qualitative Research Interviewing, Sage Publications, 1996
3. Foddy, William. Constructing Questions for Interviews, Cambridge University Press, 1993

interview: unstructured

WHAT IS IT?

Unstructured interviews are interviews where questions can be modified as needed by the researcher during the interview.

WHY USE THIS METHOD?

1. A useful technique for understanding how a subject may perform under pressure.
2. Unstructured interviews are used in ethnographies and case studies
3. Respondents may be more likely to discuss sensitive experiences.

CHALLENGES

1. Interviewer bias is unavoidable

WHEN TO USE THIS METHOD

1. Know Context
2. Know User
3. Frame insight

HOW TO USE THIS METHOD

1. Researchers need a list of topics to be covered during the interview

RESOURCES

1. Computer
2. Notebook
3. Pens
4. Video camera
5. Release forms
6. Interview plan
7. Questions, and tasks
8. Confidentiality agreement

REFERENCES

1. Rubin, Herbert and Irene Rubin. Qualitative Interviewing: The Art of Hearing Data. 2nd edition. Thousand Oaks, CA: Sage Publications, 2004. Print.
2. Kvale, Steinar. Interviews: An Introduction to Qualitative Research Interviewing, Sage Publications, 1996
3. Foddy, William. Constructing Questions for Interviews, Cambridge University Press, 1993

interview: telephone

WHAT IS IT?
With this method an interview is conducted via telephone.

WHY USE THIS METHOD?
1. Wide geographical access
2. Allows researcher to reach hard to reach people.
3. Allows researcher to access closed locations.
4. Access to dangerous or politically sensitive sites

CHALLENGES
1. Lack of communication of body language.
2. Interviewer is disconnected from context.

WHEN TO USE THIS METHOD
1. Know Context
2. Know User
3. Frame insight

HOW TO USE THIS METHOD
1. Choose a topic
2. Identify a subject.
3. Contact subject and obtain approval.
4. Prepare interview questions.
5. Conduct interview
6. Analyze data.

RESOURCES
7. Computer
8. Notebook
9. Pens

REFERENCES
1. Rubin, Herbert and Irene Rubin. Qualitative Interviewing: The Art of Hearing Data. 2nd edition. Thousand Oaks, CA: Sage Publications, 2004. Print.
2. Kvale, Steinar. Interviews: An Introduction to Qualitative Research Interviewing, Sage Publications, 1996
3. Foddy, William. Constructing Questions for Interviews, Cambridge University Press, 1993

image: Miklav | Dreamstime.com

longitudinal analysis

WHAT IS IT?

Some research requires long term studies. Longitudinal analysis focuses on studying a group of people over a long period of time The study may continue over decades. This method allows insights into a person's long term development. Longitudinal studies allow designers and researchers to distinguish short from long-term phenomena.

WHY USE THIS METHOD?

1. Longitudinal studies allow design researchers to distinguish short from long-term phenomena, such as poverty or aging.
2. Allows researchers to look at changes over tim

CHALLENGES

1. There is the risk of bias due to incomplete follow up,
2. Longitudinal studies are expensive
3. Participants drop out of the study

RESOURCES

1. Note pad
2. Computer
3. Video camera
4. Camera

WHEN TO USE THIS METHOD

1. Know Context
2. Know User
3. Frame insights

HOW TO USE THIS METHOD

Three types of longitudinal studies:
1. Panel Study: Involves sampling diverse individuals.
2. Cohort Study: Involves selecting a group based on factors such as their age or where they live.
3. Retrospective Study: Involves looking at historical records

REFERENCES

1. Carlson, Neil and et al. "Psychology the Science of Behavior", p. 361. Pearson Canada

magic thing

WHAT IS IT?

A Magic Thing is a prop that is a focus for ideas in the context where a design will be used. It can be a material such as wood or hard foam without surface detail. Participants carry a "magic thing" with them as they undertake their activities in context to imagine how a portable device could function.

WHO INVENTED IT?

Jeff Hawkins. Howard 2002. Jeff Hawkins, one of the inventors of the Palm Pilot PDA, carried a small block of wood to help him brainstorm interaction in various environments.

WHY USE THIS METHOD?

1. It is a form of physical prototype that simulates interaction when little information is available.

CHALLENGES

1. The researcher can put some imaginary constraints on the device so that it's technological capabilities are not too far from reality.

WHEN TO USE THIS METHOD

1. Know Context
2. Know User
3. Frame insights
4. Generate Concepts
5. Create Solutions

HOW TO USE THIS METHOD

1. The researcher briefs the participants on a design scenario.
2. The participants are given a prop, their magic thing.
3. The participants are briefed on the technological capabilities of the magic thing.
4. The participants and design team then act out scenarios in context.
5. The role playing is recorded by video or user diaries.
6. The material is analyzed and insights identified.

RESOURCES

1. A magic thing such as a block of wood about the size of a proposed device.
2. Video camera

REFERENCES

1. Lacucci, G., Mäkelä A., Ranta, M., Mäntylä, M., Visualizing Context, Mobility and Group Interaction: Role Games to Design Product Concepts for Mobile Communication, In: the Proceeding of COOP'2000, Designing Cooperative Systems Conference, 23-26 May 2000, IOS Press, 2000.

market segmentation

WHAT IS IT?

A market segment is a group of people with characteristics in common. A market segment is distinct from other segments, it exhibits common needs; it responds similarly to a market stimulus, and it can be reached by a market intervention.

WHO INVENTED IT?

Wendel Smith 1956

WHY USE THIS METHOD?

1. The purpose for segmenting a market is to allow you to focus on people that are "most likely" to use your design.
2. This will help optimize your return on investment.

CHALLENGES

1. Everyone is different.
2. Market segmentation assumes uniformity.
3. Internet based techniques will allow marketing to be done on a customized individual basis.

WHEN TO USE THIS METHOD

1. Know Context
2. Know User
3. Frame insights
4. Generate Concepts
5. Create Solutions

HOW TO USE THIS METHOD

1. Based on what people do
Use and behavior, activities or interests
2. Based on who people are
3. Based on how people think or feel
Attitudes,Needs behaviors and motivations
4. A combination of factors

REFERENCES

1. What is geographic segmentation' Kotler, Philip, and Kevin Lane Keller. Marketing Management. Prentice Hall, 2006. ISBN 978-0-13-145757-7
2. Goldstein, Doug. "What is Customer Segmentation?" Mind of Marketing.net, May 2007. New York, NY.
3. Sheth-Voss, Pieter. Carreras, Ismael. How Informative is Your Segmentation? A simple new metric yields surprising results, Marketing Research, pages 8-13, Winter 2010, American Marketing Association

mobile ethnography

WHAT IS IT?

Widespread use of mobile devices including laptops, tablets and digital cameras smart phone has enabled new ways of undertaking research and connecting with people with people in their everyday context.

WHY USE THIS METHOD?

1. Can be faster and less expensive than non-digital methods.
2. Data collected real time
3. Access to people may be easier
4. People carry digital devices such as smart phones, cameras, laptops and tablets
5. Data can be gathered in context

CHALLENGES

1. Can miss non verbal feedback.
2. Technology may be unreliable
3. Devices may be expensive

WHEN TO USE THIS METHOD

4. Define intent
5. Know Context
6. Know User
7. Frame insights
8. Explore Concepts
9. Make Plans
10. Deliver Offering

HOW TO USE THIS METHOD

There are many different methods which use or access:

1. Audio conferences
2. Web conferences
3. Virtual in depth interviews
4. Virtual Focus groups
5. Mobile diaries

RESOURCES

1. Smart phones,
2. Cameras,
3. Laptops and tablets
4. Mobile software applications

REFERENCES

1. Coover, R. (2004) 'Using Digital Media Tools and Cross-Cultural Research,Analysis and Representation', Visual Studies19(1): 6—25.
2. Dicks, B., B. Mason, A. Coffey and P. Atkinson (2005) Qualitative Research and Hypermedia: Ethnography for the Digital Age. London: SAGE.
3. Kozinets R.V. (2010a), Netnography. Doing Ethnographic Research Online, Sage, London.

mobile diary study

WHAT IS IT?

A mobile diary studies is a method that uses portable devices to capture a person's experiences in context when and where they happen such as their work place or home. Participants can create diary entries from their location on mobile phones or tablets.

WHY USE THIS METHOD?

1. Most people carry a mobile phone.
2. It is a convenient method of recording diary entries.
3. It is easier to collect the data than collecting written diaries.
4. Collection of data happens in real time.
5. Mobile devices have camera, voice and written capability.

CHALLENGES

1. Can miss non verbal feedback.
2. Technology may be unreliable

WHEN TO USE THIS METHOD

1. Know Context
2. Know User
3. Frame insights

HOW TO USE THIS METHOD

1. Define intent
2. Define audience
3. Define context
4. Define technology
5. Automated text messages are sent to participants to prompt an entry.
6. Analyze data

RESOURCES

1. Smart phones,
2. Cameras,
3. Laptops and
4. Tablets

REFERENCES

1. Coover, R. (2004) 'Using Digital Media Tools and Cross-Cultural Research,Analysis and Representation', Visual Studies19(1): 6—25.
2. Dicks, B., B. Mason, A. Coffey and P. Atkinson (2005) Qualitative Research and Hypermedia: Ethnography for the Digital Age. London: SAGE.
3. Kozinets R.V. (2010a), Netnography. Doing Ethnographic Research Online, Sage, London.

image: © Adamr | Dreamstime.com

mystery shopper

WHAT IS IT?
Mystery shopping tool used to collect information about products and services. Mystery shoppers perform tasks including purchasing a product, submitting complaints, and then produce feedback.

Mystery shopping is also known as:
1. Secret Shopping
2. Experience Evaluation
3. Mystery Customers
4. Spotters
5. Digital Customers
6. Evaluations of employee interactions
7. Audits of employee performance
8. Telephone Checks

WHO INVENTED IT?
It was first used around 1953

WHY USE THIS METHOD?
1. Provides information performance
2. Produces actionable insights.
3. Increases employee and customer levels of satisfaction

CHALLENGES
1. Can be expensive, time consuming and not supported by employees.
2. Ethical issues

WHEN TO USE THIS METHOD
1. Know Context
2. Know User
3. Frame insights

HOW TO USE THIS METHOD
1. Form objectives
2. Create evaluation form for mystery shopper
3. Recruit mystery shoppers. Can be internal or external personnel.
4. Train mystery shoppers
5. Conduct evaluation.
6. Analyze results.
7. Formulate conclusions and actions needed.
8. Implement Actions.

RESOURCES
1. Evaluation form
2. Video camera
3. Notebook
4. Digital still camera.

REFERENCES
1. Health Care Taps 'Mystery Shoppers' at Wall Street Journal, August 8, 2006
2. C. Erlich, "Mystery Shopping," Competitive Intelligence Magazine 10(2007): 43-44.
3. Ton Van Der Wiele, Martin Hesselink, and Jos Van Iwaarden, "Mystery Shopping: A Tool to Develop Insight into Customer Service Provision," Total Quality Management 16(2005): 529-541.

network map

WHAT IS IT?

This is a method which maps and helps the researcher understand systems or services that involve many stakeholders. The map identifies the stakeholders, their links, influence and goals.

WHO INVENTED IT?

Eva Schiffer 2004 to 2008

WHY USE THIS METHOD?

1. Inexpensive and fast.
2. Connects to existing research tools and methods
3. Makes implicit knowledge explicit
4. Structures complex reality
5. Flexible for use in different contexts.

RESOURCES

1. Large sheets of paper for network map
2. Felt pens for drawing links
3. Adhesive paper as actor cards
4. Flat discs for building Influence-towers
5. Actor figurines

WHEN TO USE THIS METHOD

1. Know Context
2. Know User
3. Frame insights

HOW TO USE THIS METHOD

1. Define problems and goals.
2. Recruit participants
3. Define interview questions
4. Define network links to study
5. Ask participant to go through the process in detail.
6. Make a card with the name and description of each stakeholder. Place the cards on your map.
7. Show links between the stakeholders as lines on the map.
8. Number the links.
9. Create a legend describing each link.
10. Setting up influence towers:
11. Describe the influence of each stakeholder.?
12. Quantify the strength of influence of each stakeholder.
13. Stack discs next to each stakeholder card showing the relative level of influence.
14. Write descriptions of perceived problems next to each stakeholder.

REFERENCES

1. Eva Schiffer http://netmap.wordpress.com/process-net-map

INTERVIEW PROCESS

Question 1: Who is involved?

Ask: "Who is involved in this process?"Write names on actor cards (with different colors of cards for different groups of actors) and distribute on empty Net-Map sheet.

Question 2: How are they linked?

Ask: "Who is linked to whom?" Go through the different kinds of links one by one Draw arrows between actor cards according to interviewee directions. If two actors exchange something draw double headed arrows. If actors exchange more than one thing, add differently colored arrow heads to existing links.

Question 3: How influential are they?

Ask: "How strongly can actors influence (our complex issue)?" Explain / agree on a definition of influence with your interviewee, clarify that this is about influence only and not influence in the world at large. Ask interviewee to assign influence towers to actors: The higher the influence on the issue at stake, the higher the tower. Towers of different actors can be of the same height. Actors with no influence can be put on ground level. Towers can be as high as participants want. Place influence towers next to actor cards. Verbalize set-up and give interviewee the chance to adjust towers before noting height of tower on the Net-Map.

Question 4: What are their goals?

Ask according to pre-defined goals, actor by actor, e.g. "Does this actor support environmental, developmental goals or both?" Note abbreviations for goals next to actor cards, allow for multiple goals where appropriate, by noting more than one goal next to the actor.

Discussion

Discuss the result with your interview partners. Depending on the goal of this specific mapping process, you might ask your participants to think strategically about the network and develop ideas to improve the situation in the future.

Source: Eva Schiffer http://netmap.wordpress.com/process-net-map

observation

WHAT IS IT?

This method involves observing people in their natural activities and usual context such as work environment. With direct observation the researcher is present and indirect observation the activities may be recorded by means such as video or digital voice recording.

WHY USE THIS METHOD?

1. Allows the observer to view what users actually do in context.
2. Indirect observation uncovers activity that may have previously gone unnoticed

CHALLENGES

1. Observation does not explain the cause of behavior.
2. Obtrusive observation may cause participants to alter their behavior.
3. Analysis can be time consuming.
4. Observer bias can cause the researcher to look only where they think they will see useful information.

WHEN TO USE THIS METHOD

1. Know Context
2. Know User
3. Frame insights

HOW TO USE THIS METHOD

1. Define objectives
2. Define participants and obtain their cooperation.
3. Define The context of the observation: time and place.
4. In some countries the law requires that you obtain written consent to video people.
5. Define the method of observation and the method of recording information. Common methods are taking written notes, video or audio recording.
6. Run a test session.
7. Hypothesize an explanation for the phenomenon
8. Predict a logical consequence of the hypothesis
9. Test your hypothesis by observation
10. Analyze the data gathered and create a list of insights derived from the observations.

RESOURCES

1. Note pad
2. Pens
3. Camera
4. Video camera
5. Digital voice recorder

REFERENCES

1. Kosso, Peter (2011). A Summary of Scientific Method. Springer. pp. 9. ISBN 9400716133,

open card sort

WHAT IS IT?

This is a method for discovering the relationships of a list of items. Participants asked to arrange individual, unsorted items into groups. For an open card sort the user defines the groups rather than the researcher.

Card sorting is applied when:

1. When there is a large number of items.
2. The items are similar and difficult to organize into categories.
3. Users may have different perceptions related to organizing the items.

WHO INVENTED IT?

Jastrow 1886
Nielsen & Sano 1995

WHY USE THIS METHOD?

1. It is a simple method using index cards,
2. Used to provide insights for interface design.

CHALLENGES

1. Ask participants to fill ot a second card if they feel it belongs in two groups.
2. There are a number of online card sorting tools available.

RESOURCES

1. Post cards
2. Pens
3. Post-it-notes
4. Laptop computer
5. A table

WHEN TO USE THIS METHOD

1. Know Context
2. Know User
3. Frame insights
4. Explore Concepts

HOW TO USE THIS METHOD

1. Recruit between 5 and 15 participants representative of your user group.
2. Provide a small deck of cards.
3. Provide clear instructions. Ask your participants to arrange the cards in ways that make sense to them. 100 cards takes about 1 hour to sort.
4. The user sorts labelled cards into groups by that they define themselves.
5. The user can generate more card labels.
6. If users do not understand a card ask them to exclude it. Ask participants for their rationale for any dual placements of cards.
7. Analyze the piles of cards and create a list of insights derived from the card sort.
8. Analyze the data. Proximity or similarity matrixes, dendrograms, and tree diagrams help create a taxonomical hierarchy for the items being grouped

REFERENCES

1. Jakob Nielsen (May 1995). "Card Sorting to Discover the Users' Model of the Information Space".
2. Jakob Nielsen (July 19, 2004). "Card Sorting: How Many Users to Test"

personal inventory

WHAT IS IT?

This method involves studying the contents of a research subject's purse, or wallet. Study the things that they carry everyday.

WHO INVENTED IT?

Rachel Strickland and Doreen Nelson 1998

WHY USE THIS METHOD?

1. To provide insights into the user's lifestyle, activities, perceptions, and values.
2. To understand the needs priorities and interests

WHEN TO USE THIS METHOD

1. Know Context
2. Know User
3. Frame insights

HOW TO USE THIS METHOD

1. Formulate aims of research
2. Recruit participants carefully.
3. "the participant is asked to bring their 'most often carried bag' and lay the objects they carry on a flat surface, talking through the purpose and last-use of each item. Things to look out for where the bag is kept in the home and what is clustered around it, what is packed/ repacked on arrival/departure, and the use of different bags for different activities." *Jan Chipchase*
4. Document the contents with photographs and notes
5. Ask your research subject to talk about the objects and their meaning.
6. Analyze the data.

RESOURCES

1. Camera
2. Note pad

PERSONA

PERSONA NAME
....

DEMOGRAPHICS
....
....
....
....

CHARACTERISTIC STATEMENT
....
....
....
....
....

GOALS
....
....
....
....

AMBITIONS
....
....
....
....

INFLUENCERS AND ACTIVITIES
....
....
....
....

SCENARIOS
....
....
....
....

OTHER CHARACTERISTICS

TYPE: TYPE: TYPE: TYPE: TYPE: TYPE: TYPE: TYPE: TYPE:

personas

WHAT IS IT?

"A persona is a archetypal character that is meant to represent a group of users in a role who share common goals, attitudes and behaviors when interacting with a particular product or service Personas are user models that are presented as specific individual humans. They are not actual people, but are synthesized directly from observations of real people."(Cooper)

WHO INVENTED IT?

Alan Cooper 1998

WHY USE THIS METHOD?

1. Helps create empathy for users and reduces self reference.
2. Use as tool to analyze and gain insight into users.
3. Help in gaining buy-in from stake holders.

CHALLENGES

1. Portigal (2008) has claimed that personas give a "cloak of smug customer-centricity" while actually distancing a team from engagement with real users and their needs

REFERENCES

1. Pruitt, John & Adlin, Tamara. The Persona Lifecycle : Keeping People in Mind Throughout Product Design. Morgan Kaufmann, 2006. ISBN 0-12-566251-3

WHEN TO USE THIS METHOD

1. Know Context
2. Know User
3. Frame insights
4. Explore Concept

HOW TO USE THIS METHOD

1. Inaccurate personas can lead to a false understandings of the end users. Personas need to be created using data from real users.
2. Collect data through observation, interviews, ethnography.
3. Segment the users or customers
4. Create the Personas
5. Avoid Stereotypes
6. Each persona should be different. Avoid fringe characteristics. Personas should each have three to four life goals which are personal aspirations,
7. Personas are given a name, and photograph.
8. Design personas can be followed by building customer journeys

RESOURCES

1. Raw data on users from interviews or other research
2. Images of people similar to segmented customers.
3. Computer
4. Graphics software

picture cards

WHAT IS IT?

Picture cards is a method that involves using a collection of cards with images and words that help people talk about their life experiences

WHY USE THIS METHOD?

1. Helps people discuss their experiences and feelings relevant to the research topic.
2. It is relatively inexpensive and fast.
3. The cards may make staring in depth conversations easier.

WHEN TO USE THIS METHOD

4. Know Context
5. Know User
6. Frame insights

HOW TO USE THIS METHOD

1. 100 to 150 cards are created with images and words relevant to the research topic.
2. Prepare question guide
3. In the participant session the researcher asks the participant to recall a story about an experience to start a conversation.
4. Include cards that help the participant discuss issues relevant to proposed design.
5. Can video the session with permission.
6. Analyze the data

RESOURCES

1. Deck of picture cards
2. Video camera
3. Note pad

CRITERIA	CONCEPT 1	CONCEPT 2	CONCEPT 3	CONCEPT 4
Functionality	S	-	-	+
Cost	+	+	+	+
Aesthetics	-	S	-	+
Manufacturability	-	+	+	-
Usability	+	+	-	S
Safety	-	-	-	-
Reliability	-	S	-	-
Maintenance	+	-	-	S
Efficiency	+	+	S	+
Environmental Impact	-	+	-	-
Speed to market	S	-	+	-
Fit with Brand	+	+	-	-
TOTAL	0	2	-3	-2

pugh's matrix

WHAT IS IT?
Pugh's Method is a design evaluation method that uses criteria in an evaluation matrix to compare alternative design directions.

WHO INVENTED IT?
Stuart Pugh 1977

WHY USE THIS METHOD?
1. Overcome shortcomings of design
2. Find different ideas to satisfy criteria
3. Explore alternatives
4. This method can make subjective observations more objective.

CHALLENGES
1. Groupthink
2. Not enough good ideas
3. Taking turns
4. Freeloading
5. Inhibition
6. Lack of critical thinking
7. A group that is too large competes for attention.

WHEN TO USE THIS METHOD
1. Know Context
2. Know User
3. Frame insights
4. Explore Concepts
5. Make Plans

HOW TO USE THIS METHOD
1. Develop the evaluation criteria
2. Identify design criteria to be compared.
3. Design concepts: original design
4. Concepts brainstormed
5. Evaluation matrix: each design evaluated against a best design datum
6. Generate Scores.
7. Calculate the total score
8. Iterate, refine, optimize design
9. Document results

EVALUATION SCALE
+ means substantially better
− means clearly worse
S means more or less the same

RESOURCES
1. White board
2. Dry-erase markers
3. Pens
4. Paper
5. Design Team, 4 to 12 cross disciplinary members
6. Room with privacy

REFERENCES
1. Stuart Pugh, Don Clausing, Ron Andrade, (April 24, 1996). Creating Innovative Products Using Total Design. Addison Wesley Longman. ISBN 0-201-63485-6
2. S. Pugh (1981) Concept selection: a method that works. In: Hubka, V. (ed.), Review of design methodology. Proceedings interna-tional conference on engineering design, March 1981, Rome. Zürich: Heurista, 1981, blz. 497 — 506.

questionnaires

WHAT IS IT?

A questionnaire is a research tool made up of a number of questions. Questionnaires may be designed for statistical analysis. This is a primary research method.

WHY USE THIS METHOD?

1. Easy to analyze
2. Large sample at relatively low cost.
3. Simple to manage
4. Familiar format
5. Quick to complete
6. Can be used for sensitive topics
7. Respondents have flexibility in time to complete.

WHO INVENTED IT?

Sir Francis Galton 1800s

WHEN TO USE THIS METHOD

1. Know Context
2. Know User
3. Frame insights

CHALLENGES

1. Avoid complex questions
2. Avoid leading questions
3. Avoid jargon
4. Avoid bias
5. Have standard procedure
6. Ask one information at a time
7. Be as simple as possible
8. Adjust the style of the questions to the target audience

HOW TO USE THIS METHOD

1. Define the questions to research
2. Select the participants
3. Prepare the questions
4. Use closed questions with multiple predefined choices or open questions to allow respondents to respond in their own words.
5. Two common closed formats are: the Likert 7 point format: strongly agree, agree, undecided, disagree, strongly disagree. Or 4 point Forced choice format, Strongly agree, agree, disagree, strongly disagree.
6. Pretest the questionnaire
7. Refine the questionnaire
8. Questions should flow logically

REFERENCES

1. Gillham, B. (2008). Developing a questionnaire (2nd ed.). London, UK: Continuum International Publishing Group Ltd
2. Oppenheim, A. N. (2000). Questionnaire design, interviewing and attitude measurement (New ed.). London, UK: Continuum International Publishing Group Ltd.

remote evaluation

WHAT IS IT?
Remote evaluation is any usability testing method where the researcher and participant are not in the same location. Remote evaluation may be moderated, or unmoderated.

WHO INVENTED IT?
First published Hartson Castillo Kelson and Neale 1996

WHY USE THIS METHOD?
1. Captures rich feedback
2. Users are in own context
3. Can use for single or multiple participants.
4. May be less expensive and faster.
5. Good for Geographically dispersed user groups.
6. The participant records the data.
7. Face to face evaluation can be expensive, It may be difficult to access participants. and requires a dedicated space.

CHALLENGES
1. You can read body language with in person testing.
2. Difficult to build relationship with participants.
3. Difficult to ensure security of information.
4. Technology can present problems.

WHEN TO USE THIS METHOD
1. Know Context
2. Know User
3. Frame insights

HOW TO USE THIS METHOD
1. Define focus of study.
2. Recruit participants.
3. Typically 5 to 5 participants are used in each iteration of testing.
4. Schedule the evaluation.
5. Brief the participants
6. Run a pilot test.
7. Instruct the participants to say what they are thinking and doing doing and why out loud repeatedly.
8. Users undertake the tasks.
9. Participants undertake a short questionnaire.
10. Researcher review the data and analyzes most common participant problems.
11. Designer implements the changes to the the design based on participant feedback.

RESOURCES
1. Computers
2. Research software

REFERENCES
1. Chalil Madathil, Kapil; Joel S. Greenstein (May 2011). "Synchronous remote usability testing: a new approach facilitated by virtual worlds". Proceedings of the 2011 annual conference on Human factors in computing systems. CHI '11: 2225—2234.
2. Dray, Susan; Siegel, David (March 2004). "Remote possibilities?: international usability testing at a distance". Interactions 11 (2): 10—17. doi:10.1145/971258.971264.

shadowing

WHAT IS IT?

Shadowing is observing people in context. The researcher accompanies the user and observes user experiences and activities. It allows the researcher and designer to develop design insights through observation and shared experiences with users.

WHO INVENTED IT?

Alex Bavelas 1944
Lucy Vernile, Robert A. Monteiro 1991

WHY USE THIS METHOD?

1. This method can help determine the difference between what subjects say they do and what they really do.
2. It helps in understanding the point of view of people. Successful design results from knowing the users.
3. Define intent
4. Can be used to evaluate concepts.

CHALLENGES

1. Selecting the wrong people to shadow.
2. Hawthorne Effect, The observer can influence the daily activities under being studied.

WHEN TO USE THIS METHOD

1. Know Context
2. Know User
3. Frame insights
4. Generate Concepts

HOW TO USE THIS METHOD

1. Prepare
2. Select carefully who to shadow.
3. Observe people in context by members of your design team.
4. Capture behaviors that relate to product function.
5. Identify issues and user needs.
6. Create design solutions based on observed and experienced user needs.
7. Typical periods can be one day to one week.

RESOURCES

1. Video camera
2. Digital still camera
3. Note pad
4. Laptop Computer

SEE ALSO

1. Day in the life
2. Fly on the wall

REFERENCES

1. McDonald, Seonaidh. "Studying Actions in Context: A Qualitative Shadowing Method for Organizational Research." Qualitative Research. The Robert Gordon University. SAGE Publications. London. 2005. p455-473.
2. Alan Bryman, Emma Bell. Business Research Meythods. Oxford University Press 2007 ISBN 978-0-19-928498-6

image: © Vwimage | Dreamstime.com

PATIENT STAKEHOLDER MAP

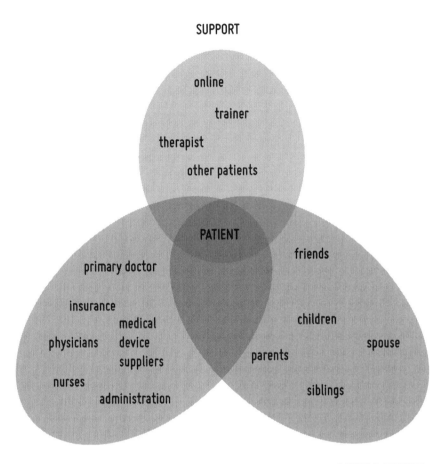

SUPPORT

online

trainer

therapist

other patients

PATIENT

friends

primary doctor

insurance

children

medical

physicians device spouse

suppliers parents

nurses

siblings

administration

HEALTH CARE

FAMILY & FRIENDS

stakeholder map

WHAT IS IT?

Stakeholders maps are used to document the key stake holders and their relationship. They can include end users, those who will benefit, those who may be adversely affected, those who hold power and those who may sabotage design outcomes. At the beginning of a design project it is important to identify the key stake holders and their relationships. The map serves as a reference for the design team.

WHO INVENTED IT?

Mitchell 1997

WHY USE THIS METHOD?

1. Stakeholder mapping helps discover ways to influence other stakeholders.
2. Stakeholder mapping helps discover risks.
3. Stakeholder mapping helps discover positive stakeholders to involve in the design process.

CHALLENGES

1. Stakeholder mapping helps discover negative stakeholders and their associated risks.

RESOURCES

1. White board
2. Post-it-notes
3. Pens
4. Dry-erase markers
5. Interview data

WHEN TO USE THIS METHOD

1. Define intent
2. Know Context
3. Know User
4. Frame insights

HOW TO USE THIS METHOD

1. Develop a categorized list of the members of the stakeholder community.
2. Assign priorities
3. Map the 'highest priority' stakeholders.
4. Can initially be documented on a white board, cards, post-it-notes and consolidated as a diagram through several iterations showing hierarchy and relationships.

Some of the commonly used 'dimensions' include:

1. Power (three levels)
2. Support (three levels)
3. Influence (three levels)
4. Need (three levels)

REFERENCES

1. Mitchell, R. K., B. R. Agle, and D.J. Wood. (1997). "Toward a Theory of Stakeholder Identification and Salience: Defining the Principle of Who and What really Counts." in: Academy of Management Review 22(4): 853 - 888
2. Savage, G. T., T. W. Nix, Whitehead and Blair. (1991). "Strategies for assessing and managing organizational stakeholders." In: Academy of Management Executive 5(2): 61 — 75.

STORYBOARD

PROJECT

NAME

DATE

PAGE

DIALOGUE

ACTION

DIALOGUE

ACTION

DIALOGUE

ACTION

storyboards

WHAT IS IT?

The storyboard is a narrative tool derived from cinema. A storyboard is a form of prototyping which communicates each step of an activity, experience or interaction. Used in films and multimedia as well as product and UX design. Storyboards consists of a number of 'frames' that communicate a sequence of events in context.

WHO INVENTED IT?

Invented by Walt Disney in 1927. Disney credited animator Webb Smith with creating the first storyboard. By 1937–38 all studios were using storyboards.

WHY USE THIS METHOD?

1. Can help gain insightful user feedback.
2. Conveys an experience.
3. Can use a storyboard to communicate a complex task as a series of steps.
4. Allows the proposed activities to be discussed and refined.
5. Storyboards can be used to help designers identify opportunities or use problems.

CHALLENGES

1. Interaction between the storyboard and a user is limited (Landay & Myers, 1996).
2. Participants may not be able to draw well.
3. There haven't been conclusive studies about the effectiveness of storyboards for some design activities.
4. Storyboarding is linear.
5. Not useful for detailed design.

WHEN TO USE THIS METHOD

1. Generate Concepts
2. Create Solutions

HOW TO USE THIS METHOD

1. Decide what story you want to describe.
2. Choose a story and a message: what do you want the storyboard to express?
3. Create your characters
4. Think about the whole story first rather than one panel at a time.
5. Create the drafts and refine them through an iterative process. Refine.
6. Illustrations can be sketches or photographs.
7. Consider: Visual elements, level of detail, text, experiences and emotions, number of frames, and flow of time.
8. Keep text short and informative.
9. 6 to 12 frames.
10. Tell your story efficiently and effectively.
11. Brainstorm your ideas.

RESOURCES

1. Pens
2. Digital camera
3. Storyboard templates
4. Comic books for inspiration

REFERENCES

1. Giuseppe Cristiano Storyboard Design Course: Principles, Practice, and Technique Barron's Educational Series (October 1, 2007) ISBN-10: 0764137328

surveys

WHAT IS IT?
Surveys are a method of collecting information. Surveys collect data usually from a large number of participants. A survey may be undertaken to study objects or animals as well as people. Surveys may take the form of a questionnaire or a face to face interview.

WHO INVENTED IT?
Sir Francis Galton 1800s

WHY USE THIS METHOD?
1. Easy to analyze
2. Large sample at relatively low cost.
3. Simple to manage
4. Familiar format
5. Quick to complete
6. Can be used for sensitive topics
7. Respondents have flexibility in time to complete.

CHALLENGES
1. Avoid complex questions
2. Avoid leading questions
3. Avoid jargon
4. Avoid bias
5. Have standard procedure
6. Ask one information at a time
7. Be as simple as possible
8. Adjust the style of the questions to the target audience

WHEN TO USE THIS METHOD
1. Know Context
2. Know User
3. Frame insights

HOW TO USE THIS METHOD
1. Define topics for research
2. Define the participants
3. Prepare the questions
4. Use closed questions with multiple predefined choices or open questions to allow respondents to respond in their own words.
5. Two common closed formats are: the Likert 7 point format: strongly agree, agree, undecided, disagree, strongly disagree. Or 4 point Forced choice format, Strongly agree, agree, disagree, strongly disagree.
6. Pretest the questionnaire
7. Refine the questionnaire
8. Questions should flow logically

REFERENCES
1. Gillham, B. (2008). Developing a questionnaire (2nd ed.). London, UK: Continuum International Publishing Group Ltd
2. Oppenheim, A. N. (2000). Questionnaire design, interviewing and attitude measurement (New ed.). London, UK: Continuum International Publishing Group Ltd.

BLUEPRINT

ACTIVITY PHASE	CUSTOMER ACTIONS	TOUCHPOINTS	LINE OF INTERACTION	DIRECT CONTACT	LINE OF VISIBILITY	BACK OFFICE	EMOTIONAL EXPERIENCE

swimlanes

WHAT IS IT?

Diagram that shows parallel streams for user, business, and technical process flows. You can include a storyboard lane. Create a blueprint for each persona, interaction or scenario. Provides a focus for discussion and refinement of services or experiences. They may document activities over time such as:

1. Customer Actions
2. Touch points
3. Direct Contact visible to customers
4. Invisible back office actions
5. Support Processes
6. Physical Evidence
7. Emotional Experience for customer.

WHO INVENTED IT?

Lynn Shostack 1983

WHY USE THIS METHOD?

1. Can be used for design or improvement of existing services or experiences.
2. Is more tangible than intuition.
3. Makes the process of service development more efficient.
4. A common point of reference for stakeholders for planning and discussion.
5. Tool to assess the impact of change.

WHEN TO USE THIS METHOD

1. Know Context
2. Know User
3. Frame insights

HOW TO USE THIS METHOD

1. Define the service or experience to focus on.
2. A blueprint can be created in a brainstorming session with stakeholders.
3. Define the customer demographic.
4. See though the customer's eyes.
5. Define the activities and phases of activity under each heading.
6. Link the contact or customer touchpoints to the needed support functions
7. Use post-it-notes on a white board for initial descriptions and rearrange as necessary drawing lines to show the links.
8. Create the blueprint then refine iteratively.

RESOURCES

1. Paper
2. Pens
3. White board
4. Dry-erase markers
5. Camera
6. Blueprint templates
7. Post-it-notes

REFERENCES

1. (1991) G. Hollins, W. Hollins, Total Design: Managing the design process in the service sector, Trans Atlantic Publications
2. (2004) R. Kalakota, M.Robinson, Services Blueprint: Roadmap for Execution, Addison-Wesley, Boston.

talk out loud protocol

WHAT IS IT?

Think aloud or thinking out loud protocols involve participants verbalizing their thoughts while performing a set of tasks. Users are asked to say whatever they are looking at, thinking, doing, and experiencing. A related method is the think-aloud protocol where subjects also explain their actions.

WHO INVENTED IT?

Clayton Lewis IBM 1993

WHY USE THIS METHOD?

1. Provides an understanding of the user's mental model and interaction with the product.
2. Enables observers to see first-hand the process of task completion
3. The terminology the user uses to express an idea or function the design or and documentation.
4. Allows testers to understand how the user approaches the system.

CHALLENGES

1. The design team needs to be composed of people with a variety of skills.

WHEN TO USE THIS METHOD

1. Know Context
2. Know User
3. Frame insights
4. Explore Concepts

HOW TO USE THIS METHOD

1. Identify users.
2. Choose representative tasks.
3. Create a mock-up or prototype.
4. Select participants.
5. Provide the test users with the system or prototype to be tested and tasks.
6. Brief participants.
7. Take notes of everything that users say, without attempting to interpret their actions and words.
8. Iterate
9. Videotape the tests, then analyze the videotapes.

RESOURCES

1. Computer
2. Video camera
3. Note pad
4. Pens

taxonomies

WHAT IS IT?

A taxonomy is a method of organizing groups of items based on their characteristics. It is a way of organizing a large number of ideas or things. Tagging items on the web is a form of taxonomy. Taxonomies are becoming more important as access to information increases. A taxonomy provides a way to describe content.

WHO INVENTED IT?

Taxonomy has been called "the world's oldest profession", One of the earliest recorded was written by Shen Nung, Emperor of China c. 3000 BC. The most widely-known and used taxonomy system is named for the Swedish biologist Carolus Linnaeus.

WHY USE THIS METHOD?

1. A taxonomy is useful to understand the relationships between a group of objects, living organisms or ideas.
2. A taxonomy makes it easier to find an item

WHEN TO USE THIS METHOD

1. Define intent
2. Know Context
3. Know User
4. Frame insights
5. Explore Concepts

HOW TO USE THIS METHOD

1. A taxonomy needs to be relevant to stakeholders.
2. Define the subject of the field or discipline or domain
3. Create tentative list of terms for your taxonomy
4. Organize the information into main categories
5. Identify synonyms
6. Look for gaps
7. Capture the knowledge of users and experts.

RESOURCES

1. Paper
2. Pens
3. White board
4. Dry-erase markers

REFERENCES

1. McGarty, C. (1999). Categorization in Social Psychology, SAGE Publications.
2. Manktelow, M. (2010) History of Taxonomy. Lecture from Dept. of Systematic Biology, Uppsala University. atbi.eu/summerschool/files/summerschool/Manktelow_Syllabus.pdf
3. McGarty, C. (1999). Categorization in Social Psychology, SAGE Publications.

through other eyes

WHAT IS IT?

At several times during a design project it is useful to invite an outside group to review the state of the design and to tell your design team if they think that your design direction is real and good.

WHY USE THIS METHOD?

1. A design team can follow design directions that seem unworkable or unrealistic to end users because they may be remote from the end users of a product or service.

WHEN TO USE THIS METHOD

1. Explore concepts

RESOURCES

1. Pen
2. Paper
3. White board
4. Dry erase markers

HOW TO USE THIS METHOD

1. Define your design problem clearly
2. Select a group of outside people who are representative of the end users of a product or service.
3. Prepare a presentation that may include prototypes or images and statements that clearly communicate the favored concept direction.
4. Prepare a question guide to help your design team obtain useful feedback
5. Review your design with the outside group.
6. Refine your design based on the feedback
7. Provide feedback to the outside reviewers to let them know how their input has been useful.
8. It may be necessary to ask the external participants to sign a non disclosure agreement before to the design review.

unfocus group

WHAT IS IT?

Unfocus groups is a qualitative research method in which interviewers hold group interviews where the subjects are selected based on diverse viewpoints and backgrounds The participants may not be users of the product or service.

WHO INVENTED IT?

Uses methods pioneered by Liz Sanders and the consulting firm IDEO circa 2001

WHY USE THIS METHOD?

1.

WHEN TO USE THIS METHOD

1. Define intent
2. Know Context
3. Know User
4. Frame insights
5. Explore Concepts
6. Make Plans

HOW TO USE THIS METHOD

1. Assemble a diverse group of participants. Choose Diverse Participants Who:
   - Are not likely to use the product or service,
   - Are highly motivated.
   - Are extreme users of the product
   - Have a tangential connection with the product
   - Don't want the product.
2. Select a good moderator.
3. Prepare a screening questionnaire.
4. Decide incentives for participants.
5. Select facility.
6. Recruit participants.
7. Provide refreshments.
8. Prepare the space. Participants should sit around a large table.
9. Describe rules.
10. First question should encourage talking and participation.
11. Provide simple materials such as paper and ask the participants to create crude prototypes for discussion.
12. Ask participants to act out ideas.
13. Record the feedback for idea generation phase.
14. Follow discussion guide.
15. At end of focus group summarize key points.
16. Moderator collects forms and debriefs focus group.

teachback

WHAT IS IT?

In the teachback method an expert explains a concept to a non-expert. The non-expert then tries to teach back what the expert had explained. During the teachback session, the expert corrects any misunderstandings.

WHY USE THIS METHOD?

1. Teachback is a way to confirm that you have explained what needs to be known in a manner that is understood.
2. The method can highlight concepts that are hard to understand.
3. Everyone benefits from clear information.
4. A chance to check for understanding and, if necessary, re-teach the information.

CHALLENGES

1. The teachback method is not highly structured.
2. It is hard to identify people at risk of misunderstanding.

WHEN TO USE THIS METHOD

1. Know Context
2. Know User
3. Frame insights
4. Deliver Offering

HOW TO USE THIS METHOD

1. Use Plain Language, avoid technical terms, talk slowly, break it down into short statements, focus on the 2 or 3 most important concepts.
2. Ask the subject to repeat in his or her own words how he or she understands the concept explained. If a process was demonstrated to the subject ask the subject to demonstrate it, "I want to be sure I explained everything clearly. Can you please explain it back to me so I can be sure I did?"
3. Ask the subject to verbalize their understanding to ensure that it is correct.
4. Repeat Steps 2 and 3 as necessary.
5. Ask the subject to explain or demonstrate how they will undertake an activity.

REFERENCES

1. Johnson, L. & Johnson, N.E., (1987). Knowledge Elicitation Involving Teachback Interviewing in Kidd, A.L., (Ed.), 1987, Knowledge Acquisition for Expert

think out loud protocol

WHAT IS IT?

Think aloud or thinking out loud protocols involve participants verbalizing their thoughts while performing a set of tasks. Users are asked to say whatever they are looking at, thinking, doing, and feeling.

A related but method is the talk-aloud protocol. where participants describe their activities but do not give explanations. This method is thought to be more objective

WHO INVENTED IT?

Clayton Lewis IBM 1993

WHY USE THIS METHOD?

1. Helps a researcher understand interaction with a product or service,.
2. Enables observers to see first-hand the process of task completion
3. The terminology the user uses to express an idea or function the design or and documentation.
4. Allows testers to understand how the user approaches the system.

CHALLENGES

1. The design team needs to be composed of persons with a variety of skills.
2. Pick a diverse, cross disciplinary team.

WHEN TO USE THIS METHOD

1. Know Context
2. Know User
3. Frame insights
4. Explore Concepts

HOW TO USE THIS METHOD

1. Identify users.
2. Choose Representative Tasks.
3. Create a Mock-Up or Prototype.
4. Select Participants.
5. Provide the test users with the system or prototype to be tested and tasks.
6. Brief participants.
7. Take notes of everything that users say, without attempting to interpret their actions and words.
8. Iterate
9. Videotape the tests, then analyze the videotapes.

RESOURCES

1. Computer
2. Video camera
3. Note pad
4. Pens

REFERENCES

1. Lewis, C. H. (1982). Using the "Thinking Aloud" Method In Cognitive Interface Design (Technical report). RC-9265.

triangulation

WHAT IS IT?

Triangulation is a research method where the researcher uses more than two research methods in one study to see if the different methods give similar findings. One example of triangulation is to compare observed behavior with the responses of a survey.

WHO INVENTED IT?

The comes from surveying where triangles are used to create a map.

WHY USE THIS METHOD?

1. Useful when analyzing large data sets.
2. It is employed in quantitative and qualitative research.
3. Helps overcome bias of a single method.
4. It may help the credibility of research conclusions.

CHALLENGES

1. There may be more than one valid conclusion from studying real world people and contexts.

WHEN TO USE THIS METHOD

1. Know Context
2. Know User
3. Frame insights

HOW TO USE THIS METHOD

Types of triangulation approaches include:

1. Dat triangulation where the researcher uses several different strategies for collecting data.
2. Researcher triangulation where more than one researcher is used
3. Method triangulation where more than one method is used to gather data.

REFERENCES

1. Denzin, N. (2006). Sociological Methods: A Sourcebook. Aldine Transaction. ISBN 978-0-202-30840-1. (5th edition).

wizard of oz

WHAT IS IT?

Wizard of Oz method is a research method in which research participants interact with a computer interface that subjects believe to be responding to their input, but which is being operated by an unseen person. The unseen operator is sometimes called the "wizard"

WHO INVENTED IT?

John F. Kelley
Johns Hopkins University. 1980 USA
Nigel Cross

WHY USE THIS METHOD?

1. Wizard of Oz is good for the testing of preliminary interface prototypes.
2. A relatively inexpensive type of simulation
3. Identify problems with an interface concept
4. Investigate visual affordance of an interface.

CHALLENGES

1. Requires training for the wizard.
2. It is difficult for wizards to provide consistent responses across sessions.
3. Computers respond differently than humans
4. It is difficult to evaluate systems with a complex interface using this method.

WHEN TO USE THIS METHOD

1. Know Context
2. Know User
3. Frame insights
4. Explore Concepts

HOW TO USE THIS METHOD

1. The wizard sits in a place not visible to the research participant.
2. The wizard observes the user's actions, and initiates the system's responses.
3. The "wizard" watches live video from a camera focused on the participant's hands and simulate the effects of the participant's actions.
4. Users are unaware that the actions of the system are being produced by the wizard.

RESOURCES

1. Video camera
2. Software interface prototype
3. Computers

REFERENCES

1. Höysniemi, J., Hämäläinen, P., and Turkki, L. 2004. Wizard of Oz prototyping of computer vision based action games for children. In Proceeding of the 2004 Conference on interaction Design and Children: Building A Community (Maryland, June 1—03, 2004). IDC '04. ACM Press, New York, NY, 27–34

Photo: photocase.com – el raph

Chapter 6
Frame insights
this is what we discovered

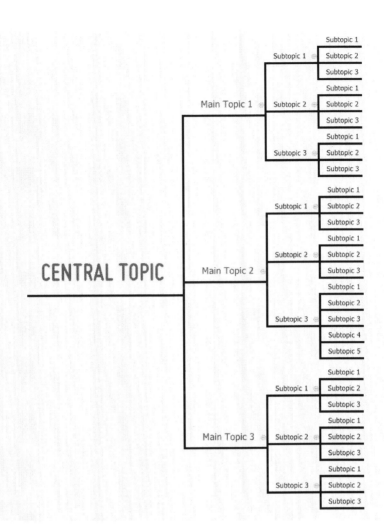

dendrogram

WHAT IS IT?

A dendrogram is a tree diagram used to illustrate hierarchical clustering. The distance of one group from the other groups indicates the degree of relationship

WHO INVENTED IT?

Carl Lamanna and M. Frank Mallette 1953

WHY USE THIS METHOD?

1. It is a visual method of displaying and communicating the relationship between a group of items or ideas.

WHEN TO USE THIS METHOD

1. Know Context
2. Know User
3. Frame insights

RESOURCES

1. Paper
2. Pen
3. White board
4. Dry-erase markers.

HOW TO USE THIS METHOD

1. Write down all of the items.
2. Determine how to cluster the items.
3. Name each group.
4. Connect the groups with lines.

Connect the larger groups and continue the process till the dendrogram is complete.

REFERENCES

1. Analyzing Animal Societies: Quantitative Methods for Vertebrate Social Analysis Hal Whitehead University of Chicago Press, Jul 15, 2008

Infographic elements

Statistics

Lorem ipsum dolor sit amet, consectetur adipiscing elit. Phasellus laoreet rhoncus massa, rhoncus consequat enim tempor at.

Lorem ipsum dolor sit amet, consectetur adipiscing elit. Phasellus laoreet rhoncus massa, rhoncus consequat enim tempor at. Nunc ultricies varius sollicitudin. In id ullamcorper leo.

75% **67%** **69%** **75%**

Lorem ipsum dolor sit amet
Consectetur adipiscing elit.
Phasellus laoreet
Rhoncus massa
Rhoncus consequat
Nunc ultricies sollicitudin
In id ullamcorper leo

Human Resources

Energy Used

Lorem ipsum dolor sit amet, consectetur adipiscing elit. Phasellus laoreet rhoncus massa, rhoncus consequat enim tempor at.

Lorem ipsum dolor sit amet, consectetur adipiscing elit. Phasellus laoreet rhoncus massa, rhoncus consequat enim tempor at. Nunc ultricies varius sollicitudin. In id ullamcorper leo.

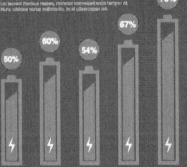

50% 60% 54% 67% 75%
2011 2012 2013 2014 2015

Analytics

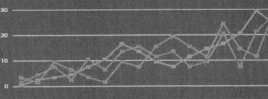
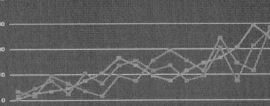

Donec volutpat, lacus id dignissim dictum, ante quam sempe nec scelerisque ligula arcu in mi. Nullam eget tempus dolor.

WAR

Lorem ipsum dolor sit amet, consectetur adipiscing elit. Phasellus laoreet rhoncus massa, rhoncus consequat enim tempor at.

PEACE

Lorem ipsum dolor sit amet, consectetur adipiscing elit. Phasellus laoreet rhoncus massa, rhoncus consequat enim tempor at.

Statistics (drinks)

Lorem ipsum dolor sit amet, consectetur adipiscing elit. Phasellus laoreet rhoncus massa, rhoncus consequat enim tempor at. Nunc ultricies varius sollicitudin. In id ullamcorper leo.

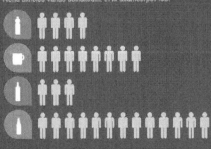

Appreciated:

55% 7% 38%

Lorem ipsum dolor sit amet, consectetur adipiscing elit. Phasellus laoreet rhoncus massa, rhoncus consequat enim tempor at.

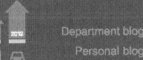

67% 75% 69%

Media Stats

Department blog	23%
Personal blog	27%
Company website	
Podcasts	16%
Overviews	38%
Journals	25%
Social media	26%
Newspapers	17%

infographic

WHAT IS IT?
An infographic is a graphic that displays information. The aim of an infographic is to present complex information and clearly communicate the significance of the data.

WHO INVENTED IT?
Some prehistoric cave paintings may have functioned as infographics.

WHY USE THIS METHOD?
1. Use infographics to communicate complex information

WHEN TO USE THIS METHOD
1. Frame insights

RESOURCES
1. Infographic vector elements
2. Computer graphics software
3. Computer

REFERENCES
1. John Emerson (2008). Visualizing Information for Advocacy: An Introduction to Information Design. New York: OSI.
2. Sandra Rendgen, Julius Wiedemann (2012). Information Graphics. Taschen Publishing. ISBN 978-3836528795

gantt chart

WHAT IS IT?

A Gantt chart is a bar chart that shows the tasks of a project, the start time and the time from start to completion of each task.

This method is used widely in industry to ensure that activities are completed on time and on budget.

WHO INVENTED IT?

Henry Gantt first published in "Organizing for Work 1919.

WHY USE THIS METHOD?

1. Use to track a design project
2. Use to ensure that tasks are completed on time.

WHEN TO USE THIS METHOD

1. Define intent
2. Know Context
3. Know User
4. Frame insights
5. Explore Concepts
6. Make Plans
7. Deliver Offering

RESOURCES

1. Pen
2. Paper
3. Gantt Chart software

HOW TO USE THIS METHOD

1. Identify the tasks
2. Identify the milestones in the project.
3. Identify the time required for each task.
4. Identify the order and dependencies of each task.
5. Identify the tasks that can be undertaken in parallel
6. Draw a horizontal time axis along the top or bottom of a page.
7. Draw a list of tasks in order down the left hand side of the page in the order that they should be undertaken.
8. Draw a diamond for tasks that are short in duration such as a meeting
9. For longer activities draw a horizontal bar indicating the planned duration.

REFERENCES

1. Gantt, Henry L., A graphical daily balance in manufacture, Transactions of the American Society of Mechanical Engineers, VolumeXIV, pages 1322—1336, 1903.
2. Gerard Blokdijk, Project Management 100 Success Secrets, Lulu.com, 2007

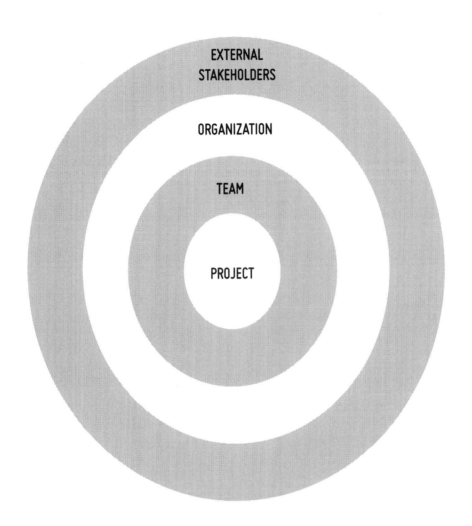

onion map

WHAT IS IT?

An onion map is a chart that shows dependencies of a system. The items in each circle depend on the items in the smaller circle.

WHO INVENTED IT?

Onion models have been used for centuries to indicate hierarchical levels of dependency. Peter Apian's 1539 Cosmographia used an onion model to illustrate the pre-Copernican model of the universe.

WHY USE THIS METHOD?

1. It is an effective way of describing complex relationships
2. It provides a focus for team discussion and alignment
3. It is fast
4. It is inexpensive.

WHEN TO USE THIS METHOD

1. Know Context
2. Know User
3. Frame insights

HOW TO USE THIS METHOD

1. Define the system to be represented by the onion diagram.
2. Create a circle to define the innermost level of dependency
3. Create concentric circles around the inner circle to represent progressively higher levels of dependency
4. Name the levels.

RESOURCES

1. Pen
2. Paper
3. Software
4. Computer
5. White board
6. Dry-erase markers

REFERENCES

1. Hofstede, G. (1992). Culture and Organisations: Software of the Mind. McGraw Hill, Maidenhead

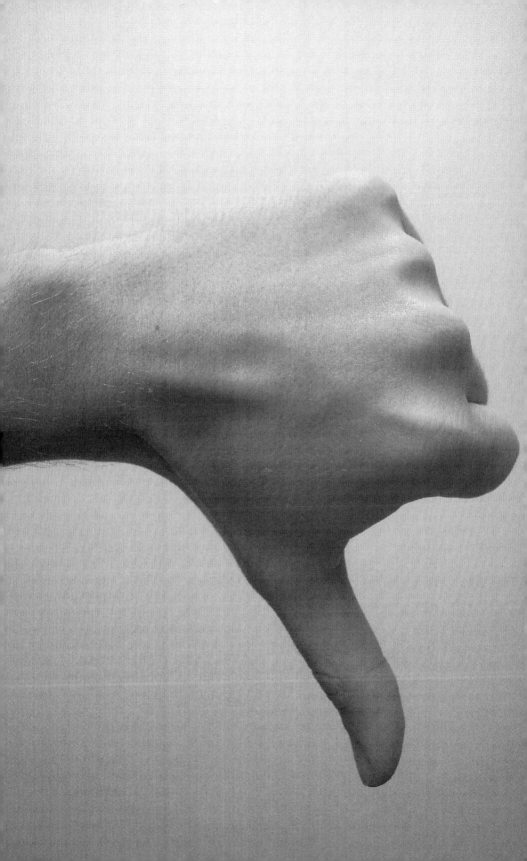

point of view

WHAT IS IT?

A point of view statement is a combination of user needs and insights gained in initial research. It is a re framing of a design challenge into an actionable problem statement.

WHO INVENTED IT?

Part of Design Thinking process methodology.

WHY USE THIS METHOD?

1. It is necessary to have a point of view statement because it is not possible to design for everyone and every need.
2. It is necessary to focus on one.

WHEN TO USE THIS METHOD

1. Know Context
2. Know User
3. Frame insights
4. Explore Concepts

HOW TO USE THIS METHOD

1. Develop user insights from workarounds, human behavior and interactions.
2. Use a brainstorming session with your team to identify a point of view that is actionable and potentially generative based on the user insights.
3. Use point of view as the starting place for design ideation of possible design solutions.

RESOURCES

1. Pens
2. Paper
3. White board
4. Dry erase markers

Photo: photocase.com – AndreasF

RADAR CHART

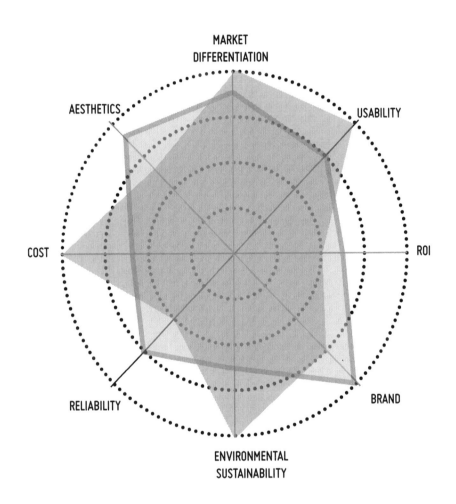

radar chart

WHAT IS IT?

The radar chart is a star shape chart that allows information to be logged radially for a number of variables. The radar chart is also known as a web chart, spider chart, star chart, star plot, cobweb chart, irregular polygon, polar chart, or kiviat diagram.

WHO INVENTED IT?

Georg von Mayr 1877

CHALLENGES

1. Radar charts may not provide information for trade off decisions.

WHY USE THIS METHOD?

1. A spider diagram is a way of displaying a great deal of information in a condensed form,

WHEN TO USE THIS METHOD

1. Know Context
2. Know User
3. Frame insights

HOW TO USE THIS METHOD

1. Draw a circle on a flipchart paper
2. For each item to evaluate draw a line from the center to the circle.
3. Write the item on the intersection between the line and the circle.
4. Draw spider lines from the inside to the outside of the circle (see photo).
5. Gather the participants around the flipchart.
6. Ask them to put one dot for each item: If highly ranked the dot should be close top the center; if poorly ranked the dot should be close to the circle.
7. Present and discuss the result with the group.

RESOURCES

1. Paper
2. Pens
3. Computer
4. Graphic software

REFERENCES

1. Chambers, John, William Cleveland, Beat Kleiner, and Paul Tukey, (1983). Graphical Methods for Data Analysis. Wadsworth. pp. 158-162

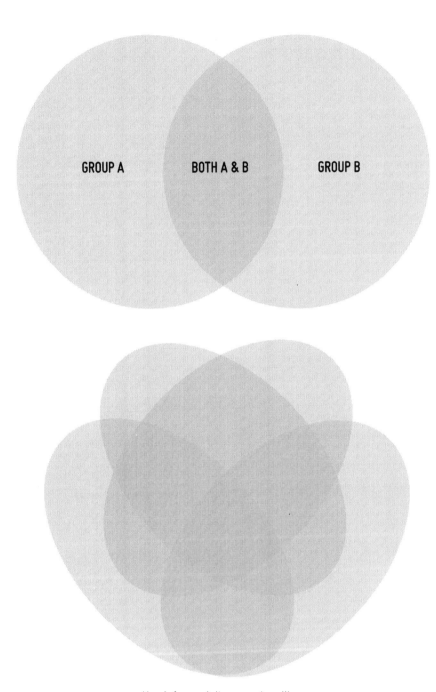

GROUP A   BOTH A & B   GROUP B

Venn's four-set diagram using ellipses

venn diagram

WHAT IS IT?

Venn diagrams normally are constructed from overlapping circles. The interior of the circle and the areas of overlap symbolically represents the elements of discreet sets.

WHO INVENTED IT?

John Venn 1880

WHY USE THIS METHOD?

1. A useful tool for simplifying and communicating data related to user populations and design features

WHEN TO USE THIS METHOD

1. Know Context
2. Know User
3. Frame insights

RESOURCES

1. Paper
2. Pens
3. Software

REFERENCES

1. Grimaldi, Ralph P. (2004). Discrete and combinatorial mathematics. Boston: Addison-Wesley. p. 143. ISBN 0-201-72634-3.
2. Edwards, A.W.F. (2004). Cogwheels of the mind: the story of Venn diagrams. JHU Press. ISBN 978-0-8018-7434-5.

Chapter 7
Explore ideas
how is this idea to start?

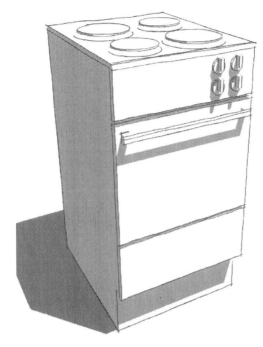

The position of the control knobs suggests which hotplate which each knob controls

This alternate design provides less guidance or affordance on the relationship between the knobs and hotplates

affordance

WHAT IS IT?

Affordance is the way an object communicates to people how it should be used.

"The perceived and actual properties of the thing, primarily those fundamental properties that determine just how the thing can be used" *Don Norman*.

WHO INVENTED IT?

J. J. Gibson 1977

WHY USE THIS METHOD?

1. It improves the usability of an object, service or system.
2. It reduces error.
3. It increases safety.

WHEN TO USE THIS METHOD

1. Define intent
2. Know Context
3. Know User
4. Frame insights
5. Explore Concepts
6. Make Plans
7. Deliver Offering

CHALLENGES

1. A false affordance is an apparent affordance that suggests actions that are invalid.

HOW TO USE THIS METHOD

Four principles of affordance:

1. Follow conventional usage
2. Use words to describe the desired action
3. Use metaphor.
4. Design the system, product or experience so that once part of the interaction is learned, the same principles apply to other parts.

REFERENCES

1. Gibson, J. J. (1979). The Ecological Approach to Visual Perception. Boston: Houghton Mifflin.
2. Norman, D. A. (1988). The psychology of everyday things. New York: Basic Books.
3. Norman, D. A. (1990). The design of everyday things. New York: Doubleday.
4. James J. Gibson (1977), The Theory of Affordances. In Perceiving, Acting, and Knowing, Eds. Robert Shaw and John Bransford, ISBN 0-470-99014-7.
5. Norman D. A. (1999). Affordances, Conventions and Design. Interactions 6(3):38-43, May 1999, ACM Press.

attribute scoring

WHAT IS IT?

This method is a way of selecting a concept direction from a number of alternatives based on the preferences of your design team. Each participant allocates a number of points to each of a number of attributes of a concept design

WHY USE THIS METHOD?

1. It is a fast and effective way of selecting the best concepts to develop further.

CHALLENGES

1. Can be subjective
2. Team members can influence voting by the strength of their personality.

WHEN TO USE THIS METHOD

1. Explore Concepts

RESOURCES

1. Pen
2. Paper
3. White board
4. Dry erase markers

HOW TO USE THIS METHOD

1. Assemble your design team.
2. Brainstorm concepts
3. Pin the concepts on a wall
4. Team members present their ideas to the group.
5. Each team member allocates between one and five points to each concept according to a number of design attributes.
6. This method works best if your team is between 4 and 12 people and a diverse cross disciplinary team
7. For a manufactured product these attributes could be headings such as
   ○ Return on Investment
   ○ Usability
   ○ Aesthetic appeal
   ○ Functionality
   ○ Brand conformance
   ○ Innovation
   ○ Safety
   ○ Environmental sustainability
8. Team members shouldn't vote for their own ideas.
9. Total the points and develop the ideas with most points in a further brainstorming session.

five points

WHAT IS IT?

This method is a way of selecting a concept direction from a number of alternatives based on the preferences of your design team. Each participant is given five points to distribute between the concepts they like the most.

WHY USE THIS METHOD?

1. It is a fast and effective way of selecting the best concepts to develop.

CHALLENGES

1. Can be subjective
2. Team members can influence voting by the strength of their personality.

WHEN TO USE THIS METHOD

1. Explore Concepts

RESOURCES

1. Pen
2. Paper
3. White board
4. Dry erase markers

HOW TO USE THIS METHOD

1. Assemble your design team.
2. Brainstorm concepts
3. Pin the concepts on a wall
4. Team members present their ideas to the group.
5. Each team member is given five points to allocate to the concepts
6. This method works best if your team is between 4 and 12 people and a diverse cross disciplinary team
7. Each team member has five points to allocate.
8. They can allocate them all to one idea or distribute the points between several ideas.
9. Team members shouldn't vote for their own ideas.
10. Total the points and develop the ideas with most points in a further brainstorming session.

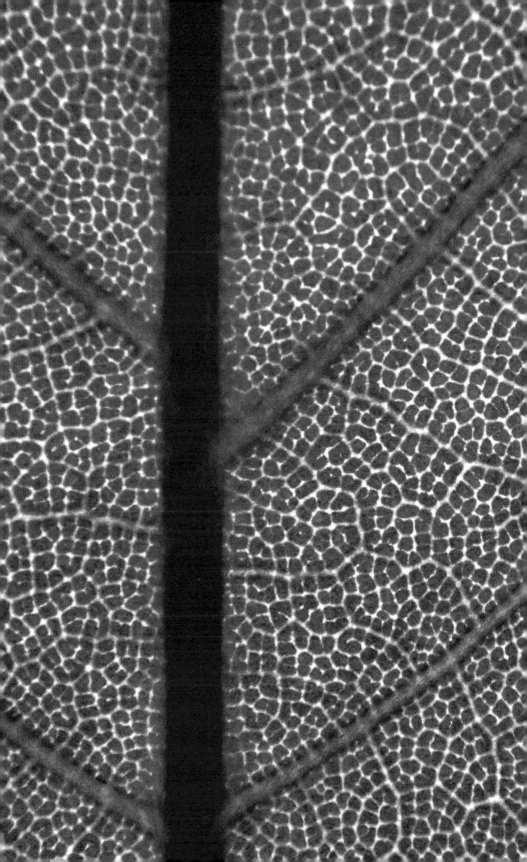

biomimicry

WHAT IS IT?

Biomimicry or biometics is taking inspiration from nature to solve human problems,

WHO INVENTED IT?

Philip Steadman 1979. Popularized by Janine Benyus in her book Biomimicry 1997

WHY USE THIS METHOD?

1. For billions of years nature has evolved and refined living things, systems and materials.
2. Humans have been inspired by nature throughout our existence.
3. Solutions inspired by nature are often better solutions than we can come up with on our own.

CHALLENGES

1. Using a biomimicry may lead you into unknown territory.
2. Our system of business woks independently and sometimes in conflict with nature.

WHEN TO USE THIS METHOD

1. Define intent
2. Know Context
3. Know User
4. Frame insights
5. Explore Concepts
6. Make Plans
7. Deliver Offering

HOW TO USE THIS METHOD

1. Develop the problem
2. Translate the brief into biological parameters.
3. Research natural models that may relate to the design problem.
4. Identify patterns.
5. Create solutions based on nature.
6. Review solutions against natural principles
7. Use nature to stimulate ideas.

RESOURCES

1. Camera
2. Video camera
3. Note pad
4. White board
5. Dry-erase pens

REFERENCES

1. Benyus, Janine (1997). Biomimicry: Innovation Inspired by Nature. New York, NY, USA: William Morrow & Company, Inc. ISBN 978-0-688-16099-9.
2. Hargroves, K. D. & Smith, M. H. (2006). Innovation inspired by nature Biomimicry. Ecos, (129), 27-28.
3. Vogel, S., Cats' Paws and Catapults: Mechanical Worlds of Nature and People. Norton & co. 2000.
4. Pyper, W. (2006). Emulating nature: The rise of industrial ecology. Ecos, (129), 22-26.

Photo: photocase.com – akai

brainstorming

WHAT IS IT?
Brainstorming is one of the oldest, fastest and most widely used creativity methods. Brainstorming does need to be undertaken by experts. It can be undertaken as a group or individually. Osborn believed that brainstorming as a group was most effective. Recent research has questioned this assumption. It should be used to address a single problem. Brainstorming is worthwhile when it is part of a larger process of design.

WHO INVENTED IT?
Alex Faickney Osborn 1953

WHY USE THIS METHOD?
1. It is useful for generating new types of solutions to problems.
2. Brainstorming allows each person in a group to better understand a problem.
3. It can be used to overcome creative blocks.
4. There is group buy-in to a design direction.

CHALLENGES
1. Groupthink
2. Not enough good ideas
3. Taking turns
4. Freeloading
5. Inhibition
6. Lack of critical thinking
7. A group that is too large competes for attention.

WHEN TO USE THIS METHOD
1. Explore Concepts

HOW TO USE THIS METHOD
1. A facilitator explains the problem to be explored and the process.
2. The problem can be written in a place where it can be seen by everyone participating
3. Defer judgment
4. Build on ideas to make them better.
5. Don't ridicule any idea.
6. One person speaking at a time.
7. Go for quantity the more ideas the better
8. No idea is too wild.
9. Stay focused on the problem
10. Be visual
11. Record everything.
12. Don't edit during a brainstorm
13. Preferred group size is from 2 to 12
14. A good facilitator should keep the ideas flowing.
15. Give a number of ideas to be generated for example 10 and time limit such as 30 minutes.
16. Analyze the results.

RESOURCES
1. Pens
2. Post-it-notes
3. A flip chart
4. White board or wall
5. Refreshments.

REFERENCES
1. Clark , Charles Hutchinson. Brainstorming: The Dynamic New Way to Create Successful Ideas Publisher: Classic Business Bookshelf (November 23, 2010) ISBN-10: 1608425614 ISBN-13: 978-1608425617
2. Rawlinson J. Geoffrey Creative Thinking and Brainstorming. Jaico Publishing House (April 30, 2005) ISBN-10: 8172243480 ISBN-13: 978-8172243487

brainstorming: aoki method

WHAT IS IT?
The Aoki or MBS method is a structured brainstorming method that stresses input by all team members.

WHO INVENTED IT?
Sadami Aoki. Used by Mitsubishi

WHY USE THIS METHOD?
1. There is a hierarchy of ideas
2. This method requires that a quantity of ideas is generated.
3. shifts you from reacting to a static snapshot of the problem and broadens your perspective toward the problem and the relationships and connections between its components

CHALLENGES
1. Groupthink
2. Not enough good ideas
3. Taking turns
4. Freeloading
5. Inhibition
6. Lack of critical thinking
7. A group that is too large competes for attention.

WHEN TO USE THIS METHOD
1. Explore Concepts

RESOURCES
1. Paper
2. Pens
3. White board
4. Dry-erase markers
5. Post-it-notes.

HOW TO USE THIS METHOD
6. Warm Up: Participants generate ideas for 15 minutes.
7. Participants present their ideas verbally to the larger group.
8. The larger group continues to generate ideas during the individual presentations.
9. For one hour the individual team members further explain their ideas to the group
10. Idea maps are created by the moderator.

REFERENCES
1. Clark , Charles Hutchinson. Brainstorming: The Dynamic New Way to Create Successful Ideas Publisher: Classic Business Bookshelf (November 23, 2010) ISBN-10: 1608425614 ISBN-13: 978-1608425617
2. Rawlinson J. Geoffrey Creative Thinking and Brainstorming. Jaico Publishing House (April 30, 2005) ISBN-10: 8172243480 ISBN-13: 978-8172243487

brainstorming: brainwriting

WHAT IS IT?

Brainwriting is an alternative to brainstorming generating ideas by asking people to write down their ideas rather than presenting them verbally.

WHO INVENTED IT?

Brahm & Kleiner, 1996

WHY USE THIS METHOD?

1. Moderation of Brainwriting is easier than brainstorming.
2. Brainwriting tends to produce more ideas than brainstorming
3. Can be conducted in 15 to 30 minutes
4. Brainwriting is better if participants are shy or from cultures where group interaction is more guarded.
5. Brainwriting reduces the problems of groupthink.

CHALLENGES

1. Not enough good ideas
2. Freeloading
3. Inhibition
4. Lack of critical thinking

WHEN TO USE THIS METHOD

1. Explore Concepts

SEE ALSO

Explore Concepts

HOW TO USE THIS METHOD

1. Define the problem
2. Each participant should brainstorm three solutions in two minutes in written form.
3. Then have them pass the sheet of paper to their left.
4. Have the participants add to or build upon the existing suggestions by writing their own ideas underneath the original solutions. Allow 3 minutes.
5. The process should be repeated as many times as there are people around the table allowing an additional minute each time.
6. When you've finished post the ideas on a wall.
7. Get the group to vote on the most promising ideas.

RESOURCES

1. Pens
2. Post-it-notes
3. A flip chart
4. White board or wall
5. Refreshments.

REFERENCES

1. Clark , Charles Hutchinson. Brainstorming: The Dynamic New Way to Create Successful Ideas Publisher: Classic Business Bookshelf (November 23, 2010) ISBN-10: 1608425614 ISBN-13: 978-1608425617
2. Rawlinson J. Geoffrey Creative Thinking and Brainstorming. Jaico Publishing House (April 30, 2005) ISBN-10: 8172243480 ISBN-13: 978-8172243487

brainstorming: digital method

WHAT IS IT?

This brainstorming method uses an electronic meeting system or e-mail.

WHY USE THIS METHOD?

1. Ideas are automatically recorded.
2. This method requires that a quantity of ideas is generated.
3. The session can be a short duration such as 30 minutes or over a long duration such as 2 weeks.
4. Enables much larger groups to brainstorm on a topic than would normally be productive in a traditional brainstorming session

CHALLENGES

1. Groupthink
2. Not enough good ideas
3. Taking turns
4. Freeloading
5. Inhibition
6. Lack of critical thinking

WHEN TO USE THIS METHOD

1. Explore Concepts

RESOURCES

1. Computer
2. Internet connection
3. Brainstorming software
4. E-mail
5. Electronic meeting system.

HOW TO USE THIS METHOD

1. Define a problem to be explored
2. Appoint a moderator.
3. Each participant connects through an electronic meeting system
4. Participants share ideas
5. Ideas are immediately visible to the group
6. Ideas are often anonymously posted or through avatars.
7. Review the contributions.

brainstorming: journey method

WHAT IS IT?
This is a brainstorming method that uses flexible geographic perspectives to look at a design problem.

WHO INVENTED IT?
Alex Faickney Osborn 1953

WHY USE THIS METHOD?
1. Leverages the diverse experiences of a team.
2. Makes group problem solving fun.
3. Helps build team cohesion.
4. Everyone can participate.

CHALLENGES
1. Some ideas that you generate using the tool may be impractical.
2. Best used with other creativity methods

WHEN TO USE THIS METHOD
1. Generate concepts

HOW TO USE THIS METHOD
1. Define a problem
2. Select a diverse design team of 4 to 12 people and a moderator.
3. Ask team how they would deal with the problem if they were in a different place.
4. Analyze results and prioritize.
5. Develop actionable ideas.

RESOURCES
1. Pens
2. Post-it-notes
3. A flip chart
4. White board or wall
5. Refreshments

REFERENCES
1. Clark , Charles Hutchinson. Brainstorming: The Dynamic New Way to Create Successful Ideas Publisher: Classic Business Bookshelf (November 23, 2010) ISBN-10: 1608425614 ISBN-13: 978-1608425617
2. Rawlinson J. Geoffrey Creative Thinking and Brainstorming. Jaico Publishing House (April 30, 2005) ISBN-10: 8172243480 ISBN-13: 978-8172243487

brainstorming: kj method

WHAT IS IT?

The KJ method is a form of brainstorming. The KJ method places emphasis on the most important ideas. It is one of the seven tools of Japanese quality management and incorporates the Buddhist value of structured meditation.

WHO INVENTED IT?

Kawakita Jiro

WHY USE THIS METHOD?

1. There is a hierarchy of ideas
2. This method generates many ideas.
3. This method highlights the connections between ideas which is the starting point for a design solution.

CHALLENGES

1. Groupthink
2. Not enough good ideas
3. Taking turns
4. Freeloading
5. Inhibition
6. Lack of critical thinking
7. A group that is too large competes for attention.

RESOURCES

1. Paper
2. Pens
3. White board
4. Dry-erase markers
5. Post-it-notes.

WHEN TO USE THIS METHOD

1. Explore Concepts

HOW TO USE THIS METHOD

1. The moderator frames the design challenge.
2. Team members generate ideas in up to 25 words on post-it notes.
3. Cards are shuffled and then handed out again to the participants.
4. Each participant should not gat any of their own cards back.
5. Each post-it note is read out by the participants, and all participants review the post-it notes that they hold to find any that seem to go with the one read out, so building a 'group'.
6. Organise post-it notes into groups.
7. Group the groups until you have no more than ten groups.
8. Sort categories into subcategories of 20-30 cards.
9. Refine groups into 10 post-it notes or less.
10. Use a white board or smooth wall.
11. Write the individual post-it notes arranged in groups on the white board or arrange the post-it notes on a wall.
12. The moderator will read out the groups and record the participant's ideas about the relationships and meaning of the information gathered.

brainstorming: merlin

WHAT IS IT?

The merlin method is a brainstorming method that seeks to develop ideas for improving a product, service or experience by imagining changes in size use or function.

WHY USE THIS METHOD?

1. There is a hierarchy of ideas
2. This method generates many ideas.
3. This method highlights the connections between ideas which is the starting point for design solutions.

WHO INVENTED IT?

Alex Faickney Osborn 1953

CHALLENGES

1. Groupthink
2. Not enough good ideas
3. Taking turns
4. Freeloading
5. Inhibition
6. Lack of critical thinking
7. A group that is too large competes for attention.

WHEN TO USE THIS METHOD

1. Explore Concepts

HOW TO USE THIS METHOD

1. The moderator frames the design challenge.
2. On a whiteboard or flipchart write four headings: enlarge reduce eliminate, reverse.
3. Work for ten minutes with your team under each heading
4. Review the lists, create hierarchy of solutions.

RESOURCES

1. Paper
2. Pens
3. White board
4. Dry-erase markers
5. Post-it-notes.

REFERENCES

1. Clark , Charles Hutchinson. Brainstorming: The Dynamic New Way to Create Successful Ideas Publisher: Classic Business Bookshelf (November 23, 2010) ISBN-10: 1608425614 ISBN-13: 978-1608425617
2. Rawlinson J. Geoffrey Creative Thinking and Brainstorming. Jaico Publishing House (April 30, 2005) ISBN-10: 8172243480 ISBN-13: 978-8172243487

brainstorming: nyaka

WHAT IS IT?

The Nyaka method is a form of brainstorming. The Nyaka method places emphasis on exploring problems and solutions to problems.

WHY USE THIS METHOD?

1. There is a hierarchy of ideas
2. This method generates many ideas.

CHALLENGES

1. Groupthink
2. Not enough good ideas
3. Taking turns
4. Freeloading
5. Inhibition
6. Lack of critical thinking
7. A group that is too large competes for attention.

RESOURCES

1. Paper
2. Pens
3. White board
4. Dry-erase markers
5. Post-it-notes.

WHEN TO USE THIS METHOD

1. Explore Concepts

HOW TO USE THIS METHOD

1. Define a moderator
2. The moderator draws a vertical line on a whiteboard.
3. Time limit of 30 minutes
4. The moderator asks the team to define as many things that are wrong with a design or service or experience as possible.
5. The moderator asks the team to define solutions for as many of the problems defined as possible.
6. Create a hierarchy of problems and a hierarchy of solutions for each problem.
7. A group size of 4 to 20 people is optimum.
8. For larger groups the moderator can break the group into groups of 4 or 5 people.

REFERENCES

1. Clark , Charles Hutchinson. Brainstorming: The Dynamic New Way to Create Successful Ideas Publisher: Classic Business Bookshelf (November 23, 2010) ISBN-10: 1608425614 ISBN-13: 978-1608425617
2. Rawlinson J. Geoffrey Creative Thinking and Brainstorming. Jaico Publishing House (April 30, 2005) ISBN-10: 8172243480 ISBN-13: 978-8172243487

brainstorming: personal

WHAT IS IT?

Recent research has suggested that some individuals are more creative working alone for brainstorming sessions rather than in groups. In this case the divergent idea generation is done by an individual and the convergent phase is done by the team.

WHO INVENTED IT?

Alex Faickney Osborn 1953

WHY USE THIS METHOD?

1. Leverages the diverse experiences of a team.
2. Uses the creativity of the individual free from distractions.
3. Helps build empathy.

CHALLENGES

1. Some ideas that you generate using the tool may be impractical.
2. Best used with other creativity methods

WHEN TO USE THIS METHOD

1. Generate concepts

HOW TO USE THIS METHOD

1. Define a problem
2. Find a quiet place
3. Generate as many ideas as possible in 30 minutes.
4. Get the team together and present the ideas to them.
5. Get the team to vote on which ideas they like the most. Two votes per person.
6. Analyze results and prioritize.
7. Develop actionable ideas.

RESOURCES

1. Pens
2. Post-it-notes
3. A flip chart
4. White board or wall
5. Refreshments

REFERENCES

1. Clark , Charles Hutchinson. Brainstorming: The Dynamic New Way to Create Successful Ideas Publisher: Classic Business Bookshelf (November 23, 2010) ISBN-10: 1608425614 ISBN-13: 978-1608425617
2. Rawlinson J. Geoffrey Creative Thinking and Brainstorming. Jaico Publishing House (April 30, 2005) ISBN-10: 8172243480 ISBN-13: 978-8172243487

brainstorming: personas

WHAT IS IT?

This is a brainstorming method that uses the imagined perspectives of an identified persona or group identified as one of your client's customer groups such as students look at a design problem.

WHO INVENTED IT?

Alex Faickney Osborn 1953

WHY USE THIS METHOD?

1. Leverages the diverse experiences of a team.
2. Helps build empathy.
3. Makes group problem solving fun.
4. Helps build team cohesion.
5. Everyone can participate.

CHALLENGES

1. Some ideas that you generate using the tool may be impractical.
2. Best used with other creativity methods

WHEN TO USE THIS METHOD

1. Generate concepts

HOW TO USE THIS METHOD

1. Define a problem
2. Select a diverse design team of 4 to 12 people and a moderator.
3. Identify a persona to focus on. See personas.
4. Ask the team how they would deal with the problem if they were the persona
5. Analyze results and prioritize.
6. Develop actionable ideas.

RESOURCES

1. Pens
2. Post-it-notes
3. A flip chart
4. White board or wall
5. Refreshments

REFERENCES

1. Clark , Charles Hutchinson. Brainstorming: The Dynamic New Way to Create Successful Ideas Publisher: Classic Business Bookshelf (November 23, 2010) ISBN-10: 1608425614 ISBN-13: 978-1608425617
2. Rawlinson J. Geoffrey Creative Thinking and Brainstorming. Jaico Publishing House (April 30, 2005) ISBN-10: 8172243480 ISBN-13: 978-8172243487

brainstorming: nhk method

WHAT IS IT?
The NHK method is a rigorous iterative process of brainstorming of ideas following a predetermined structure.

WHO INVENTED IT?
Hiroshi Takahashi

WHY USE THIS METHOD?
1. This method requires that a quantity of ideas is generated.

CHALLENGES
1. Groupthink
2. Not enough good ideas
3. Taking turns
4. Freeloading
5. Inhibition
6. Lack of critical thinking
7. A group that is too large competes for attention.

WHEN TO USE THIS METHOD
1. Explore Concepts

RESOURCES
1. Paper
2. Pens
3. White board
4. Dry-erase markers
5. Post-it-notes.

HOW TO USE THIS METHOD
1. Define problem statement.
1. Each participant writes down five ideas on five separate cards.
2. Create groups of five participants
3. While each person explains their ideas, the others continue to record new ideas.
4. Collect, and create groups of related concepts.
5. Form new groups of two or three people Brainstorm for half an hour.
6. Groups organize ideas and present them to the larger group.
7. Record all ideas on the white board.
8. Form larger groups of ten people and work further brainstorm each of the ideas on the white board.

REFERENCES
1. Clark , Charles Hutchinson. Brainstorming: The Dynamic New Way to Create Successful Ideas Publisher: Classic Business Bookshelf (November 23, 2010) ISBN-10: 1608425614 ISBN-13: 978-1608425617
2. Rawlinson J. Geoffrey Creative Thinking and Brainstorming. Jaico Publishing House (April 30, 2005) ISBN-10: 8172243480 ISBN-13: 978-8172243487

brainstorming: sensorial method

WHAT IS IT?
Design in northern Europe and the United States focuses on the visual sense which is only a component of the design experience. A design such as an Italian sports car gives greater consideration to other senses such as hearing, smell touch to give a consistent experience of through all senses to a product user.

WHO INVENTED IT?
Rob Curedale 1995

WHY USE THIS METHOD?
1. It gives a design a greater experience of quality than a design that focuses on the visual sense.
2. It gives a consistent experience.
3. It provides a more stimulating experience than a design that focuses on the visual experience.

CHALLENGES
1. Groupthink
2. Not enough good ideas
3. Taking turns
4. Freeloading
5. Inhibition
6. Lack of critical thinking
7. A group that is too large competes for attention.

WHEN TO USE THIS METHOD
1. Explore Concepts

HOW TO USE THIS METHOD
1. The moderator frames the design challenge.
2. Team members generate ideas on post-it notes.
3. The team works through 20 minute brainstorming sessions in each sense, Vision, smell, touch hearing, taste.
4. Ask team members to generate 6 to 10 ideas each under each category.
5. Use up to 25 words for non visual senses and simple sketches for the visual ideas.
6. Organise post-it notes into groups through discussion with five concepts in each group, one idea from each sense group or five different senses in each group.
7. Ask team to vote on which groups have the most potential for further development.

RESOURCES
1. Paper
2. Pens
3. White board
4. Dry-erase markers
5. Post-it-notes.

brainstorming: scamper

WHAT IS IT?
SCAMPER is a brainstorming technique and creativity method that uses seven words as prompts.
1. Substitute.
2. Combine.
3. Adapt.
4. Modify.
5. Put to another use.
6. Eliminate.
7. Reverse.

WHO INVENTED IT?
Bob Eberle based on work by Alex Osborne

WHY USE THIS METHOD?
1. Scamper is a method that can help generate innovative solutions to a problem.
2. Leverages the diverse experiences of a team.
3. Makes group problem solving fun.
4. Helps get buy in from all team members for solution chosen.
5. Helps build team cohesion.
6. Everyone can participate.

CHALLENGES
1. Some ideas that you generate using the tool may be impractical.
2. Best used with other creativity methods

SEE ALSO
1. Brainstorming

WHEN TO USE THIS METHOD
1. Generate concepts

HOW TO USE THIS METHOD
1. Select a product or service to apply the method.
2. Select a diverse design team of 4 to 12 people and a moderator.
3. Ask questions about the product you identified, using the SCAMPER mnemonic to guide you.
4. Create as many ideas as you can.
5. Analyze
6. Prioritize.
7. Select the best single or several ideas to further brainstorm.

RESOURCES
1. Pens
2. Post-it-notes
3. A flip chart
4. White board or wall
5. Refreshments

REFERENCES
1. Scamper: Creative Games and Activities for Imagination Development. Bob Eberle April 1, 1997 ISBN-10: 1882664248 ISBN-13: 978-1882664245

SCAMPER QUESTIONS

SUBSTITUTE
1. What materials or resources can you substitute or swap to improve the product?
2. What other product or process could you substitute?
3. What rules could you use?
4. Can you use this product in another situation?

COMBINE
1. Could you combine this product with another product?
2. Could you combine several goals?
3. Could you combine the use of the product with another use?
4. Could you join resources with someone else?

ADAPT
1. How could you adapt or readjust this product to serve another purpose or use?
2. What else is the product like?
3. What could you imitate to adapt this product?
4. What exists that is like the product?
5. Could the product adapt to another context?

MODIFY
1. How could you change the appearance of the product?
2. What could you change ?
3. What could you focus on to create more return on investment?
4. Could you change part of the product?

PUT TO ANOTHER USE
1. Can you use this product in another situation?
2. Who would find this product useful?
3. How would this product function in a new context?
4. Could you recycle parts of this product to create a new product?

ELIMINATE
1. How could you make the product simpler?
2. What features, parts, could you eliminate?
3. What could you understate or tone down?
4. Could you make the product smaller or more efficient?
5. Would the product function differently if you removed part of the product?

REVERSE
1. What would happen if you changed the operation sequence?
2. What if you do the reverse of what you are trying to do?
3. What components could you substitute to change the order of this product?
4. What roles could you change?

brainstorming: resources

WHAT IS IT?
This is a brainstorming method that uses the availability of resources to look at a design problem.

WHO INVENTED IT?
Alex Faickney Osborn 1953

WHY USE THIS METHOD?
1. Leverages the diverse experiences of a team.
2. Helps build empathy.
3. Makes group problem solving fun.
4. Helps build team cohesion.
5. Everyone can participate.

CHALLENGES
1. Some ideas that you generate using the tool may be impractical.
2. Best used with other creativity methods

REFERENCES
1. Clark , Charles Hutchinson. Brainstorming: The Dynamic New Way to Create Successful Ideas Publisher: Classic Business Bookshelf (November 23, 2010) ISBN-10: 1608425614 ISBN-13: 978-1608425617
2. Rawlinson J. Geoffrey Creative Thinking and Brainstorming. Jaico Publishing House (April 30, 2005) ISBN-10: 8172243480 ISBN-13: 978-8172243487

WHEN TO USE THIS METHOD
1. Generate concepts

HOW TO USE THIS METHOD
1. Define a problem
2. Select a diverse design team of 4 to 12 people and a moderator.
3. Identify a resource to limit or make more available such as finance, time, people, materials or process.
4. Ask the team how they would deal with the problem if the resource was changed as proposed
5. Analyze results and prioritize.
6. Develop actionable ideas.

RESOURCES
1. Pens
2. Post-it-notes
3. A flip chart
4. White board or wall
5. Refreshments

brainstorming: thought leader

WHAT IS IT?

This is a brainstorming method that brainstorms imagined solutions that may be proposed by some of the most thoughtful people who have lived.

WHO INVENTED IT?

Alex Faickney Osborn 1953

WHY USE THIS METHOD?

1. Leverages the diverse experiences of a team.
2. Helps build empathy.
3. Makes group problem solving fun.
4. Helps build team cohesion.
5. Everyone can participate.

CHALLENGES

1. Some ideas that you generate using the tool may be impractical.
2. Best used with other creativity methods

REFERENCES

1. Clark , Charles Hutchinson. Brainstorming: The Dynamic New Way to Create Successful Ideas Publisher: Classic Business Bookshelf (November 23, 2010) ISBN-10: 1608425614 ISBN-13: 978-1608425617
2. Rawlinson J. Geoffrey Creative Thinking and Brainstorming. Jaico Publishing House (April 30, 2005) ISBN-10: 8172243480 ISBN-13: 978-8172243487

WHEN TO USE THIS METHOD

1. Generate concepts

HOW TO USE THIS METHOD

1. Define a problem
2. Select a diverse design team of 4 to 12 people and a moderator.
3. Identify a thought leader to focus on to explore the solutions such as Steve Jobs, James Dyson, Thomas Edison, Bill Gates, Henry Ford, Steven Spielberg, Albert Einstein, Richard Branson or Leonardo Da Vinci.
4. The moderator asks the group how they imagine that this person may solve the problem.
5. Analyze results and prioritize.
6. Develop actionable ideas.

RESOURCES

1. Pens
2. Post-it-notes
3. A flip chart
4. White board or wall
5. Refreshments

brainstorming: time machine

WHAT IS IT?

This is a brainstorming method that uses flexible time perspectives to look at a design problem.

WHO INVENTED IT?

Alex Faickney Osborn 1953

WHY USE THIS METHOD?

1. Leverages the diverse experiences of a team.
2. Makes group problem solving fun.
3. Helps build team cohesion.
4. Everyone can participate.

CHALLENGES

1. Some ideas that you generate using the tool may be impractical.
2. Best used with other creativity methods

REFERENCES

1. Clark , Charles Hutchinson. Brainstorming: The Dynamic New Way to Create Successful Ideas Publisher: Classic Business Bookshelf (November 23, 2010) ISBN-10: 1608425614 ISBN-13: 978-1608425617
2. Rawlinson J. Geoffrey Creative Thinking and Brainstorming. Jaico Publishing House (April 30, 2005) ISBN-10: 8172243480 ISBN-13: 978-8172243487

WHEN TO USE THIS METHOD

1. Generate concepts

HOW TO USE THIS METHOD

1. Define a problem
2. Select a diverse design team of 4 to 12 people and a moderator.
3. Ask team how they would deal with the problem if they were living 10 years ago, 1000 years ago, 10,000 years ago?
4. Ask the team how they would dal with the problem if they were living 5 years in the future, ten years, 100 years 1,000 years in the future?
5. Analyze results and prioritize.
6. Develop actionable ideas.

RESOURCES

1. Pens
2. Post-it-notes
3. A flip chart
4. White board or wall
5. Refreshments

brainstorming: trigger method

WHAT IS IT?

Iteration is important at all stages of the design process. This method takes the ideas of an initial brainstorming session and uses these ideas to build upon in a second session.

WHO INVENTED IT?

Alex Faickney Osborn 1953

WHY USE THIS METHOD?

1. Leverages the diverse experiences of a team.
2. Iteration allows refinement or ideas.
3. Makes group problem solving fun.
4. Helps build team cohesion.
5. Everyone can participate.

CHALLENGES

1. Some ideas that you generate using the tool may be impractical.
2. Best used with other creativity methods

REFERENCES

1. Clark , Charles Hutchinson. Brainstorming: The Dynamic New Way to Create Successful Ideas Publisher: Classic Business Bookshelf (November 23, 2010) ISBN-10: 1608425614 ISBN-13: 978-1608425617
2. Rawlinson J. Geoffrey Creative Thinking and Brainstorming. Jaico Publishing House (April 30, 2005) ISBN-10: 8172243480 ISBN-13: 978-8172243487

WHEN TO USE THIS METHOD

1. Generate concepts

HOW TO USE THIS METHOD

1. Ideas from a first brainstorming session are presented to the group.
2. The group creates a hierarchy by voting for the favored ideas.
3. The one or 3 ideas are selected as the basis for the brainstorming session.
4. Analyze results and prioritize.
5. Develop actionable ideas.

RESOURCES

1. Pens
2. Post-it-notes
3. A flip chart
4. White board or wall
5. Refreshments

brainstorming: 101 method

WHAT IS IT?
This is a brainstorming method focuses on creating volumes of ideas

WHY USE THIS METHOD?
1. Leverages the diverse experiences of a team.
2. A large volume of ideas helps overcome people's inhibitions to innovating.
3. Makes group problem solving fun.
4. Helps build team cohesion.
5. Everyone can participate.

CHALLENGES
1. Because the focus is on volume some ideas will not be useful.
2. Best used with other creativity methods

REFERENCES
1. Clark , Charles Hutchinson. Brainstorming: The Dynamic New Way to Create Successful Ideas Publisher: Classic Business Bookshelf (November 23, 2010) ISBN-10: 1608425614 ISBN-13: 978-1608425617
2. Rawlinson J. Geoffrey Creative Thinking and Brainstorming. Jaico Publishing House (April 30, 2005) ISBN-10: 8172243480 ISBN-13: 978-8172243487

WHEN TO USE THIS METHOD
1. Generate concepts

HOW TO USE THIS METHOD
1. Define a problem
2. Select a moderator
3. Select a diverse design team of 4 to 12 people and a moderator.
4. The moderator asks the team to each generate 101 solutions to the design problem in a defined time. Allow 30 to 60 minutes.
5. Analyze results and prioritize.
6. Develop actionable ideas.

RESOURCES
1. Pens
2. Post-it-notes
3. A flip chart
4. White board or wall
5. Refreshments

brainstorming: method 635

WHAT IS IT?

Method 635 is a structured form of brain-storming. "

Here six participant gain a thorough under-standing of the task at hand and them sepa-rately writes three rough ideas for solution. These three ideas are then passed on the one of the other participants who read and add three additional ideas or modifications. This process continues until all participants have expanded or revised all original ideas. Six participants, three ideas, five rounds of supplements" (Löwgren and Stolterman 2004).

WHO INVENTED IT?

Professor Bernd Rohrbach 1968

WHY USE THIS METHOD?

1. Can generate a lot of ideas quickly
2. Participants can build on each others ideas
3. Ideas are recorded by the participants
4. Democratic method.
5. Ideas are contributed privately.

SEE ALSO

1. Brainwriting
2. Dot voting

WHEN TO USE THIS METHOD

1. Frame insights
2. Explore Concepts

HOW TO USE THIS METHOD

1. Your team should sit around a table.
2. Each team member is given a sheet of paper with the design objective written at the top.
3. Each team member is given three minutes to generate three ideas.
4. Your participants then pass the sheet of paper to the person sitting on their left.
5. Each participant must come up with three new ideas.
6. The process can stop when sheets come around the table.
7. Repeat until ideas are exhausted. No discussion at any stage.
8. No discussion.
9. Analyze ideas as a group,

RESOURCES

1. Paper
2. Pens
3. White board
4. Large table

REFERENCES

1. Rohrbach, Bernd: Creativity by rules – Method 635, a new technique for solving problems first published in the German sales magazine "Absatzwirtschaft", Volume 12, 1969. p73–75 and Volume 19, 1 October 1969.

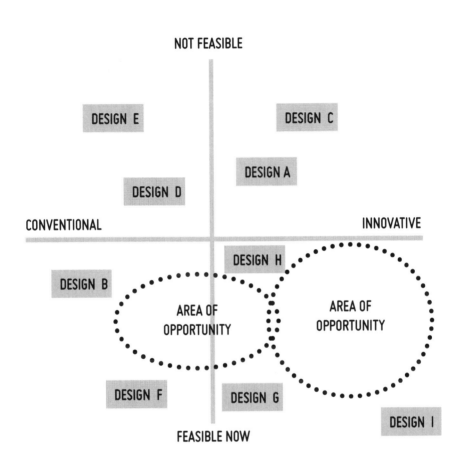

c-box

WHAT IS IT?

A c-box is a type of perceptual map that allows comparison and evaluation of a large number of ideas generated in a brainstorming session by a design team. The method allows everyone to contribute in a democratic way. It can be used to identify the most feasible and innovative ideas. It is up to your team to decide the level of innovation that they would like to carry forward from the idea generation or divergent phase of the project to the convergent or refinement and implementation phases.

WHO INVENTED IT?

Marc Tassoul, Delft 2009

WHY USE THIS METHOD?

1. It is democratic
2. It is quick and productive
3. It is inexpensive

WHEN TO USE THIS METHOD

1. Frame insights
2. Explore Concepts

REFERENCES

Tassoul, M. (2006) Creative Facilitation: a Delft Approach, Delft: VSSD.

HOW TO USE THIS METHOD

1. The moderator defines the design problem
2. You group can be optimally from 4 to 20 people.
3. On a white board or large sheet of paper create two axes. You can also use tape on a large wall.
4. The team should sit around a table facing the wall.
5. Innovation on the horizontal and feasibility on the vertical axes creating 4 quadrants
6. The scale on the innovation ranges from not innovative at the left hand to highly innovative on the right hand end.
7. Alternative axes are attractiveness and functionality.
8. The scale for feasibility runs from not feasible now at the bottom to immediately feasible at the top.
9. Hand out ten post-it-notes to each member of your team.
10. Brainstorm concepts. Each team member to generate 5 to 10 concepts over 30 minutes. One idea per post-it note. Hand out more post-it notes if required.
11. Concepts can be simple sketches or written ideas or a combination of the two.
12. Each team member then presents each idea taking one to three minutes per idea depending on time available.
13. With the group's input discuss the ideas and precise position on the map.
14. Position each post-it-note according to the group consensus.

chance arrangements

WHAT IS IT?

Chance arrangements is a creativity method that uses chance arrangements to develop product or service concepts.

WHY USE THIS METHOD?

1. This method requires that a quantity of ideas is generated.

WHEN TO USE THIS METHOD

1. Explore Concepts

RESOURCES

1. Paper
2. Pens
3. White board
4. Dry-erase markers
5. Post-it-notes.

HOW TO USE THIS METHOD

1. Define problem statement.
2. Define team.
3. Distribute five blank postcards to each participant
4. Ask each participant to describe a feature that they would like to see as part of the product or service.
5. Collect the cards
6. Shuffle the cards
7. Hand back five cards with ideas to each participant.
8. Ask each participant to create three products or services based on the ideas contained in the five cars that they have received. Allow 30 minutes.
9. Collect the cards and shuffle them repeat stages 7 and 8.
10. Each participant presents their concepts to the group.
11. The group votes on their favored ideas from those created.

chips analysis

WHAT IS IT?

Chips analysis is a way of presenting a new idea to a group who want to be assured that change is the best strategy.

WHY USE THIS METHOD?

1. It is a way of demonstrating how change will be beneficial

CHALLENGES

1. Managers and engineers are often cautious and want evidence that a change has been considered.

WHEN TO USE THIS METHOD

1. Explore Concepts

RESOURCES

1. Pen
2. Paper
3. White board
4. Dry erase markers

HOW TO USE THIS METHOD

1. In a brainstorming session with your team work through these headings with each concept to help select the favored concept direction.
2. Costs: Return on Investment
3. Help: How can managers be involved and help ensure success?
4. Innovation: Positive aspects of the innovation.
5. Prestige: How ill this make the organization and people look good?
6. Security. Why is the idea a safe bet?

co-creation

WHAT IS IT?
Co-creation involves working on new product, service or experience with stakeholders. The quality of design increases if the stakeholders interests are considered in the design process. Co-creation differs from crowdsourcing where the design ideas are produced by the crowd without collaboration with the designer.

WHO INVENTED IT?
Credit Agricole in 1890s

WHY USE THIS METHOD?
1. Designers do not have all the answers.
2. Designers are often not part of the group that they are designing for.
3. Designers may not fully understand the perspectives or context of a large number of diverse users.
4. Many people who do not work for your organization have good ideas.

CHALLENGES
1. Need effective methods and incentives for keeping the community energized.
2. Less than 1% of people in a community generate the creative output.

WHEN TO USE THIS METHOD
1. Define intent
2. Know Context
3. Know User
4. Frame insights
5. Explore Concepts
6. Make Plans
7. Deliver Offering

HOW TO USE THIS METHOD
1. Define your problem
2. Define your use of the crowd
3. Identify incentives to crowd.
4. Identify mechanism to reach the crowd.
5. Inspire participation.
6. Distribute call to the crowd
7. Enable people to work together
8. Connect to creative people.
9. Analyze results.
10. Select the best.
11. Create preferred design solution.
12. Share results
13. Iterate above stages as necessary to refine the design.

RESOURCES
1. A social or other network
2. Crowdsourcing site or interface
3. A mechanism to reach the crowd.
4. An incentive for the crowd.
5. A crowd

REFERENCES
1. Füller, J. (Winter 2010). "Refining Virtual Co-Creation from a Consumer Perspective". California Management Review. Volume 52, Number 2. pp. 98—122.
2. Potts, J.; et al. (October 2008) "Consumer Co-creation and Situated Creativity" Industry and Innovation. Volume 15, Number 5. pp. 459—474

co-discovery

WHAT IS IT?

Two participants perform an activity and help each other as they would naturally. They are encouraged to explain what they are thinking about while working on the tasks.

WHY USE THIS METHOD?

1. Compared to thinking-aloud protocol, this technique makes it more natural for the test users to verbalize their thoughts during the test.

CHALLENGES

1. It is preferable to pair two users who know each other into one group.

WHEN TO USE THIS METHOD

1. Frame insights
2. Explore Concepts
3. Make Plans
4. Deliver Offering

RESOURCES

1. Computers
2. Workstations
3. Video cameras
4. Note pad
5. Pens

HOW TO USE THIS METHOD

1. Select participants who are representative of end users.
2. Pair the test users into groups of two.
3. Provide the users with the system to be tested and a scenario of tasks to perform.
4. Request that the subjects perform the activity.
5. During a usability test, two test users perform tasks together while being observed.
6. They are to help each other in the same manner as they would if they were working together.
7. Encourage the participants to explain what they are thinking about while undertaking the tasks.
8. Video the session
9. Analyze
10. Refine the prototype.
11. Iterate

SEE ALSO

1. Think out Loud
2. Talk out loud

REFERENCES

3. J. Nielsen "Usability Engineering" p.198, Academic Press, 1993.
4. Dumas and Redish, A Practical Guide to Usability Testing, Ablex Publishing. p. 31, "Co-discovery".
5. Rubin, J. Handbook of Usability Testing. John Wiley & Sons. p. 240, "Testing two participants at a time."

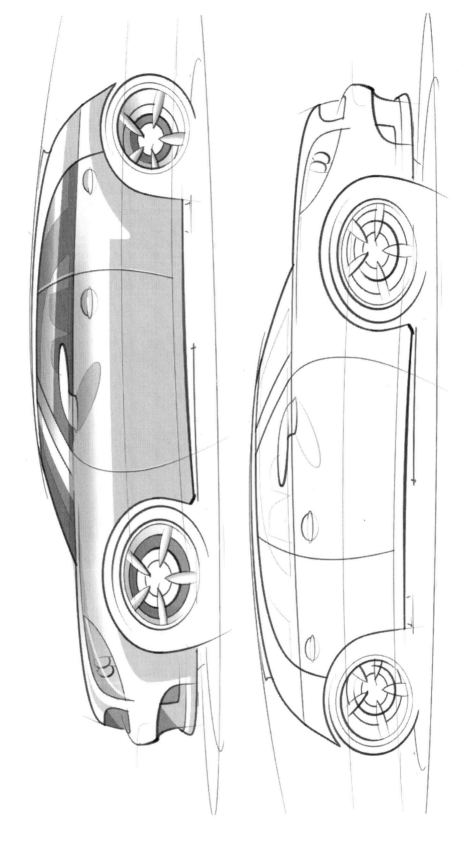

concept sketch

WHAT IS IT?
A sketch is a fast freehand drawing.

WHY USE THIS METHOD?
1. Sketches are a form of prototyping and recording ideas
2. Sketches are the first stage of making ideas real.
3. A sketch is a way of communicating and idea.
4. Sketches allow a design team to discuss and compare ideas
5. Fast and inexpensive method
6. It is iterative

CHALLENGES
1. Sketching requires investment in training.
2. Sketches can make a bad idea look good
3. The skill of sketching may exclude un-trained people with good ideas.
4. People may fall in love with a sketch to the point that they place more emphasis on the sketch than the final idea.
5. Sketching should be fast. The activity can be time consuming

RESOURCES
1. Prismacolor pencils Pencil sharpener
2. Grey markers 10%, 30%, 50%
3. Black fineliners, sharpies and ballpoints
4. Paper
5. Gel pens
6. Digital drawing tablet Sketch software
7. Computer
8. Alvin ellipse guides, Copenhagen ship curves

image: © Norebbo | Dreamstime.com

WHEN TO USE THIS METHOD
1. Explore Concepts

HOW TO USE THIS METHOD
1. Select a design problem to explore.
2. The moderator briefs the design team
3. Individual designers generate 10 sketches in 30 minutes
4. The sketches are pinned to a wall.
5. Each designer presents their ideas to the group.
6. The group votes on which ideas they think have most promise. 2 votes per person. Must vote for other person's ideas.
7. Select the three ideas that get the most votes.
8. The design team explores those ideas by each generating 10 sketches of develop-ments of the existing ideas over 30 minutes.
9. The team votes
10. Iterate as necessary.
11. Drawings should be numbered to aid dis-cussion, dated and signed by the designer.

REFERENCES
1. Design Sketching by Erik Olofsson and Klara Sjolen.
2. Learning Curves by Klara Sjolen and Allan Macdonald
3. Sketching: Drawing Techniques for Prod-uct Designers by Koos Eissen and Roselien Steur.
4. Analog Dreams by Michale DiTullo
5. Sketching Videos from Feng Zhu's FZD Design School
6. Presentation Techniques by Dick Powell.

concept selection

WHAT IS IT?

When you have developed a number of ideas how do you select the best idea or combination of ideas to move forward to prototyping and testing with people?

WHY USE THIS METHOD?

It is a method of selecting a favored idea by collective rather than individual judgment. It is a fast method that allows a design to progress. It leverages the strengths of diverse team member viewpoints and experiences.

CHALLENGES

1. The assessment is subjective.
2. Groupthink
3. Not enough good ideas
4. Inhibition
5. Lack of critical thinking

WHEN TO USE THIS METHOD

1. Explore Concepts
2. Make Plans

REFERENCES

1. Dotmocracy handbook Jason Diceman Version 2.2 March 2010 ISBN 45152708X EAN-13 9781451527087

HOW TO USE THIS METHOD

1. Pin the concept sketches to a large wall.
2. Select a small group of stakeholders to discuss and evaluate the ideas.
3. Discuss and rate each idea according to the following criteria:
   ◦ Brand fit
   ◦ Desirability
   ◦ Technical feasibility
   ◦ Business viability
   ◦ Return on Investment
   ◦ Time to launch
   ◦ Current economic environment
   ◦ Ability to get feedback prior to release
   ◦ Differentiation from competitors
4. You can use the dot voting method or evaluate each idea on the above criteria on a one to five point scale and total the score for each idea.
5. Take the top idea for further development.
6. If you have time and resources take the top three ideas and develop more themes and variations of those ideas then vote again.

RESOURCES

1. Paper
2. Pens
3. Large wall or table
4. Pins

crowd funding

WHAT IS IT?
Crowdfunding is asking a crowd of people to donate a defined amount of money for a specific cause or project in exchange for various rewards. There are three general categories crowdfunding can fall under: Equity, Donation, and Debt.

1. Equity-based crowdfunding
2. Donation-based crowdfunding
3. Debt-based crowdfunding

WHO INVENTED IT?
In 1997, fans financed a U.S. tour for the British rock group Marillion,

WHY USE THIS METHOD?
1. Relatively low risk for designer and founder.
2. Allows designers to create and make their own products.
3. Fast and efficient.

CHALLENGES
1. Intellectual property protection can be more complicated.
2. Platforms may limit the funds that you can receive.
3. New regulations and tax considerations
4. Clearly articulate what it is you're trying to accomplish in a way that inspires people to want to back it.
5. Define a compelling reward for the members of the crowd.

WHEN TO USE THIS METHOD
1. Deliver Offering

HOW TO USE THIS METHOD
Instructions for Kickstarter.com:
1. A designer visits a site and proposes an idea
2. The community reviews the proposal,
3. The idea is accepted or rejected.
4. The designer launches their project.
5. The designer creates a video to communicate the idea.
6. The designer structures a reward for backers.
7. This is often one of what is being created.
8. In film, dance or theater the reward may be a ticket.

REFERENCES
1. The Geography of Crowdfunding, NET Institute Working Paper No. 10-08, Oct 2010
2. Ordanini, A.; Miceli, L.; Pizzetti, M.; Parasuraman, A. (2011). "Crowd-funding: Transforming customers into investors through innovative service platforms". Journal of Service Management 22 (4): 443.

crowd sourcing

WHAT IS IT?

Crowd sourcing involves out sourcing a task to a dispersed group of people. It usually refers to tasks undertaken by an undefined public group rather than paid employees.

Types of crowd sourcing include:

1. Crowd funding
2. Crowd purchasing
3. Micro work

The incentives for crowd sourcing can include: immediate payoffs, delayed payoffs, and social motivation, skill variety, task identity, task autonomy, direct feedback from the job

WHO INVENTED IT?

Jeff Howe first used the term in a June 2006 Wired magazine article "The Rise of Crowd sourcing"

WHY USE THIS METHOD?

1. Crowd sourcing can obtain large numbers of alternative solutions.
2. It is relatively fast
3. Inexpensive.
4. Diverse solutions.
5. group of people is sometimes more intelligent than an individual

CHALLENGES

1. A faulty results caused by targeted, malicious work efforts
2. Ethical concerns
3. Difficulties in collaboration and team activity of crowd members.
4. Lack of monetary motivation

WHEN TO USE THIS METHOD

1. Define intent
2. Know Context
3. Know User
4. Frame insights
5. Explore Concepts
6. Make Plans
7. Deliver Offering

HOW TO USE THIS METHOD

1. Define your problem
2. Define your use of the crowd
3. Identify incentives.
4. Identify mechanism to reach the crowd.
5. Inspire your users to create
6. Distribute brief to the crowd
7. Analyze results.
8. Create preferred design solution.
9. Repeat above stages as necessary to refine the design.

RESOURCES

1. A social or other network
2. Crowd sourcing site or interface
3. A mechanism to reach the crowd.
4. An incentive for the crowd.
5. A crowd

REFERENCES

1. Jeff Howe (2006). "The Rise of Crowd sourcing". Wired.
2. Howe, Jeff (2008), "Crowd sourcing: Why the Power of the Crowd is Driving the Future of Business", The International Achievement Institute.

desktop walkthrough

WHAT IS IT?

A desktop walkthrough is the method of acting out activities of stakeholders or personas while interacting with product or service. It is a form of prototyping, in a particular future context. The focus is on people and often small figures and construction kits are used are used to represent the people and context.

WHY USE THIS METHOD?

1. Role playing helps a designer gain empathy and insights into the experience of the user.
2. Useful for unfamiliar situations.
3. It is a physical activity so may uncover insights not apparent when using story boarding
4. It encourages designers to consider the end users, and their context
5. Fast and low cost method

CHALLENGES

1. It is sometimes hard to envision misuse scenarios for new products.
2. Some people feel self conscious when asked to role play

WHEN TO USE THIS METHOD

1. Know Context
2. Know User
3. Frame insights
4. Generate Concepts
5. Create Solutions
6. © Pixelbrat | Dreamstime.com

HOW TO USE THIS METHOD

1. Identify the context.
2. Identify scenarios and tasks users undertake.
3. Create storyboards.
4. Assign roles.
5. Isolate moments where the users interact with the product or service.
6. Use your own intuitive responses to iterate and refine the design.
7. Construct environments using toy figures and building kits.
8. Act out the tasks in the environments or context of use.
9. Photograph the key actions.
10. Consider typical misuse cases.
11. Discuss insights.

RESOURCES

1. Camera
2. Toy Figures to represent people
3. Toy construction kit for environments

REFERENCES

1. Greenberg, J. (1993). The role of role playing in organizational research. Journal of Management, 19(2), 221-241.Duncombe, S., & Heikkinen, M. H. (1990). Role-playing for different viewpoints. The Social Studies (Washington, D.C.)

dot voting

WHAT IS IT?

This method is a collective way of prioritizing and converging on a design solution that uses group wisdom. Concepts can be individually scored against selection criteria such as the business proposition, ease of manufacturing, cost and usability. Each participant scores each concept against a list of assessment criteria and the scores are totaled to determine the favored ideas.

WHY USE THIS METHOD?

It is a method of selecting a favored idea by collective rather than individual judgment. It is a fast method that allows a design to progress. It leverages the strengths of diverse team member viewpoints and experiences.

CHALLENGES

1. The assessment is subjective.
2. Groupthink
3. Not enough good ideas
4. Inhibition
5. Lack of critical thinking

RESOURCES

1. Large wall
2. Adhesive dots

REFERENCES

1. Dotmocracy handbook Jason Diceman Version 2.2 March 2010 ISBN 45152708X EAN-13 9781451527087

WHEN TO USE THIS METHOD

1. Define intent
2. Know Context
3. Know User
4. Frame insights
5. Explore Concepts
6. Make Plans
7. Deliver Offering

HOW TO USE THIS METHOD

1. Select a team of between 4 and 20 cross disciplinary participants.
2. Brainstorm ideas for example ask each team member to generate six ideas as sketches.
3. Each idea should be presented on one post it note or page.
4. Each designer should quickly explain each idea to the group before the group votes.
5. Spread the ideas over a wall or table.
6. Ask the team to group the ideas by similarity or affinity.
7. Ask the team to vote on their two or three favorite ideas and total the votes. You can use sticky dots or colored pins to indicate a vote or a moderator can tally the scores.
8. Rearrange the ideas so that the ideas with the dots are grouped together, ranked from most dots to least.
9. Talk about the ideas that received the most votes and see if there is a general level of comfort with taking one or more of those ideas to the next step.

evidence based design

WHAT IS IT?
Evidence based design is the approach of basing design decisions on research findings. Evidence-based design has been applied for the measuring of the efficacy of a building design.

WHY USE THIS METHOD?
1. A designer's intuition can be wrong.
2. Designers rarely belong to the groups that we are designing for.
3. Designers need to use research to see through the eyes of those people we are designing for.
4. When doing cross cultural design it is particularly important to use evidence based design.
5. Managers and financial officers have more confidence in evidence based design than in a designers intuition.
6. Designers often design because we believe something is awesome based on a hunch this is not a good basis success.

WHEN TO USE THIS METHOD
1. Define intent
2. Know Context
3. Know User
4. Frame insights
5. Explore Concepts
6. Make Plans
7. Deliver Offering

HOW TO USE THIS METHOD
1. Start by identifying people's problems.
2. Have a cross disciplinary team
3. Use the methods in this book
4. Maintain a people centered approach
5. Use strategic partnerships.

REFERENCES
1. HALL C.R., CHD rolls out evidence-based design accreditation and certification, in Health Facilities Management. July 2009
2. A Practitioner's Guide to Evidence-Based Design by Debra D. Harris, PhD, Anjali Joseph, PhD, Franklin Becker, PhD, Kirk Hamilton, FAIA, FACHA, Mardelle McCuskey Shepley, AIA, D.Arch

generative research

WHAT IS IT?

Collections of modular objects that can be used for participatory modeling and prototyping to inform and inspire design teams. Often used in creative codesign workshops. It is a generative design method which facilitates creative play. The elements can be reused in a number of research sessions in different geographic locations.

WHO INVENTED IT?

Pioneered by Liz Sanders and Lego Johan Roos and Bart Victor 1990s.

WHY USE THIS METHOD?

Helps develop:

1. Problem solving
2. Change management
3. Strategic thinking
4. Decision making
5. Services, product and experience redesign
6. Can be fun
7. Identify opportunities
8. Re frame challenges
9. Leverages creative thinking of the team

WHEN TO USE THIS METHOD

1. Know Context
2. Know User
3. Frame insights
4. Explore Concepts

HOW TO USE THIS METHOD

1. Form cross-disciplinary team 5 to 20 members. It's best to have teams of not more than 8
2. Identify design problem. Create agenda.
3. Start with a warming up exercise.
4. Write design problem in visible location such as white board.
5. Workshop participants first build individual prototypes exploring the problem.
6. Divide larger group into smaller work groups of 3 to 5 participants.
7. Ask each participant to develop between 1 and 5 design solutions.
8. Through internal discussion each group should select their preferred group design solution.
9. The group builds a collective model incorporating the individual contributions.
10. Each group build a physical model of preferred solution and presents it to larger group.
11. Larger group selects their preferred design solutions by discussion and voting.
12. Capture process and ideas with video or photographs.
13. Debriefing and harvest of ideas.

REFERENCES

1. Statler, M., Roos, J., and B. Victor, 2009, 'Ain't Misbehavin': Taking Play Seriously in Organizations,' Journal of Change Management, 9(1): 87-107.

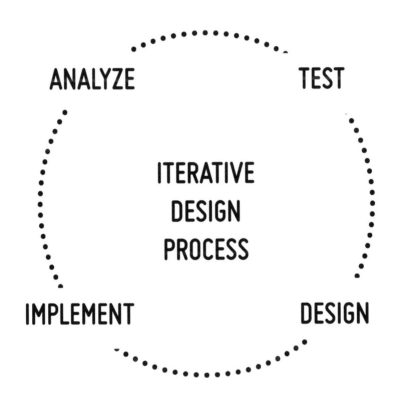

guided iteration

WHAT IS IT?

Guided iteration is a systematic approach to the design process that uses a series of divergent and convergent phases.

WHY USE THIS METHOD?

1. Guided iteration is the best proven process for design.

WHEN TO USE THIS METHOD

2. Define intent
3. Know Context
4. Know User
5. Frame insights
6. Explore Concepts
7. Make Plans
8. Deliver Offering

HOW TO USE THIS METHOD

1. Define the design problem
2. Should be a written document
3. Generate a number of alternative solutions.
4. Evaluate the solutions using methods such as Pugh's method or dot voting by your design team.
5. Redesign and refine based on your evaluation.
6. Modify Existing Alternatives
7. Create New alternatives based on your evaluation.

RESOURCES

1. Pens
2. Paper
3. White board
4. Post-it notes

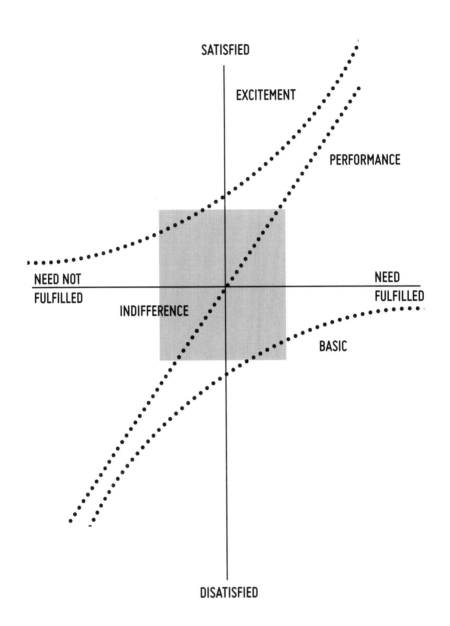

315

kano analysis

WHAT IS IT?
The Kano model of customer satisfaction classifies product attributes based on customer perception and satisfaction.

WHO INVENTED IT?
Dr Noriaki Kano 1980s

WHY USE THIS METHOD?
Strategically guides design decisions
Identifies customer needs
Determines functional requirements
Useful for concept development
Analyzing competitive products

CHALLENGES
1. Shouldn't be applied after the design is complete
2. Prioritization matrices help in understanding what excites the customer.

WHEN TO USE THIS METHOD
3. Know Context
4. Know User
5. Frame insights
6. Explore Concepts

HOW TO USE THIS METHOD
Ask customers:
1. Rate your satisfaction with this attribute?
2. Rate your satisfaction without this attribute?

Customers should select one of the following responses:
1. Satisfied;
2. Neutral (Its normally that way);
3. Dissatisfied;
4. Don't care.

REFERENCES
1. Kano, Noriaki; Nobuhiku Seraku, Fumio Takahashi, Shinichi Tsuji (April 1984). "Attractive quality and must-be quality" (in Japanese). Journal of the Japanese Society for Quality Control 14 (2): 39–48. ISSN 0386-8230.
2. Bartikowski, B., Llosa, S. (2003). Identifying Satisfiers, Dissatisfiers, Criticals and Neutrals in Customer Satisfaction. Working Paper n° 05-2003, Mai 2003. Euromed – Ecole de Management. Marseille.

if i were you

WHAT IS IT?
This is a method used to explore scenarios based on methods used by actors that allows refinement of ideas by a design team.

WHO INVENTED IT?
Gerber, E 2009

WHY USE THIS METHOD?
1. Does not require a lot of training.
2. Can take ideas into new areas.

CHALLENGES
1. Needs good moderator.

WHEN TO USE THIS METHOD
1. Know Context
2. Know User
3. Frame insights
4. Explore Concepts

HOW TO USE THIS METHOD
1. Moderator defines scenario.
2. Can use props or empathy tools.
3. Can videotape session.
4. Group sits around a table or on chairs in a circle.
5. Moderator introduces idea or scenario. Each participant in turn adds something to the idea prefixed by the statement "If I was you I would."
6. Statements should be positive

A1	A2	A3	B1	B2	B3	C1	C2	C3
A4	**A**	A5	B4	**B**	B5	C4	**C**	C5
A6	A7	A8	B6	B7	B8	C6	C7	C8
D1	D2	D3	**A**	**B**	**C**	E1	E2	E3
D4	**D**	D5	**D**	■	**E**	E4	**E**	E5
D6	D7	D8	**F**	**G**	**H**	E6	E7	E8
F1	F2	F3	G1	G2	G3	H1	H2	H3
F4	**F**	F5	G4	**G**	G5	H4	**H**	H5
F6	F7	F8	G6	G7	G8	H6	H7	H8

lotus blossom

WHAT IS IT?

The lotus blossom is a creativity technique that consists a framework for idea generation that starts by generating eight concept themes based on a central theme. Each concept then serves as the basis for eight further theme explorations or variations.

WHO INVENTED IT?

Yasuo Matsumura, Director of the Clover Management Research

WHY USE THIS METHOD?

1. There is a hierarchy of ideas
2. This method requires that a quantity of ideas is generated.
3. shifts you from reacting to a static snapshot of the problem and broadens your perspective toward the problem and the relationships and connections between its components

CHALLENGES

1. It is a somewhat rigid model. Not every problem will require the same number of concepts to be developed.

WHEN TO USE THIS METHOD

1. Explore Concepts

HOW TO USE THIS METHOD

1. Draw up a lotus blossom diagram made up of a square in the center of the diagram and eight circles surrounding the square;
2. Write the problem in the center box of the diagram.
3. Write eight related ideas around the center.
4. Each idea then becomes the central idea of a new theme or blossom.
5. Follow step 3 with all central ideas.

RESOURCES

1. Paper
2. Pens
3. White board
4. Dry-erase markers
5. Post-it-notes.

REFERENCES

1. Michalko M., Thinkpak, Berkeley, California, Ten Speed Press, 1994.
2. Michalko, Michael, Thinkertoys: A handbook of creative-thinking techniques, Second Edition, Ten Speed Press, 2006, Toronto;
3. Sloane, Paul. The Leader's Guide to Lateral Thinking Skills: Unlocking the Creativity and Innovation in You and Your Team (Paperback - 3 Sep 2006);

misuse scenarios

WHAT IS IT?

This is a method that focuses on possible misuse, both unintentional and malicious, of a product or service. The method involves use of scenarios and personas to envision possible misuse cases. These may be:

1. Typical scenarios
2. Atypical scenarios
3. Extreme scenarios

WHO INVENTED IT?

Ian Alexander 2003

WHY USE THIS METHOD?

1. Considering misuse reduces the possibility that a product will fail in use.
2. Consider on projects where there is potential for misuse.
3. High volume manufactured products have high potential for misuse.

CHALLENGES

1. Use customer service feedback to construct misuse scenarios.
2. It is sometimes hard to envision misuse scenarios for new products.

WHEN TO USE THIS METHOD

1. Know Context
2. Know User
3. Frame insights
4. Explore Concepts

HOW TO USE THIS METHOD

1. Think of various types of scenarios and when they may become misuse scenarios.
2. Talk to experts and ask them to provide scenarios of misuse.
3. Consider the context of use and how that may influence misuse.
4. Brainstorm with team to create scenarios of misuse.
5. Create a list of misuse scenarios.
6. Brainstorm remedies for misuse and modify design to remedy misuse.

RESOURCES

1. Pen
2. Paper
3. White board
4. Dry-erase markers
5. Camera

REFERENCES

1. Alexander, Ian, Use/Misuse Case Analysis Elicits Non-Functional Requirements, Computing & Control Engineering Journal, Vol 14, 1, pp 40–45, February 2003
2. Sindre, Guttorm and Andreas L. Opdahl, Templates for Misuse Case Description, Proc. 7th Intl Workshop on Requirements Engineering, Foundation for Software Quality (REFSQ'2001), Interlaken, Switzerland, 4–5 June 2001

Photo: photocase.com – kallejipp

mood board

WHAT IS IT?

A mood board is a collage made of images and words and may include sample of colors and fabrics or other materials. They are used to convey the emotional communication of an intended design

WHO INVENTED IT?

Possibly Terence Conran 1991

WHY USE THIS METHOD?

1. A mood board helps convey complex emotional ideas at an early stage in design project
2. Provides a focus for team discussion and alignment.
3. It is fast
4. Inexpensive
5. A form of visual prototype of a perceptual experience

CHALLENGES

1. It is subjective,

WHEN TO USE THIS METHOD

1. Define intent

HOW TO USE THIS METHOD

A mood board can include

1. Colors
2. Forms
3. Cultures
4. Materials
5. Finishes
6. Textures

RESOURCES

1. Graphic programs
2. Print Magazines
3. Digital images
4. Fabric swatches
5. Color swatches
6. Graphics software
7. Computer

REFERENCES

1. Kathryn McKelvey, Janine Munslow Fashion Forecasting :Page 150 2008
2. Product Design: Practical Methods for systematic Development of New Products By Mike Baxter 1995

now and new now

WHAT IS IT?

New and New Now is a simple planning tool that gives output like Blueprint Modelling developed by Giulia Piu

WHO INVENTED IT?

Giulia Piu

WHY USE THIS METHOD?

1. This exercise allows entrepreneurs to
2. Think about their personal strengths.
3. What additional skills or knowledge may be necessary for success
4. Strategic partnerships.
5. What steps are needed to achieve success.

WHEN TO USE THIS METHOD

1. Define intent

HOW TO USE THIS METHOD

1. The exercise can be done by one person or by a design team.
2. List the skills and attributes you have already
3. List the skills and activities you need to get from where you are to where you want to be.
4. List the skills that you consider most important for success.

Giulia Piu

RESOURCES

1. Pens
2. Paper
3. White Board
4. Dry erase markers
5. Post-it notes

participatory budgeting

WHAT IS IT?

A process of democratic decision-making, in which people decide how to allocate a budget.

WHO INVENTED IT?

It was first implemented in Porto Alegre, Brazil, in 1990.

WHY USE THIS METHOD?

1. Higher public satisfaction with design decisions More transparent decision making More accountable managers and government officials, Better design decisions

WHEN TO USE THIS METHOD

1. Define intent
2. Know Context
3. Know User
4. Frame insights
5. Explore Concepts
6. Make Plans
7. Deliver Offering

HOW TO USE THIS METHOD

1. Develop participatory budgeting process. Set clear rules.
2. Approve the amount of the budget
3. Assemblies are organized and meet and who will be making project proposals to the community
4. Proposals are developed in collaboration with, technical experts.
5. Proposals are presented, publicized, discussed and voted on.
6. Evaluate
7. Work with architects and other design professionals to implement the proposals.

RESOURCES

1. Private space
2. White boards
3. Dry-erase markers
4. Pens
5. Paper

REFERENCES

1. YES Magazine, 2010 Apr. 10, "Chicago's $1.3 Million Experiment in Democracy; For the First Time in the U.S., the City's 49th Ward Lets Taxpayers Directly Decide How Public Money is Spent,"

related contexts

WHAT IS IT?

A method that involves discovering and projecting the thinking of another sector, brand, organization or context onto a design problem.

WHY USE THIS METHOD?

A method of discovering affinities that can facilitate innovative thinking and solutions.

1. Scenarios become a focus for discussion which helps evaluate and refine concepts.
2. Usability issues can be explored.
3. Scenarios help us create an end to end experience.
4. Personas give us a framework to evaluate possible solutions.

CHALLENGES

1. Strong personalities can influence the group in negative ways.
2. Include problem situations
3. Hard to envision misuse scenarios.

WHEN TO USE THIS METHOD

1. Know Context
2. Know User
3. Frame insights
4. Generate Concepts

HOW TO USE THIS METHOD

1. Identify a design problem
2. Put together a design team of 4 to 12 members with a moderator.
3. Brainstorm a list of sectors, organizations, or contexts that may imply a different approach or thinking to your design problem.
4. Imagine your design problem with the associated list.
5. Generate concepts for each relationship
6. Vote for favored directions using dot voting method.
7. Analyze and summarize insights.

RESOURCES

1. Post-it notes
2. White board
3. Paper
4. Pens
5. Dry-erase markers

REFERENCES

1. "Scenarios," IDEO Method Cards. ISBN 0-9544132-1-0
2. Carroll, John M. Making Use: Scenario-based design of human-computer interactions. MIT Press, 2000.
3. Carroll J. M. Five Reasons for Scenario Based Design. Elsevier Science B. V. 2000.

role playing

WHAT IS IT?

Role playing is a research method where the researcher physically acts out the interaction or experience of the user of a product, service or experience. It is a type of prototyping, a narrative or story about how people may experience a design in a particular future context. Role playing can be used to predict or explore future interactions with concept products or services.

WHY USE THIS METHOD?

1. Role playing helps a designer gain empathy and insights into the experience of the user.
2. Useful for unfamiliar situations.
3. It is a physical activity so may uncover insights not apparent when using storyboarding
4. It helps designers empathize with the intended users and their context.
5. Is an inexpensive method requiring few resources.

CHALLENGES

1. It is difficult to envision all the ways a product or service could be misused.
2. Some people feel self conscious when asked to role play

RESOURCES

1. Note pad
2. Pens
3. Video camera
4. Empathy tools

image: © Wavebreakm. | Dreamstime.com

WHEN TO USE THIS METHOD

1. Know Context
2. Know User
3. Frame insights
4. Generate Concepts
5. Create Solutions

HOW TO USE THIS METHOD

1. Identify the situation.
2. Identify scenarios and tasks users undertake.
3. Create storyboards.
4. Assign roles.
5. Isolate moments where the users interact with the product or service.
6. Use your own intuitive responses to iterate and refine the design.
7. This method can be used to test physical prototypes.
8. You can act out the tasks in the environments or context of use.
9. You can use empathy tools such as glasses to simulate the effects of age or a wheelchair.
10. Consider typical misuse cases.
11. Discuss insights.

REFERENCES

1. Greenberg, J. (1993). The role of role playing in organizational research. Journal of Management, 19(2), 221-241.
2. Duncombe, S., & Heikkinen, M. H. (1990). Role-playing for different viewpoints. The Social Studies (Washington, D.C.)

scenarios

WHAT IS IT?

A scenario is a narrative or story about how people may experience a design in a particular future context of use. They can be used to predict or explore future interactions with concept products or services. Scenarios can be presented by media such as storyboards or video or be written. They can feature single or multiple actors participating in product or service interactions.

WHO INVENTED IT?

Herman Kahn, Rand Corporation 1950, USA

WHY USE THIS METHOD?

1. Scenarios become a focus for discussion which helps evaluate and refine concepts.
2. Usability issues can be explored at a very early stage in the design process.
3. The are useful tool to align a team vision.
4. Scenarios help us create an end to end experience.
5. Interactive experiences involve the dimension of time.
6. Personas give us a framework to evaluate possible solutions.

CHALLENGES

1. Generate scenarios for a range of situations.
2. Include problem situations
3. Hard to envision misuse scenarios.

WHEN TO USE THIS METHOD

1. Frame insights
2. Generate Concepts
3. Create Solutions

HOW TO USE THIS METHOD

1. Identify the question to investigate.
2. Decide time and scope for the scenario process.
3. Identify stake holders and uncertainties.
4. Define the scenarios.
5. Create storyboards of users goals, activities, motivations and tasks.
6. Act out the scenarios.
7. The session can be videotaped.
8. Analyze the scenarios through discussion.
9. Summarize insights

RESOURCES

1. Storyboard templates
2. Pens
3. Video cameras
4. Props
5. White board
6. Dry-erase markers

REFERENCES

1. "Scenarios," IDEO Method Cards. ISBN 0-9544132-1-0
2. Carroll, John M. Making Use: Scenario-based design of human-computer interactions. MIT Press, 2000.
3. Carroll J. M. Five Reasons for Scenario Based Design. Elsevier Science B. V. 2000.
4. Carroll, John M. Scenario-Based Design: Envisioning Work and Technology in System Development.

six thinking hats

WHAT IS IT?

Six thinking hats is a tool for thinking described in a book by the same name by Edward de Bono. It can help a design team understand the effects of decisions from different viewpoints.

1. White Hat thinking is information, numbers, data needs and gaps.
2. Red Hat thinking is intuition, desires and emotion.
3. Black Hat thinking is the hat of judgment and care.
4. Yellow Hat thinking is the logical positive.
5. Green Hat thinking is the hat of creativity, alternatives, proposals, provocations and change.
6. Blue Hat thinking is the overview or process control.

WHO INVENTED IT?

Edward de Bono 1985

CHALLENGES

1. When describing your concept, be specific about your goal.
2. Utilize your thinking for practical solutions.
3. Always think in the style of the hat you're wearing.
4. Stick to the rules.

WHY USE THIS METHOD?

The key theoretical reasons to use the Six Thinking Hats are to:

1. Encourage Parallel Thinking
2. Encourage full-spectrum thinking
3. Separate ego from performance
4. Encourage critical thinking.

Image Copyright Olga Popova, 2012 Used under license from Shutterstock.com

WHEN TO USE THIS METHOD

1. Know Context
2. Know User
3. Frame insights
4. Generate Concepts
5. Create Solutions

HOW TO USE THIS METHOD

1. Optimum number of participants is 4 to 8.
2. Present the facts White Hat.
3. Generate ideas on how the issue should be handled Green Hat.
4. Evaluate the ideas. Yellow Hat.
5. List the drawbacks Black Hat.
6. Get the feelings about alternatives Red Hat.
7. Summarize and finish the meeting. Blue Hat.
8. Time required 90 minutes.

RESOURCES

1. Paper and
2. Pens,
3. Descriptions of different hats
4. Symbols of hats
5. Space to sit in the circle

REFERENCES

1. de Bono, Edward (1985). Six Thinking Hats: An Essential Approach to Business Management. Little, Brown, & Company. ISBN 0-316-17791-1 (hardback) and 0316178314 (paperback).
2. Moseley, D., Baumfield, V., Elliott, J., Gregson, M., Higgins, S., Miller, J., Newton, D. (2005). "De Bono's lateral and parallel thinking tools", in ed. Moseley, David: Frameworks for Thinking. Cambridge University Press.

skunkworks

WHAT IS IT?

The term "skunk works", or "skunkworks", describes a group within an organization given a high degree of autonomy and unhampered by bureaucracy, working on advanced innovative projects. The term was invented by Lockheed during WW2. Their secret laboratory was nicknamed "Skunk Works" because of an odor from an adjacent plastics factory that reminded the engineers of the "Skonk Works" distillery in a popular cartoon.

WHO INVENTED IT?

Kelly Johnson Lockheed 1943
Burbank, California

WHY USE THIS METHOD?

1. Can lead to innovation

CHALLENGES

1. Skunk works can become isolated or withdrawn,
2. Can destroy trust and inhibit collaboration, co-creation, innovation, and implementation. with other design staff.
3. This division can retard necessary innovation and change.
4. The knowledge of how to pull off breakthrough innovation tends to get stuck inside the group

WHEN TO USE THIS METHOD

1. Define intent
2. Know Context
3. Know User
4. Frame insights
5. Explore Concepts
6. Make Plans

HOW TO USE THIS METHOD

1. Only involve small number of people who care. Create the team from the right people.
2. Reports directly to senior executive,
3. Identify corporate resources
4. Start small and build
5. Learn from your mistakes
6. Maintain low visibility
7. Manage the approvals process and risks.
8. Do not threaten the internal establishment.

REFERENCES

1. Bennis, Warren and Patricia Ward Biederman. Organizing Genius: The Secrets of Creative Collaboration, p. 117. Perseus Books, 1997.
2. Miller, Jay. Lockheed Martin's Skunk Works: The Official History, Updated Edition. Aerofax, 1995. ISBN 1-85780-037-0.
3. Rich, Ben, Leo Janos. (1996) Skunk Works. Little, Brown & Company, ISBN 0-316-74300-3

synectics

WHAT IS IT?

Synectics is a structured creativity method that is based on analogy. Synectics is based on observations collected during thousands of hours of group process and group problem solving and decision making activities (Nolan 1989)The word synectics combines derives from Greek "the bringing together of diverse elements."

WHO INVENTED IT?

George Prince and William Gordon 1976

WHY USE THIS METHOD?

1. Use to stimulate creative thinking and generate new problem solving approaches.
2. Synectics provides an environment in which risk taking is validated.
3. Synectics can be fun and productive.

CHALLENGES

1. Synectics is more demanding than brainstorming,
2. If the analogy is too obvious, then it may not promote innovative thinking.
3. Synectics works best as a group process.

WHEN TO USE THIS METHOD

1. Frame insights
2. Generate Concepts

HOW TO USE THIS METHOD

1. Problem definition.
2. Create an analogy. Use ideas from the natural or man-made world, connections with historical events, your location, etc.
3. Use this Sentence Stem: An is a lot like a y because...
4. Use a syntectic trigger mechanism like a picture, poem, song, drawing etc. to start your analogical reasoning.
5. The group generates as many solution approaches, called springboards, as possible.
6. Idea selection.
7. Excursions – Structured side trips.
8. Develop the selected ideas into concepts.
9. Analyze the connections in the analogy you have created.

RESOURCES

1. Paper
2. Pens
3. White board
4. Dry-erase markers

REFERENCES

1. Gordon, William J.J. Synectics: The Development of Creative Capacity. (New York: Harper and row, Publishers, 1961
2. Nolan, Vincent. "Whatever Happened to Synectics?" Creativity and Innovation Management, v. 21 n.1 (2003): 25.

written scenario

WHAT IS IT?
Scenarios are stories that describe a possible future event. Scenarios are used by organizations to understand different ways that future events might unfold

WHO INVENTED THIS METHOD?
Herman Kahn RAND 1950s

WHY USE THIS METHOD?
1. A written scenario helps a designer understand interactions of an intended user with a product service or experience.
2. Scenarios can also be used for evaluating an intended design.

WHEN TO USE THIS METHOD
1. Define intent
2. Know Context
3. Know User
4. Frame insights
5. Explore Concepts
6. Make Plans

CHALLENGES
1. Work in small groups
2. Avoid identifying one solution
3. Keep focussed on the problem.

HOW TO USE THIS METHOD
1. Decide on the key question to be answered.
2. Determine the time and scope of the scenario.
3. Determine the stakeholders or actors.
4. Determine the goals the actor has to complete.
5. Map basic trends and driving forces.
6. Consider key uncertainties.
7. Determine a starting point of the scenario: a trigger or an event.
8. You need to have an understanding of the users and the context of use.
9. Brainstorm possible solutions.
10. Produce 7 to 9 initial mini-scenarios
11. Reduce to 2 to 3 scenarios
12. You can use story boarding.
13. In simple language describe the interactions.
14. Assess the scenarios. Identify the issues arising.

RESOURCES
1. Paper
2. Pens

REFERENCES
1. Schoemaker, Paul J.H. "Scenario Planning: A Tool for Strategic Thinking," Sloan Management Review. Winter: 1995, pp. 25-40.
2. M. Lindgren & H. Bandhold, Scenario planning — the link between future and strategy, Palgrave Macmillan, 2003

Chapter 8
Prototype and iterate
how can we make it better?

low fidelity prototyping

WHAT IS IT?

Cardboard prototyping is a quick and cheap way of gaining insight and informing decision making without the need for costly investment. Simulates function but not aesthetics of proposed design. Prototypes help compare alternatives and help answer questions about interactions or experiences.

WHY USE THIS METHOD?

1. May provide the proof of concept
2. It is physical and visible
3. Inexpensive and fast.
4. Useful for refining functional and perceptual interactions.
5. Assists to identify any problems with the design.
6. Helps to reduce the risks
7. Helps members of team to be in alignment on an idea.
8. Helps make abstract ideas concrete.
9. Feedback can be gained from the user

CHALLENGES

1. Producer might get too attached to prototype and it becomes jewelry because it is beautiful rather than a design tool.

WHEN TO USE THIS METHOD

1. Know Context
2. Know User
3. Frame insights
4. Explore Concepts

Image Copyright Liudmila P. Sundikova, 2012
Used under license from Shutterstock.com

HOW TO USE THIS METHOD

1. Construct models, not illustrations
2. Select the important tasks, interactions or experiences to be prototyped.
3. Build to understand problems.
4. If it is beautiful you have invested too much.
5. Make it simple
6. Assemble a kit of inexpensive materials
7. Preparing for a test
8. Select users
9. Conduct test
10. Record notes on the 8x5 cards.
11. Evaluate the results
12. Iterate

RESOURCES

1. Paper
2. Cardboard
3. Wire
4. Foam board,
5. Post-it-notes
6. Hot melt glue

REFERENCES

1. Sefelin, R., Tscheligi, M., & Gukker, V. (2003). Paper Prototyping — What is it good for? A Comparison of paper — and Computer — based Low fidelity Prototyping, CHI 2003, 778-779
2. Snyder, Carolyn (2003). Paper Prototyping: the fast and easy way to design and refine user interfaces. San Francisco, CA: Morgan Kaufmann

high fidelity prototype

WHAT IS IT?

High fidelity prototyping is a prototype that looks like and may work like the finished design. It simulates the aesthetics of proposed design.

WHY USE THIS METHOD?

1. May provide the proof of concept
2. It is physical and visible
3. Useful for refining functional and perceptual interactions.
4. Assists to identify any problems with the design.
5. Helps to reduce the risks
6. Helps members of team to be in alignment on an idea.
7. Helps make abstract ideas concrete.
8. Feedback can be gained from the user

CHALLENGES

1. Expensive and slow.
2. People may become attached a high fidelity prototype and not wish to change the design so it should be produced only when iteration and refinement stages are complete.
3. Producer might get too attached to prototype and it becomes jewelry because it is beautiful rather than a design tool.

WHEN TO USE THIS METHOD

1. Make plans
2. Deliver offering

HOW TO USE THIS METHOD

1. Create final design through guided iterative process.
2. There are various methods for prototyping designs in different fields of design.
3. Create engineering database.
4. Build prototype
5. Preparing for a test
6. Select users
7. Conduct test
8. Record notes on the 8x5 cards.
9. Evaluate the results

RESOURCES

1. Rapid prototyping facility
2. Model shop
3. Spray paint
4. Engineering database
5. Many other resources depending on what is being prototyped

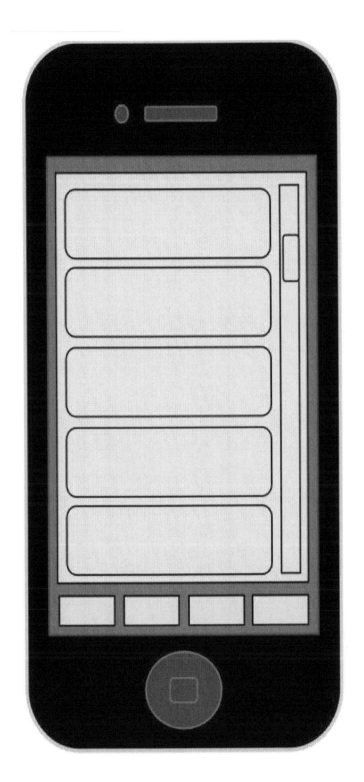

wireframe

WHAT IS IT?
Website wireframes are a simplified outline of the elements of a web page. They are useful for communicating the functionality of a website in order to get feedback on the design. The wireframe depicts the page layout, interface and navigation, and how these elements interact in use.

WHO INVENTED IT?
Matthew Van Horn claims to have invented the term around 1994 in New York.

WHY USE THIS METHOD?
1. Wireframes are useful for getting feedback on a design.
2. Wireframes can speed up the iteration process of a website design.
3. Enable online collaboration
4. Helps Identify needed changes early on in the development.
5. Wireframes are low cost

CHALLENGES
1. Notes to explain behavior are usefull
2. Wireframes do not explain interactive details involving movement.
3.

WHEN TO USE THIS METHOD
1. Define intent
2. Know Context
3. Know User
4. Frame insights
5. Explore Concepts

HOW TO USE THIS METHOD
1. There are a several ways to create wireframes. These include drawing by hand. Using Adobe Photoshop or Illustrator and using wireframe software.
2. Start by listing all of the elements that you want on your website.
3. Use simple boxes or outlines of the shape of elements, and name them. These elements can include: navigation: buttons, Company logo: can just be represented by a box, content areas and search box.
4. Review your design and adjust as necessary.
5. Make wireframe for each page in your site.

RESOURCES
1. Paper
2. Pens
3. Wireframe software
4. Computer

REFERENCES
1. Brown, Dan M. (2011). Communicating Design: Developing Web Site Documentation for Design and Planning, Second Edition. New Riders. ISBN 978-0-13-138539-9.
2. Wodtke, Christina; Govella, Austin (2009). Information Architecture: Blueprints for the Web, Second Edition. New Riders. ISBN 978-0-321-59199-9.

Chapter 9
Deliver offering
let's make and sell it

IMPORTANT

ACTIVITY A

ACTIVITY I

ACTIVITY B

ACTIVITY H

ACTIVITY C

URGENT

NOT URGENT

ACTIVITY F

ACTIVITY G

ACTIVITY D

ACTIVITY E

NOT IMPORTANT

eisenhower map

WHAT IS IT?

The Eisenhower map is a simple tool that helps you manage your time effectively. also called "Eisenhower matrix", "Eisenhower principle", "Eisenhower grid" Eisenhower is quoted as saying, "What is important is seldom urgent and what is urgent is seldom important."

WHO INVENTED IT?

US President Dwight D. Eisenhower

WHY USE THIS METHOD?

1.   Aids communication and discussion within the organization.
2.   It is human nature to do tasks which are not most urgent first.
3.   To gain competitive advantage,
4.   Helps build competitive strategy
5.   Helps build communication strategy
6.   Helps manage time effectively

CHALLENGES

1.   Can be subjective

WHEN TO USE THIS METHOD

1.   Know Context
2.   Know User
3.   Frame insights
4.   Explore Concepts

HOW TO USE THIS METHOD

1.   Moderator draws grid on whiteboard or flip chart.
2.   At the end of each project meeting the team brainstorms the tasks that need to be completed and places each task by consensus on the map.
3.   Map individual tasks.
4.   Interpret the map.
5.   Create strategy.
6.   Tasks which are important and urgent are given immediate resources.

RESOURCES

1.   Pen
2.   Paper
3.   White board
4.   Dry erase markers

agile development

WHAT IS IT?

Agile software development is a group of software development methods based on iterative collaboration between cross-functional teams. It features methods that help rapid and flexible response to change. Iterative methods are favored that involve stakeholders.

Agile manifesto 2001:

1. Individuals and interactions over processes and tools
2. Working software over comprehensive documentation
3. Customer collaboration over contract negotiation
4. Responding to change over following a plan

WHO INVENTED IT?

Bernie Dimsdale at IBM 1957

CHALLENGES

Opponents of the use of this method claim weaknesses of the methods are :

1. Claimed universality
2. Claimed infallibility
3. Ritual activity
4. Has it's own jargon
5. The administration minimize diversity of opinion

WHEN TO USE THIS METHOD

1. Define intent
2. Know Context
3. Know User
4. Frame insights
5. Generate Concepts
6. Create Solutions
7. Implement solutions

HOW TO USE THIS METHOD

Twelve principles underlie the Agile Manifesto:

1. Satisfied customers
2. Welcome change at all stages of design.
3. Working software is delivered often.
4. Working software measures progress
5. Sustainable development,
6. Close, daily cooperation between business people and developers
7. Face-to-face conversation where possible
8. Use motivated people,
9. Attention to good design
10. Simplicity
11. Self-organizing teams
12. Regular adaptation to changing circumstances.

REFERENCES

1. Beck, Kent; et al. (2001). "Manifesto for Agile Software Development". Agile Alliance.
2. Shore, J., & Warden S. (2008). The Art of Agile Development. O'Reilly Media, Inc.

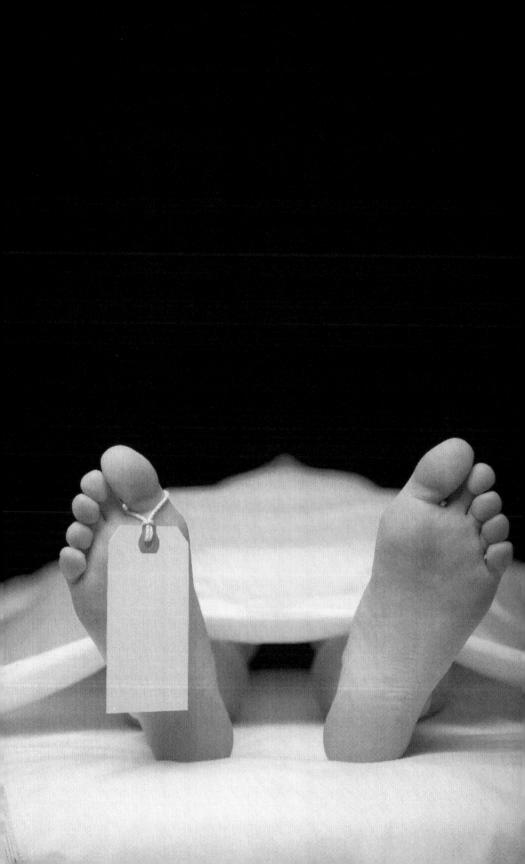

postmortem

WHAT IS IT?

This is a method for the team to evaluate after the project is completed how successful they were in meeting the initial project goals.

WHO INVENTED IT?

Booz Allen and Hamilton Consultants

WHEN TO USE THIS METHOD

1. Deliver offering

HOW TO USE THIS METHOD

1. The moderator asks each team member and or stakeholder to assign a percentage to how much they were able to meet the initial project goals. 0%, 25%, 50%, 75% 100%
2. Moderator asks "What could we have done to achieve 100% for this goal?"
3. Record the session and review it before the next project.

Annex A
Templates

BLUEPRINT

ACTIVITY PHASE	CUSTOMER ACTIONS	TOUCHPOINTS	LINE OF INTERACTION	DIRECT CONTACT	LINE OF VISIBILITY	BACK OFFICE	EMOTIONAL EXPERIENCE

635 METHOD

PROBLEM STATEMENT:	IDEA 1	IDEA 2	IDEA 3
1			
2			
3			
4			
5			
6			

CONTEXT MAP

TRENDS	POLITICAL	ECONOMIC	USER NEEDS	TECHNOLOGY	UNCERTAINTIES	TRENDS

COMPETITOR MATRIX

BRAND	BRAND A	BRAND B	BRAND C	BRAND D
BRAND STATEMENT				
VALUE PROPOSITION				
TARGET CUSTOMERS				
BUSINESS MODEL				
TECHNOLOGY				
ENVIRONMENTAL PERFORMANCE				
KEY DIFFERENTIATION				

EVALUATION MATRIX

CRITERIA	WEIGHT	DESIGN A		DESIGN B		DESIGN C		DESIGN D	
		SCORE	WEIGHTED	SCORE	WEIGHTED	SCORE	WEIGHTED	SCORE	WEIGHTED
TOTAL									

FISHBONE DIAGRAM

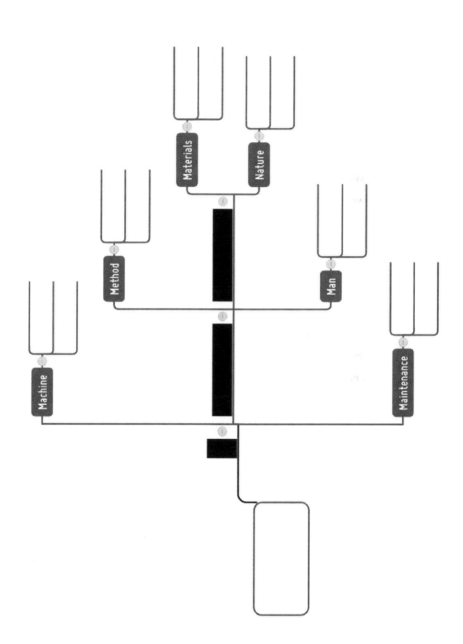

FREE LIST

Name of List ....
Prepared for ....
Date ....

Number	Name	Category	Use	Status	Checklist
1					
2					
3					
4					
5					
6					
7					
8					
9					
10					

Signature ....

363

HARRIS PROFILE

ASSESSMENT CRITERIA	-2	-1	+1	+2	-2	-1	+1	+2	-2	-1	+1	+2

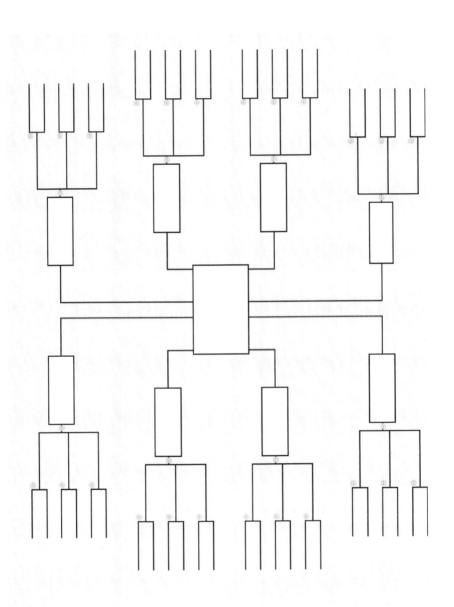

ONION MAP

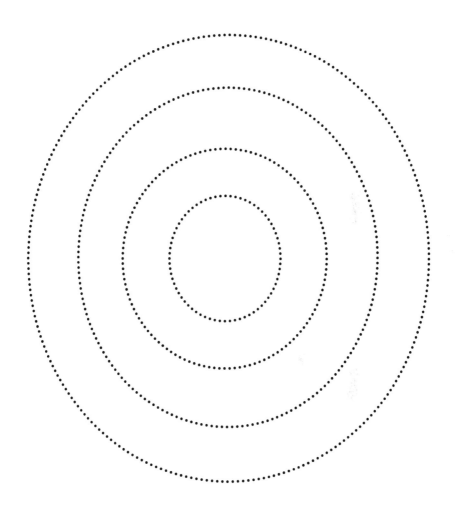

PERSONA

PERSONA NAME
....

DEMOGRAPHICS
....
....
....
....

CHARACTERISTIC STATEMENT
....
....
....
....
....

GOALS
....
....
....
....

AMBITIONS
....
....
....

INFLUENCERS AND ACTIVITIES
....
....
....
....

SCENARIOS
....
....
....
....

OTHER CHARACTERISTICS

TYPE: TYPE: TYPE: TYPE: TYPE: TYPE: TYPE: TYPE: TYPE: TYPE:

PERCEPTUAL MAP

PUGH MATRIX

CRITERIA	1	2	3	4	
TOTAL					

SPIDER DIAGRAM

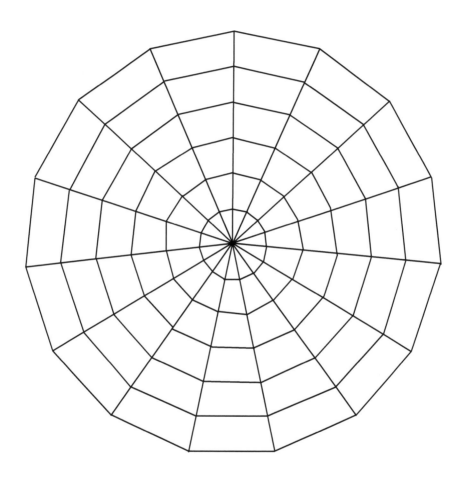

STAKEHOLDER POWER INFLUENCE MAP

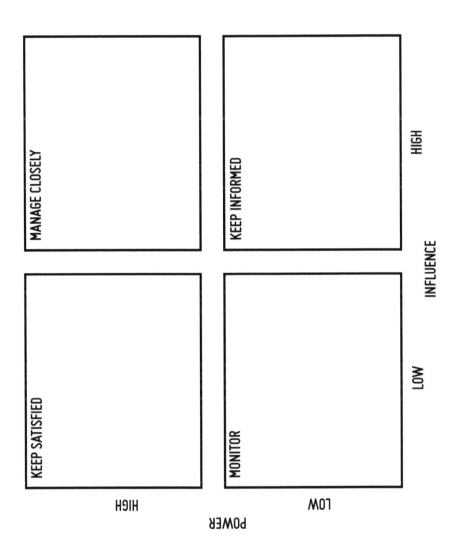

MANAGE CLOSELY

KEEP INFORMED

KEEP SATISFIED

MONITOR

HIGH

INFLUENCE

LOW

HIGH

LOW

POWER

STORYBOARD

PAGE

DATE

NAME

PROJECT

DIALOGUE

ACTION

SWOT

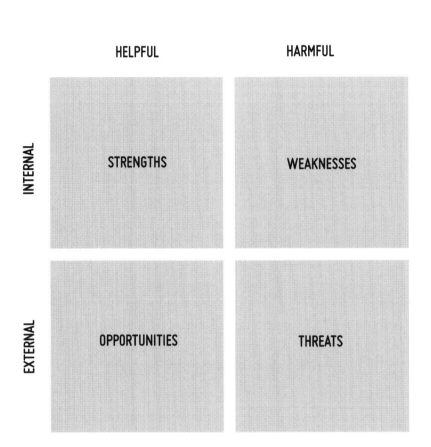

WHO DOES WHAT?

TASK	NAME	DATE	CONCERNS

index

index

index

index

other titles in this series

Design Thinking
Process and methods manual
Author: Curedale, Robert A
Publisher: Design Community College.
Edition 1 Feb 2013
ISBN-13: 978-0988236240
ISBN-10: 0988236249

Design Thinking
Pocket Guide
Author: Curedale, Robert A
Publisher: Design Community College.
Edition 1 Jun 2013
ISBN-13: 978-0-9892468-5-9
ISBN-10: 098924685X

Design Methods 2
200 more ways to apply design thinking
Author: Curedale, Robert A Publisher: Design
Community College.
Edition 1 January 2013
ISBN-13: 978-0988236240
ISBN-10: 0988236249

Design Research Methods
150 ways to inform design
Author: Curedale, Robert A
Publisher: Design Community College.
Edition 1 January 2013
ISBN-10: 0988236257
ISBN-13: 978-0-988-2362-5-7

50 Brainstorming Methods
for team and individual ideation
Author: Curedale, Robert A
Publisher: Design Community College.
Edition 1 January 2013
ISBN-10: 0988236230
ISBN-13: 978-0-9882362-3-3

50 Selected Design Methods
to inform your design
Author: Curedale, Robert A
Publisher: Design Community College.
Edition 1 January 2013
ISBN-10:0988236265 ISBN-13:978-0-9882362-6-4

Mapping Methods
for design and strategy
Curedale, Robert A
Publisher: Design Community College.
Edition 1 April 2013
ISBN-10: 0989246817
ISBN-13: 978-0-9892468-1-1

Interviews Observation and Focus Groups: 110
methods for user-centered design
Curedale, Robert A
Publisher: Design Community College.
Design Community College Inc
ISBN-13: 978-0989246835
ISBN-10: 0989246833

about the author

Rob Curedale was born in Australia and worked as a designer, director and educator in leading design offices in London, Sydney, Switzerland, Portugal, Los Angeles, Silicon Valley, Detroit, and China. He designed and managed over 1,000 products and experiences as a consultant and in-house design leader for the world's most respected brands. Rob has three decades experience in every aspect of product development, leading design teams to achieve transformational improvements in operating and financial results. He has extensive experience in forging strategic growth, competitive advantage, and a background in expanding business into emerging markets through user advocacy and extensive cross cultural expertise. Rob's designs can be found in millions of homes and workplaces around the world.

Rob works currently as a Adjunct Professor at Art Center College of Design in Pasadena and consults to organizations in the United States and internationally and presents workshops related to design. He has taught as a member of staff and presented lectures and workshops at many respected design schools and universities throughout the world including Yale, Pepperdine University, Art Center Pasadena, Loyola University, Cranbrook, Pratt, Art Center Europe; a faculty member at SCA and UTS Sydney; as Chair of Product Design and Furniture Design at the College for Creative Studies in Detroit, then the largest product design school in North America, Art Institute Hollywood, Cal State San Jose, Escola De Artes e Design in Oporto Portugal, Instituto De Artes Visuals, Design e Marketing, Lisbon, Southern Yangtze University, Jiao Tong University in Shanghai and Nanjing Arts Institute in China.

Rob's design practice experience includes projects for HP, Philips, GEC, Nokia, Sun, Apple, Canon, Motorola, Nissan, Audi VW, Disney, RTKL, Governments of the UAE,UK, Australia, Steelcase, Hon, Castelli, Hamilton Medical, Zyliss, Belkin, Gensler, Haworth, Honeywell, NEC, Hoover, Packard Bell, Dell, Black & Decker, Coleman and Harmon Kardon. Categories including furniture, healthcare, consumer electronics, sporting, homewares, military, exhibits, packaging. His products and experiences can be found in millions of homes and businesses throughout the world.

Rob established and manages the largest network of designers and architects in the world with more than 300,000 professional members working in every field of design.

37573971R00223

Made in the USA
Charleston, SC
10 January 2015